Red closet

Manchester University Press

Red closet

The hidden history of gay oppression
in the USSR

Rustam Alexander

MANCHESTER UNIVERSITY PRESS

Published by Manchester University Press
Oxford Road, Manchester M13 9PL
www.manchesteruniversitypress.co.uk

British Library Cataloguing-in-Publication Data
A catalogue record for this book is available from the British Library

ISBN   978 1 5261 6745 3   hardback

First published 2023

Typeset
by New Best-set Typesetters Ltd
Printed in Great Britain
by TJ Books Ltd, Padstow

Contents

Contents

Preface

The idea of writing a non-fiction book on the history of the oppression of Soviet gay men and lesbians, unburdened with academic jargon, came to me while I was working on my first book, *Regulating Homosexuality in Soviet Russia, 1956–91: A Different History*, based on my PhD thesis and of which the main audience was scholars in the field of Russian and LGBTQ studies. Back then I could not help but think about readers outside academia, who, despite their potential interest in the unexplored history of gay lives in the USSR, might find an academic style of writing unappealing and simply inaccessible. This is why I made a promise to myself that I would write another book, this time using accessible language and mostly based on individual stories of Soviet gay men and lesbians.

Although I wanted to write a compelling story, as a trained historian I knew I had to stay truthful to the historic sources and not distort or bend the historical evidence for the sake of the narrative. So, when writing *Red Closet: The Hidden History of Gay Oppression in the USSR*, I strove to read the available sources as closely as I could.

I should say that finding historical documents and sources in Russia on a topic as controversial as homosexuality is very difficult and sometimes almost impossible (especially after the beginning of the war in Ukraine). The most illuminating files remain classified in the archives and will remain so for at least another fifty years. Soviet people who identify as homosexuals are either too ashamed to speak about their past experiences or simply deceased. The Russian government actively prosecutes LGBTQ activists and sympathizers, bans gender studies in universities and does many other horrible things that fuel a homophobic climate. It is simply not safe to do such research in Russia.

The sources which lie at the heart of the book were acquired by me during my work on my PhD dissertation and they include archival materials, criminal "sodomy" cases, Soviet books and press, personal autobiographies of Soviet men who underwent psychotherapy for homosexuality, unpublished Soviet dissertations and many others. Some sources are more complete and intelligible than others; some of them are fragmented and hard to decipher. In the legal reports "sodomy" is used to refer to anal intercourse, though in other sources it is also often used more generally as a synonym for homosexuality.

I strove to write this book using accessible language, free of academic jargon and theoretical concepts. I did so intentionally to make the book as readable as I could to wider, non-academic audiences.

I would also like to point out that, while this book strives to discuss the experiences of both lesbian women and homosexual men, it deals predominantly with the experiences of the latter. The reason is simple: unlike male homosexuality, which was a crime in the USSR and was widely discussed by police officers, jurists, doctors and educators, lesbian relationships remained off the radar of the police and other professionals. This resulted in a veritable absence of any reliable sources on lesbian relationships in the USSR. Certainly, to be more inclusive of Soviet lesbian experiences would undoubtedly warrant a separate book to do justice to it, but to write such a book would require the author to possess adequate and sufficient historical sources. The absence of sufficient discussion of lesbian experience in the USSR in this book, for which I do apologize, is the result of the paucity of sources.

It would be impossible to write this book and omit sexual content, which is vital for our understanding of the lives of Soviet male homosexuals under oppressive conditions. I would therefore like to forewarn the reader that some chapters contain descriptions of sexual encounters between men in toilets, bathhouses and cruising places, as well as the use of sexual paraphernalia.

Preface

The true stories in this book are, as the notes indicate, based on a variety of archive and published sources, including diaries, autobiographies, medical reports and court case records, many of them not previously translated into English. Quotations from these sources appear as displayed extracts. In some cases where the sources are less detailed I have added and interspersed fictionalized expansions of what is implied in the original accounts, partly to provide a fuller cultural context for non-Russian readers and partly to try to maintain a uniform level of narrative discourse throughout the book. These expansions appear as part of the main text, with note references to indicate the source on which they are based. I have invented names for some of the people in the stories who are anonymous in the sources, and have changed the names of others for reasons of confidentiality.

I have included some comparative comments on the situation in other countries, particularly the US since it was the USSR's principal rival and opponent during the Cold War.

Some historical knowledge about homosexuality in Russia could be useful for the reader. Before the eighteenth century, homosexual behaviour in Russia was surprisingly widespread and travellers from other countries who came to visit Russia during this time, as well as Russian Orthodox churchmen, deplored its prevalence. But during the reign of Peter the Great, homosexual behaviour became the object of state regulation. In 1716, Peter the Great adopted the Military Code, which introduced corporal punishment for sodomy and the death penalty or hard labour for life if homosexual acts were accompanied by rape or violence. These military regulations, however, concerned only soldiers on active duty and did not apply to society at large.

Homosexual behaviour was criminalized for the whole of Russian society for the first time in 1832, when Nicholas I adopted a new Legal Code which contained legal punishments for male homosexuality. Article 995 made it illegal for two consenting men to have homosexual sex, while Article 996 penalized the homosexual rape and seduction of male minors. Despite the existence of a penalty for consensual homosexuality, it was rarely enforced.[1]

Preface

The Bolsheviks, who seized power in late 1917, overturned the entire Criminal Code of the Russian Empire along with the legislation prohibiting sex between consenting adult men. The new Soviet Criminal Code, created in 1922 and amended in 1926, did not criminalize sexual contacts between consenting adult men, which meant that male homosexual acts were now legal.[2] The issue of whether the Bolsheviks decriminalized male homosexuality intentionally or just overlooked it is still subject to debate among historians.[3] Nevertheless, the fact is that for more than a decade up to the early 1930s male homosexuality was legal in the USSR.

The story of this book begins in 1933, when the Soviet dictator Joseph Stalin decided to reintroduce criminal penalties for male homosexual behaviour, condemning thousands of Soviet gay and lesbian people to criminal prosecution, harassment and other forms of barbaric treatment which lasted for almost seven decades.

Abbreviations

AIDS   Acquired Immunodeficiency Syndrome

GARF   Gosudarstvennyi arkhiv Rossiiskoi Federatsii (State Archive of the Russian Federation)

GULAG   Glavnoe upravlenie lagerei (Main camp administration)

KGB   Komitet gosudarstvennoi bezopasnosti (Committee for State Security)

LGBTQ   lesbian, gay, bisexual, transsexual, queer or questioning

MVD   Ministerstvo vnutrennikh del (Ministry of Internal Affairs)

NKVD   Narodnyi komissariat vnutrennikh del (People's Commissariat for Internal Affairs)

OGPU   Ob'edinennoe gosudarstvennoe politicheskoe upravleniye (Unified State Political Administration, secret police, 1923–34)

RSFSR   Rossiiskaia Sovetskaia Federativnaia Sotsialisticheskaia Respublika (Russian Soviet Federative Socialist Republic)

STI   sexually transmitted infection

USSR   Union of Soviet Socialist Republics

Archival citations are accompanied by the following abbreviations:

f.   fond, fond

op.   opis', inventory

l., ll.   list, listy; page(s)

Global timeline
of the twentieth century

1917 – Russia decriminalizes homosexuality

1933 – Denmark decriminalizes homosexuality

1934 – The USSR recriminalizes consensual homosexual behaviour across the entire country

1942 – Switzerland decriminalizes homosexuality

1944 – Sweden decriminalizes homosexuality

1957 – The Wolfenden Committee recommends decriminalizing consensual homosexual acts between men in England and Wales

1961 – Czechoslovakia decriminalizes homosexual relations between consenting males

1961 – Hungary decriminalizes homosexual relations between men over the age of twenty

1967 – England and Wales decriminalize most adult male homosexual relations

1968 – East Germany (German Democratic Republic) decriminalizes consensual homosexual relations between men

1968 – Bulgaria decriminalizes consensual homosexual relations

1969 – West Germany (Federal Republic of Germany) allows homosexual acts between men aged twenty-one and over

1969 – The Stonewall riots take place in New York

1971 – Austria and Finland decriminalize homosexuality

1972 – Norway decriminalizes homosexuality

Global timeline

1973 – The American Psychiatric Association removes the diagnosis of "homosexuality" from the second edition of its *Diagnostic and Statistical Manual of Mental Disorders*

1975 – South Australia decriminalizes homosexuality

1979 – Spain decriminalizes homosexuality

1981 – Victoria, Australia, decriminalizes homosexuality

1983 – Portugal decriminalizes homosexuality

1984 – New South Wales, Australia, decriminalizes homosexuality

1990 – Western Australia and Queensland decriminalize homosexuality

1993 – Russia decriminalizes male consensual homosexual acts

1997 – Tasmania, Australia, formally decriminalizes homosexuality

Part I

Under Stalin

1

Stalin decides to make male homosexuality a crime

Moscow, 1933–1934

Joseph Stalin and his cronies hated homosexuals. In fact, they never called them homosexuals – instead they called them "pederasts" – a crude and vulgar Russian counterpart of the English word "queer". The ruthless Soviet leader, responsible for the death and suffering of millions of Soviet people, was unconcerned with political correctness.

The Soviet Union, the largest communist state in the world, over which Stalin presided, was slightly over a decade old when he came to power. In 1917, the Bolsheviks led by Vladimir Lenin made adroit use of the escalating political crisis, which saw the demise of the royal dynasty of the Romanovs that had ruled Russia for more than three hundred years. They then took advantage of the weak and ineffective provisional government, which they overturned in October the same year, seizing power completely.

Once in power, the Bolsheviks made short work of those who opposed them and their rule. To begin with, they removed the Romanov family from the capital and later had them all brutally murdered. Then, with the help of the hastily created secret police, they initiated mass executions of the supporters of the tsarist regime. A murderous and devastating civil war ensued: supporters of the new regime fought against those who opposed it. By 1922, the Bolsheviks, led by the ruthless Vladimir Lenin, had defeated their foes and formed the new state – the Union of Soviet Socialist Republics (USSR), which comprised Russia, Ukraine, Belarus, Georgia, Armenia and Azerbaijan. They also established the Communist Party, headed by Lenin, which now fully controlled the USSR's government.

Then, in 1924, Lenin fell into a coma and died, leaving the country in the hands of his close associates. Joseph Stalin, one of these, acted fast: eliminating his rivals one by one, he worked his way up to the pinnacle of power, replacing Lenin to become the undisputed political leader of the USSR.

Fearing foreign invasion, Stalin wanted to turn the largely agricultural Soviet Union into an industrial power. In 1928, he proclaimed the beginning of "industrialization". His plans to modernize the Soviet economy were truly ambitious and set astonishingly high goals – he demanded a 111 per cent increase in coal production, a 200 per cent increase in iron production and a 335 per cent increase in electrical power generation.[1] To ensure that these goals were met, Stalin introduced a system of harsh punishments for those who refused to work. If workers, for example, failed to reach their set targets, they would be criticized and publicly humiliated by the factory's leadership. Those who did not come to work, and with the increasing pressure and exhausting work this became a common problem, were accused of sabotaging the Five Year Plan and were either shot or sent to work themselves to death in labour camps.[2]

To feed Soviet workers in the cities and prevent food shortages Stalin decided to improve agricultural productivity. He launched a new policy called "collectivization", which coerced individual farmers and peasants in the villages into giving up their individual farms and joining large collective farms under state control. Those who resisted – and there were many farmers who did – had their land confiscated or were arrested, deported to labour camps or even shot. Stalin was particularly harsh and brutal with wealthy peasants or *kulaks*, whom he wished to liquidate as a class. The poor administration of the collectivization eventually caused mass famine in the villages and across the republic of Ukraine in particular, where millions of people were starved to death.

But Stalin did not appear concerned. Consolidating his power within the Party, he sought to promote his own cult of personality. In 1929, the whole country lavishly celebrated his fiftieth birthday, during which Stalin was proclaimed Lenin's only successor and heir.[3] In 1933, Stalin delivered a triumphal speech at the Plenum of the Central Committee of the

Communist Party, declaring the First Five Year Plan a success. Soon the press pronounced Stalin as "the inspirer of all successes" and newspapers began to feature collective letters from the masses praising and thanking him for his leadership. The official propaganda avoided the atrocities which had accompanied Stalin's push for industrialization and collectivization, and criticizing the leader was becoming increasingly dangerous.

Anybody who did not work or refused to work was a problem to be dealt with immediately. The OGPU, Stalin's secret police, were actively looking to punish such individuals and bring them into the workforce or, if they proved uncooperative, throw them into the rapidly growing system of labour camps, where people were made to work themselves to death.

The OGPU also unleashed a crackdown on so-called "social anomalies" – female prostitutes, beggars, alcoholics and homeless people, who roamed Moscow, Leningrad and other big cities. As early as 1933, the OGPU started rounding up the "undesirables" in marketplaces and railway stations, banishing them or sending them to prison without trial.

Initially, homosexuals were not classified as "social anomalies". Party leaders never discussed them in official documents and did not seem to be bothered about their existence. In fact, during the early Soviet regime and up until Stalin's decision to introduce sodomy laws, most Soviet men who desired other men experienced tolerance and even acceptance, especially if they performed politically valued work.[4] This was in contrast to the situation with homosexuals elsewhere in the world. In the US of the 1930s, for example, homosexual men and women faced the moral condemnation of churches and the possibility of being prosecuted under the existing sodomy laws. Although few men were convicted under these laws, the existing anti-homosexual legislation across the US heavily stigmatized same-sex relations.[5] Police also invoked other existing laws to crack down on the urban gay subculture in various American cities, arresting gay men and charging them with disorderly conduct, vagrancy, public lewdness and solicitation. Likewise, unlike the USSR, where a new generation of psychiatrists were now deeming homosexuality a normal variant of human sexuality, even attempting to help their patients accept it, in the US most psychiatrists classified homosexuality as a "disease".[6]

However this period of relative tolerance of homosexuality in the USSR began to subside from the early 1930s, when homosexuals started to appear on the radar of Stalin's secret police.[7]

On a warm August night in 1933, during a routine round-up in Moscow, the OGPU officers stormed into an apartment, reputed to be a brothel. Inside the apartment there was a rowdy crowd, loud music from a gramophone, alcohol and thick smoke. Those inside did not initially notice the presence of the uniformed intruders who stood at the door, observing what was happening. Straining their eyes through the smoke, at first the officers thought that the crowd consisted mainly of women. Soon however they realized that many of the people in the room were actually men dressed up as women. They had their faces painted and powdered, they seemed to be squealing and addressing each other by women's names, embracing soldiers sitting next to them.

Enraged and disgusted, the OGPU people smashed the gramophone from the table and the room went quiet. Then they swooped, wrestling men to the ground, even beating some of them, unable to contain their disgust at seeing men in women's clothing. That night the detained men were taken to the OGPU headquarters for interrogation. The investigators learned that these men did not only drink and have parties but also engaged in "perversions": men had sex with men. Forcing and beating the detained men into confessions, the investigators learned that this particular brothel was not the only one in Moscow and that there were similar establishments in other large cities.

Genrikh Yagoda, the OGPU chief and Stalin's associate notorious for orchestrating mass deportations and killing of innocent people, was informed about the raid on the same day. Yagoda immediately directed his subordinates to locate similar dens in other cities and detain as many people as possible.

On 15 September 1933, Yagoda had his secretary type a lengthy telegram to Stalin, breaking the news to him that "pederasts" were recruiting young people to their ranks in various Soviet cities. He reported that his secret police had conducted raids in Moscow and Leningrad, apprehending as many as 130 persons. According to Yagoda, all of them had established networks and dens, and were involved in espionage activities. Aware of Stalin's paranoia and his fear of foreign intrusion, Yagoda reported that the members of these circles were seeking to undermine the Soviet state and demoralize young workers, even attempting to infiltrate the army and navy.[8]

Informing Stalin of the captured groups of homosexuals, Yagoda drew his attention to the absence in Soviet legislation of sodomy laws which would let him imprison these people, and suggested that such laws be adopted immediately. After seizing power in 1917, the Bolsheviks had indeed repealed the tsarist-era legislation with its existing penalties for sodomy, thereby officially decriminalizing homosexual behaviour. Yet Yagoda's telegrams to Stalin in 1933 convinced the dictator that male homosexual behaviour had to be recriminalized. Interestingly, Yagoda did not propose to criminalize female homosexuality and did not even mention it. This was apparently because homosexual men were more likely to catch the OGPU's attention, as they met and socialized in bars, restaurants, public toilets and other places vulnerable to the raids of the secret police. Lesbians, however, tended to be more discreet.

In his telegram, Yagoda wrote that homosexuals were spies, tapping into Stalin's never-ending paranoia about foreign invasion, mainly on the part of Germany, where Hitler had come to power in early 1933. Although Stalin and his cronies believed that Hitler's rule would not last long and would pose no danger to the USSR, they were soon proved wrong.

Stalin, who was also aware of the rumours that Germans had managed to infiltrate the homosexual circles in Moscow, obtaining Soviet military information and sowing dissent in the Party, quickly responded to Yagoda's proposal to criminalize sodomy: "These scoundrels must receive exemplary punishment and a corresponding guiding decree must be introduced in our legislation". The report then landed on the desk of Vyacheslav Molotov, Stalin's close associate and member of the Politburo, the highest policy-making authority within the Communist Party, who scribbled on it, "Of course, it is necessary! Molotov." Lazar Kaganovich, another influential member of Stalin's close circle and Politburo, also signed, "Correct! L. Kaganovich."[9]

On a frigid winter day on 13 December 1933, Yagoda reported to Stalin that he and his officers had finally liquidated the gatherings of homosexuals in Moscow and Leningrad, attaching the proposal for a new sodomy law. Yagoda's law introduced punishment of up to five years in prison for sexual intercourse between two consenting men and up to eight years for "forcible" sodomy. This legislation was to be included in the laws of all the Soviet republics.

While Stalin was considering Yagoda's proposal, the OGPU chief decided to unleash purges of the prominent members of the Soviet cultural elite known to be homosexuals. In February 1934, OGPU officers discovered that the director of the State Literary Museum, Vladimir Bonch-Bruevich, had purchased the diaries and papers of a Leningrad poet, Mikhail Kuzmin, whose love affairs with men were an open secret.[10]

Kuzmin himself never shied away from depicting same-sex love in his work. The diaries and papers which Bonch-Bruevich obtained from him featured clear references to homosexual love, and OGPU officers confiscated them, hoping to learn more about homosexuals in Moscow.[11] Although Kuzmin was now in danger, he managed to escape prosecution because of the reshuffling within the OGPU, which led to a certain hiatus in his case. Kuzmin died in 1936.

Other members of the Soviet intellectual elite, like Nikolai Kliuev, were less lucky. Like Kuzmin, he did not hide his homosexuality, and one day he submitted a manuscript of a poem with homosexual themes to the editor of the journal *Novyi Mir*, Ivan Gronskii. Reading Kliuev's manuscript at breakfast in his flat with his friend Pavel, Gronskii struggled to understand the poem's meaning. The poem was about love, but it appeared that the author was in love with a young man, not a young woman as Gronskii expected. Gronskii frowned and looked in the direction of Pavel, who was reading a morning newspaper in his rocking chair.

"Pasha, have a look". He tossed Kliuev's poem to him. "I don't understand any goddamn thing here." Pavel took the piece of paper and then burst out laughing.

"What the hell are you are laughing at?"

"What do you mean you don't understand? This man is his 'wife'." Pavel's boisterous laughter now filled the room.

"Disgusting, I am not going to publish it. I feel like I need to wash my hands after that," he said and shuddered in disgust. Several weeks later, Kliuev showed up at Gronskii's office in Moscow.

"Did you get my poem?" enquired Kliuev.

"Yes," Gronskii replied.

"Are you going to print it?"

"No, we are not going to let this filth into literature. If you write normal poetry, we will be printing it. If you want to work normally, we will give you such an opportunity."

"If you don't print the poem, I will not be writing anything then," he insisted stubbornly. "You either print it, or I am not going to work for you."

"In this case, our conversation will be short. You won't stay in Moscow any more," he threatened.

"These are my terms – you either print or I am not going to work," Kliuev insisted. Kliuev indeed was not overly concerned about being published as he preferred reading his poetry to a close circle of people.[12]

Kliuev's problem was not just that he was a homosexual. His poem about his lover obviously aggravated Gronskii, but it was not as seditious as his other poems which criticized the Soviet government. Gronskii had read them without complaint but the homosexual themes in Kliuev's last poem evoked a visceral reaction of disgust, which grew into a desire to punish the poet. In 1933, Gronskii held several meetings with Stalin during which he told him about Kliuev's seditious poetry, which prompted the opening of a criminal case against the poet. Kliuev was arrested in February 1934 and eventually, in 1937, shot.

While Yagoda was going after homosexuals among members of the Soviet cultural elite, his draft law on sodomy was being approved by the highest Soviet organs in the Russian and other republics from March to April 1934. The new sodomy law was codenamed 154-a and consisted of two parts. The first criminalized consensual sex between males, making it punishable by deprivation of liberty for a term of three to five years. The second outlawed so-called "forcible" sodomy, which carried a more severe penalty of five to eight years.

Having adopted the sodomy law, Stalin and his henchmen failed to promulgate any information about this new legislation, so most men whose actions were now deemed criminal simply didn't know about its existence. This was hardly surprising because Stalin's regime preferred to be secretive and ambiguous when it came to public policy issues.[13] Instead of issuing a clear directive, Stalin preferred to give signals about what was to come. These signals included Stalin's public speeches and published articles, editorial reviews in Soviet major newspapers and, quite frequently, show trials of prominent officials associated with certain policies. Such actions indicated a turn in Soviet policies and communicated what the Party's stance was but did not give clear explanations as to what they implied or how officials and civilians should act. The historian Sheila Fitzpatrick believes that such secrecy around law-making was essential for Stalin to create an aura of mystery around his regime and thus enhance its power.[14]

When it came to the newly introduced sodomy law, similar tactics were employed. On 23 May 1934, Maksim Gorky, Soviet poet and Stalin's mouthpiece, introduced the law to the public. In his article "Proletarian Humanism", published in the major Soviet newspapers *Pravda* and *Izvestiia*, he vaguely mentioned that, unlike "cultured" Germany, the USSR punished homosexuality:

> Not tens, but hundreds of facts speak to the destructive, corruptive influence on Europe's youth. To recount the facts is disgusting, but ... I will point out the following, however, that in the country which is bravely and successfully ruled by the proletariat, homosexuality, the corruption of youth, is socially understood as a crime and punished, but in the "cultured" country of great philosophers, scientists, musicians, it exists openly and unpunished.[15]

Apart from members of the Soviet cultural elite, Kuzmin's diary, which OGPU officers confiscated from the State Literary Museum, also featured descriptions of Kuzmin's friendships with some Soviet high-ranking officials. The diary mentioned Kuzmin's ambiguous friendship with the former head of the USSR Ministry of Foreign Affairs, Georgii Chicherin.[16] Chicherin had already been retired for four years – he was often ill and led a secluded life. Maybe that is why OGPU officers decided not to touch him and allowed him to die peacefully in his bed in 1936. But the ministry over which he presided became a target. Apprehensive of possible homosexual infiltration from abroad, the OGPU officers wanted to identify as many homosexuals as possible in the ranks of Soviet diplomats.

Soon they homed in on Dmitrii Florinskii, whom Chicherin had personally invited to work for the Ministry in 1920 and whose homosexuality became soon apparent to them. The OGPU people managed to catch Florinskii's young lovers, all of whom testified against the official. They revealed that Florinskii used his former wife as bait to attract young men, promising that they could have sex with her in his presence. They also alleged that he led a promiscuous life by seducing young men and leading them down the pathway to sodomy.

Florinskii initially denied his involvement in sodomy, but the OGPU managed to beat him into incriminating himself. After his brutal interrogation, not only did he admit to committing sodomy but he also declared himself a German spy.[17] In 1939, he was shot for espionage. Florinskii's purge marked the beginning of homosexual cleansing within the Soviet's state organs.

In Stalin's Russia, nobody could be sure of their immunity and soon the author of the sodomy law, the notorious OGPU chief Genrikh Yagoda, became a victim of the purges himself. In July 1934, the OGPU, the organization he had previously headed, ceased to exist as an independent state organ and became part of the People's Commissariat for Internal Affairs (NKVD), an abbreviation that would instil fear in many people. Although Yagoda was appointed the boss within the organization, he soon fell into disfavour at the hands of his rival Nikolai Yezhov, who conspired against him to take his place. Yezhov would soon become the main mastermind of the 1937 Great Terror, in the course of which many Soviet people would be falsely charged with espionage and conspiracy against the Party and subsequently sent to labour camps or shot.

Yezhov also orchestrated Yagoda's detention, accusing him of espionage in March 1937. The NKVD officers searched Yagoda's residences and discovered that the author of the sodomy law, who was so concerned about the moral corruption of the younger generation by homosexuals, was no stranger to debauchery himself. The officers found a pornographic collection of almost four thousand photographs as well as pornographic movies and countless pieces of women's clothing – stockings, hats, silk tights. Yagoda also possessed a collection of pornographic pipes, cigarette holders and even a rubber dildo.[18]

Yagoda was sentenced to death at a show trial along with twenty other former disgraced Party functionaries in March 1938. All of them were executed on the same day. Yagoda's execution was conducted in a particularly sadistic way: he was seated in a chair and made to watch how the other twenty were shot before his own execution. His successor, Nikolai Yezhov, was present at the execution, and, before shooting Yagoda, he ordered him to be beaten to a pulp.[19]

In a rapid, but unsurprising twist of fate, Yezhov soon fell into disgrace himself. In 1939, he was charged with conspiracy against the Soviet state. Furthermore, he even admitted to having engaged in sodomy on numerous occasions from the very early stages of his career.[20] Yezhov was shot the same year. He who lives by the sword, indeed …

2

A Scottish man stands up for the rights of Soviet homosexuals

Moscow, 1934

Harry Whyte could boast of numerous professional successes, all due to his talent and hard work.[1] His father was a Scottish painter and neither of his parents had any interest in foreign languages or journalism. Despite this, young Harry learned several languages while at school, including Russian, which fascinated him the most. Then at the age of sixteen he left school to take up the job of an office boy with the *Edinburgh News*, which marked the beginning of his journalistic career.

Harry's knowledge of the Russian language fuelled his curiosity about life in the USSR, revolution and socialism. It also fuelled his desire to live in the USSR. Harry was unhappy living in Scotland for a particular reason: he could not openly meet and have romantic relationships with other men. Scottish law criminalized sodomy and branded people like Harry criminals and perverts. This mirrored the situation in the US, where during the 1930s homosexual men lived in constant fear of arrest.[2] The USSR, in contrast, did not seem to have any anti-sodomy legislation – Harry couldn't find any legislation against it in the Soviet Criminal Code. What's more, the Bolsheviks seemed far less puritanical than the Scots, and some of their prominent members, like Alexandra Kollontai, even advocated "free love".

In 1931, Harry joined the Communist Party of Great Britain, combining his journalistic and political work. In 1932, at the age of twenty-five, he was invited to Moscow to work as a staff journalist of Russia's English-language newspaper *Moscow News*. Harry readily took up the job. Going to the USSR seemed like a perfect mixture of professional and personal opportunities – working for an international newspaper of the first communist country and living out his homosexual life without fear of criminal prosecution and condemnation.

In Moscow, Harry's professional work went very well. His boss, the editor-in-chief of the newspaper, Mikhail Borodin, was impressed with Harry's dedication and work ethic, and, as early as 1933, promoted him to the post of deputy. Harry was excited – it seemed as if he had made the right choice moving to the USSR – and he even applied for a transfer from the British Communist Party to the Communist Party of the USSR.

Harry's personal life was seeing some improvements as well. Once he became familiar with the city, Harry ventured out into the public toilets and parks, where he hoped to meet other men like himself. This strategy had worked for him in Scotland and it would surely work for him in the USSR, where homosexuals lived freer lives. And indeed, he did begin to meet local men and make acquaintances among them.

One of them, Ivan, really struck his fancy. Tall with blond hair, Ivan was also in his late twenties. He had come to Moscow to study engineering. Ivan was also infatuated by Harry, whose foreign accent and neat suit with a handkerchief in his buttonhole made him seem charming and endearing. Ivan had never met a foreigner who spoke Russian, and in fact he had never met a foreigner in his life. They often went on walks together and saw each other with growing frequency.

One day in December 1933, however, Ivan disappeared.[3] On that day Harry and Ivan had agreed to meet in one of Moscow's central parks and then have a stroll around the city. But Ivan never showed up. After several days of silence, Harry resolved to give him a call. Ivan shared a flat with his sister Aleksandra, who, as Ivan had told Harry, knew about his life and disapproved of it. In order not to upset her, Ivan asked Harry not to call him and instead had said he would call Harry himself, unless something urgent happened. But Harry couldn't wait. Having found Ivan's number in his notebook, he dialled it.

Ivan's sister picked up the phone. She said that Ivan had been detained – she didn't explain on what charges and did not wish to continue their rather short conversation.[4] The news shocked Harry. Had Ivan been detained because of his homosexuality? No, it couldn't be true. The Soviet law didn't criminalize homosexuals – such individuals were free to be who they were. That was one of the reasons why Harry had come to the USSR in the first place. There was no law that could prosecute him.

Once Harry's fear and shock subsided, he collected his thoughts and decided on a course of action. He would approach the OGPU to find out what happened to his friend. He also wanted to know if there was indeed an issue with him being a homosexual, in order to avoid potential trouble in the future, because, if so, he would have to leave the country altogether.

An average Russian would have thought twice before going to the OGPU with such a matter. The organization and its headquarters on Lubyanka Square, less than a kilometre from the Kremlin, instilled fear in Moscow city dwellers. Those whom the OGPU accused of espionage or counter-revolutionary activities were interrogated in the basements of the building, and many were beaten and tortured to death. Walking through the doors of the OGPU building often meant never walking out again.

The history of the OGPU harks back to 1917, when Bolsheviks seized power and created a special state organ – Cheka, which was intended to fight the opponents of the new regime. The Cheka quickly became synonymous with terror and mass repressions. Unrestrained by the rule of law, it freely arrested, tortured and executed anybody deemed an enemy of the state. And as the Soviet regime became increasingly totalitarian, the secret police was also becoming more powerful. In an attempt to break away from its brutal reputation, the Cheka was renamed the OGPU in 1923, but this didn't change the way many people perceived it.

Obtaining the OGPU's phone number and securing an appointment was not difficult. After all, Harry was deputy editor-in-chief of *Moscow News* and he had some connections. It took him several days to secure an appointment and obtain his building pass, without which it was impossible to gain entry.

The entrance to the OGPU headquarters lay through the old building with the original doors, above which was a bas-relief depicting Karl Marx.

Harry hesitated at the entrance, collecting his thoughts and contemplating whether the subject matter was going to land him in trouble. But then again, he reminded himself that homosexuality was not a crime in the USSR, so he had nothing to fear.

Walking through the long, glum corridors of the building, he was asked to show his pass three times. Having verified the pass, the sullen security guards with rifles pointed the way. Soon he found himself in the room of one of the investigators, who agreed to talk. The man was wearing a uniform and smoking a cigarette. In the room there was a couch – an important attribute of the investigators' rooms. Very often interrogations lasted for the entire day and in between the investigator could have some rest.

The OGPU officer looked directly into Harry's eyes. Harry explained that his friend Ivan had been arrested and said that he wanted to know whether he had been detained because of his homosexuality.

The officer cleared his throat, clearly uncomfortable with the topic, and explained that Ivan could not have been arrested because of his sexual preference as it was not a punishable offence in the USSR. When Harry told the OGPU officer that he himself was a homosexual, the officer drily assured him that the OGPU had nothing against him.

Harry went back to his office, confused and still upset. His boss, Borodin, knew of Harry's homosexual lifestyle although they never discussed it in detail. On this day, however, Harry decided to share what had happened, not mentioning the fact that he went to the OGPU himself. Harry later recalled:

> Comrade Borodin said that he personally had a negative attitude towards homosexuality but at the same time he said that he considered me a good enough communist, that I could be trusted and that I could arrange my personal life as I desired.[5]

Weeks went by but Harry still had not heard anything from Ivan. Unsatisfied with the answers from the OGPU and Borodin, Harry decided to verify if something indeed had changed in the Soviet legislation. He went to the Lenin State Library in the centre of Moscow, where he consulted the *Great Soviet Encyclopaedia* – the Soviet Union's largest and most authoritative written source of knowledge.

The encyclopaedia was written, managed and edited by prominent Soviet academics and scientists, and its content was decided upon at the highest state and party level. The encyclopaedia's entries were organized alphabetically so it was not difficult for Harry to find the desired item – "homosexuality". The entry spanned several pages and the author of the entry, a distinguished Soviet psychiatrist, Mark Sereiskii, argued that homosexuality was an incurable medical condition. He also commented on its relation to the law. Sereiskii criticized the pre-revolutionary sodomy statute, calling it "absurd":

> Apart from being a piece of legislation, prohibiting biological deviation, it is absurd per se – it does not yield any results and it has an adverse influence of homosexuals' psyche. The struggle for the abolition of these hypocritical provisions is still far from over in the advanced capitalist countries.

The author essentially took pride in the fact that homosexuality was not a punishable offence in the USSR, unlike in Western countries. According to Sereiskii, not only was Soviet legislation indifferent to homosexuals (understood to be males), leaving them free to seek out men like themselves in Soviet society, but Soviet society itself was helping homosexuals to become fully fledged members of society:

> Thus it becomes clear that the Soviet stance on homosexuals' characteristics and peculiarities differs significantly from what we can observe in the West. Aware of the incorrect development of homosexuals, society does not and cannot lay the blame for this development on the bearer of these incorrect characteristics. This breaks, to a large extent, the wall that naturally springs up between the homosexual and the society and forces him to withdraw into himself. Our society… creates all the necessary conditions for the life clashes of homosexuals to be as painless as possible and for the alienation they inherently experience to dissipate in the new collective.[6]

The volume of the encyclopaedia which contained the passage on homosexuality was dated 1930, which seemingly meant that the views expressed in it were current, and not outdated. It also meant that Ivan was probably detained not on charges of sodomy but for something else. Indeed, perhaps

Ivan was engaged in some counter-revolutionary activities that he hadn't told Harry about.

Over the following months Harry was beginning to forget about Ivan's disappearance until one day in May 1934, when Borodin came to his desk. The chief editor carefully laid out several pages of an official-looking document and gestured to Harry to have a look. Harry popped on his glasses and the first two lines jumped out at him: "Article 154-a. Sexual intercourse of a man with a man (sodomy) – deprivation of liberty for a term of three to five years". Harry was both shocked and bewildered.

Here before him was what appeared to be a copy of Stalin's newest decree on sodomy. Harry read it quickly then pushed it away in disbelief. He then immediately told Borodin about the article he read in the *Great Soviet Encyclopaedia*, which stated that Soviet society was not against homosexuality. Harry later recalled how Borodin responded:

> Comrade Borodin told me that I should not attach any importance to the article on homosexuality in the *Great Soviet Encyclopaedia*, because – as he said – the author of the article was a homosexual himself and the article was published at a time when a whole series of sexual deviations had not been discovered ...[7] Comrade Borodin also pointed out to me that the fact that I am a homosexual in no way diminishes my value as a revolutionary. He confided in me by appointing me the deputy editor ... He also pointed out that my private life was not something that could in the slightest degree undermine my position as a member of the Party or a member of the Editorial Board.[8]

Harry was now both scared and enraged. This was not the Soviet Union that he wanted to live in and work in. Instead of taking the progressive path regarding sexual relations, the USSR seemed to be following in the footsteps of capitalist societies, where people like Harry were considered criminals. The fact that the *Great Soviet Encyclopaedia*, the main Soviet propaganda mouthpiece, where the articles were vetted and censored at the highest level, openly stated that homosexuals were welcome in the USSR, puzzled Harry even more. This confusion led Harry to consult a psychiatrist in Moscow, whom he had seen on several occasions before and who had assured him twice that his patients, if they were honest citizens or good communists, were free to arrange their personal lives as they pleased.[9]

After the revolution and the subsequent abolition of the tsarist-era sodomy laws, a young generation of Soviet psychiatrists were keen to explore the origins of homosexuality. In the 1920s, many of them had been aware of calls for tolerance towards such individuals in some European countries and they sought to promote the same values at home. Soviet psychiatrists did not see any problem in their patients' homosexuality as long as they were honest and hard-working individuals. In their interactions with such people, they deemed it preferable to help them accept their sexual orientation rather than try to treat it.[10] In this way, Mark Sereiskii's article which Harry read in the *Great Soviet Encyclopaedia* accurately reflected the current medical thinking on the problem.

Harry's psychiatrist at first refused to believe that a law criminalizing homosexual relations had been adopted in the USSR. Harry then produced a paper from his briefcase and pushed it towards the doctor. For a few moments, silence hung in the room. Harry's psychiatrist had nothing to say – the document explicitly said that sodomy was henceforth a crime, and it definitely bore Stalin's signature. The doctor cleared his throat and shifted in his chair and then tried to explain that he personally had nothing against homosexuals and that he still could not believe that this law existed.

Having summoned his courage, Harry resolved to seek clarification from the OGPU a second time. But, instead of going to their headquarters, he gave them a call. This time the officer's response was short and harsh: "We will strictly enforce the existing law in every uncovered case of homosexuality."[11]

Confused and astounded, Harry decided to write a letter to Stalin, hoping that Borodin would be able to hand it to the Soviet leader at one of his meetings. But Borodin flatly refused to do so and strongly advised Harry against proceeding with the matter.

But Harry wouldn't budge. He would stand his ground and send the letter to Stalin anyway. Harry's letter to Stalin was not a personal letter with demands to explain Ivan's detention, but an impassioned discussion on the role of homosexuality in Soviet society, which spanned several pages and ran to around 4500 words. Although respectful and cautious in tone, Harry's letter voiced his strong disagreement with Stalin's decision to criminalize sodomy in the USSR. Harry was treading on dangerous ground – Stalin had little tolerance for those who questioned his policies or showed disloyalty. By 1934, many of the Party officials who had expressed *any* disagreement with Stalin had already been shot or sent to the GULAG.

Many Soviet people did write to Stalin. Reading their letters enabled Stalin to understand the moods of the people. There were in fact so many letters that Stalin's officials had to set up a special department to process them. This department consisted of fifteen readers who read the letters, as well as extra staff who assisted with registering, cataloguing and archiving them. Letters considered of no interest were to be directed to the archive, while others were to be forwarded to governmental bodies or Stalin's associates and, finally, a selected group of letters landed on Stalin's desk.[12]

Harry's letter had a striking title, "Can a homosexual be a member of the Communist Party?", which immediately caught the eye of Stalin's readers. Whyte's position as a deputy editor of *Moscow News* and his foreign nationality also increased the odds of his letter landing on Stalin's desk. The letter read in part:

> Dear Comrade Stalin!
>
> Although I am a foreign communist, I think you, the leader of the world proletariat, will be able to shed light on the question, which is of great importance for a great number of communists both in the USSR and other countries of the world. The question is – can a homosexual be a member of the Communist Party? The recently promulgated sodomy law, apparently, means that a homosexual cannot be deemed worthy to bear the title of a Soviet citizen. Being personally interested in this issue, I have consulted a number of comrades from OGPU, psychiatrists and Comrade Borodin. All of them gave me contradicting opinions. Given all this lack of clarity, I am writing to you in a hope that you will have time to give your view on that.
>
> Please let me give you my interpretation of the issue. I believe that the social standing of working homosexuals is equal to that of women and people of colour in the capitalist society as well as Jews under Hitler. All these individuals face persecution and oppression in a capitalist society.

There are two types of homosexuals. Those from the first group are homosexuals from birth. Those from the second group engage in homosexuality because of vice and due to economic considerations. As for the first group of homosexuals, research has shown that the proportion of these people in every society is practically the same – it is about 2 per cent. So in the USSR alone, there are approximately two million homosexuals. I am convinced that among them there could be found people who actively participate in socialist construction. So is it really possible to convict such a great number of people? Besides, the conditions of living for homosexuals in the USSR are already difficult, by which I mean that it is really difficult to find a partner for sexual intercourse – homosexuals constitute a minority and many of them are forced to hide their genuine inclinations.

How does capitalist society regard homosexuals? It is inherently against it. Desperately needing a great army and more people for exploitation, it regards homosexuality as a threat to birth-rates. But at the same time, rapidly deteriorating conditions of workers in these societies force workers to resort to homosexuality because of their material needs. In the USSR, on the contrary, it is not an issue – in the USSR death rates are decreasing and birth-rates are increasing.

I have always considered it wrong to put forward a separate slogan for the liberation of homosexuals because I believe that the issue of homosexual liberation is inseparable from the general struggle for the liberation of the whole humankind from capitalist oppression. I have never intended to create a problem out of it. However, the current realities put forward the issue and I consider it essential to achieve fundamental clarity on it.

Comrade Borodin told me that my homosexuality does not diminish my worth as a revolutionary. Before the publication of the law, OGPU officials told me that they also had nothing against me. A psychiatrist I know refused to believe that sodomy laws existed until I showed him a copy of it. It is clear that, prior to the publication of the law, the public had not been hostile towards homosexuals. And that fact did not surprise me at all.

I have also consulted the *Great Soviet Encyclopaedia*, which contains official viewpoints of the Soviet public on various issues. Comrade Borodin pointed out to me that I should not pay much attention to the entry on homosexuality in it, because, according to him, the author was a homosexual himself. Firstly, I don't think that I should treat the history of the Communist Party with suspicion only because it was written by a communist. Secondly, I am too familiar with the rigorous political control over the press exercised in the USSR to believe that a flawed article could be allowed for publication in a book like the *Great Soviet Encyclopaedia*. Such oversight is possible in insignificant newspapers and journals, but not in the *Great Soviet Encyclopaedia*.

I have visited two psychiatrists inquiring if it was possible to get a cure for homosexuality. You will be probably surprised to hear that, but I really did not want to run afoul of the Soviet legislation. I was ready to do anything to avoid doing that. But if this type of cure really existed, everything would have been so much simpler. However, I am afraid, most people will never be normal in a sexual sense. My fears are well substantiated by the examples in history. I would like to remind you that homosexuals constitute only 2 per cent of the whole population, among whom there were people like Socrates, Leonardo da Vinci, Michelangelo, Shakespeare and Tchaikovsky. In no way am I going to defend the absurd theory thereby homosexuals are superhuman and that genius is synonymous with homosexuality. But I suppose that some talents, especially talents in the world of arts, are strikingly compatible with homosexuality and we should bear that in mind.

When both psychiatrists whom I visited admitted that there are cases of incurable homosexuality, I have finally established my own attitude towards the issue. Indeed, I think it is important to admit that there are cases of incurable homosexuality and such a minority will inevitably be part of any society. One should not, therefore, prosecute these people for their distinctive characteristics that they are in no way responsible for. They cannot get rid of them even if they wanted to.

Hence, trying to reason in accordance with the principles of Marxism-Leninism, I now realize that my arguments run against the existing legislation and it is this fact that makes me ask for your authoritative statement on this matter.

With communist greetings,

Harry Whyte[13]

Stalin did read Harry's letter. And he was not impressed. The naive Scot caused nothing but ridicule and contempt on the part of the dictator. Stalin scribbled on the letter:

IN THE ARCHIVE. IDIOT AND DEGENERATE. JOSEPH STALIN.

Devoid of sympathy to millions of people of the USSR, whom he ordered to be shot or sent to die in the GULAG, Stalin surely had no special sympathy for people like Harry.

Stalin learned about the existence of homosexuality during his stints in tsarist prisons in the early 1900s. Homosexual activity there usually occurred thus: older and more experienced prisoners brutally raped young newcomers, who then acquired the status of "pederast" – a man, sexually available to male prisoners and forced into submissive roles by them. Being on the lowest rung of the prison system, "pederasts" might also start prostituting or offering themselves to other prisoners in order to survive. There was another way to become a "pederast" – if a prisoner failed to conform to the code of prisoners' norms. Usually, such prisoners were also raped and sexually humiliated.[14]

That both Yagoda and Stalin used the word "pederasty" demonstrates the extent and perhaps limits of their knowledge on homosexuality and hints at its provenance. It also shows the associations that they had with this word and thus makes Stalin's reaction to Harry Whyte's letter hardly surprising. Stalin apparently imagined homosexuality or "sodomy" as an infection of degradation, which emerged in prisons and could spread into the army and navy.

Harry never received any response from Stalin. In 1935, he left Moscow and the USSR.

3

A young man from Siberia comes to Moscow in pursuit of his dreams

Moscow, 1937

The year 1937 was a special one for Sasha Petrov, a young man of nineteen years old.[1] This was the year Sasha was admitted to the Moscow Glazunov School, a prestigious institute for aspiring actors. Born in Blagoveshensk, a far-flung town of around sixty thousand people near Siberia's border with China, Sasha had always dreamt of leaving it as soon as possible to pursue his career as an actor in Moscow. When actors from Moscow came to Blagoveshensk on tours, Sasha always wished for them to take him with them. Sasha's parents, however, never approved of his desire to be an actor as they thought that a job like that was too precarious and, besides, they didn't want him to leave.

By the time he'd finished school, they had resigned themselves to the idea and gave him money for the train fare. In 1937, Sasha bought his train ticket and set off on the long railway journey from Siberia to Moscow, which took almost five days. As the train rattled along the track, Sasha watched the forests and sprawling fields rush by, imagining his new life in the USSR's capital.

The entrance exam for the university was an audition, during which Sasha had to read poetry and prose, dance and play music as well as showcase any other stage talent he possessed to impress the panel of distinguished actors. And Sasha did, because after the auditions he found his name on a shortlist of those who passed on the wall outside the auditorium.

The year 1937 was also one when people in Moscow and other big cities started disappearing. These night-time disappearances were caused by arrests conducted by Stalin's secret police – the NKVD. A secret-police automobile would pull up to an apartment block, under cover of darkness, and two or three men in black coats would emerge. They would silently locate the apartment in question, tap on the door and wake up the family. They would then sternly explain that a family member was accused of some political crime. They would search the apartment, turning everything upside down. Finally, they would order the accused to pick up their belongings and come with them. Many of the accused never needed any of their belongings as they were shot a few hours later. Others were sent to the camps. Those who disappeared at night generally never came back.

This period of Soviet history was dubbed the time of Great Terror, the height of which took place in 1937. The list of victims of the Great Terror ranged from high-ranking officials and military generals whom Stalin suspected of disloyalty, to ordinary people. The latter could be charged with espionage for a careless chat about foreign singers or conspiracy against the Soviet regime for something as innocuous as accidentally stepping on a piece of newspaper with Stalin's photo. Fear and suspicion were everywhere – people eavesdropped and wrote denunciations of their neighbours and friends – some thinking that it would protect them from repressions, others because it served their interests. And this was the time when Sasha was about to fulfil his dream.

The USSR was not the only country in the 1930s where terror and mass arrests of innocent people were occurring. In 1933, the Nazis under Adolf Hitler came to power and unleashed mass repressions of anyone deemed "dangerous" to the new regime: political opponents, German Jews, Jehovah's Witnesses and homosexuals. The Nazi government closed most bars for homosexual men and women, shut down the homosexual publishing industry and sent thousands of homosexual men to prisons and concentration camps.[2] Apart from establishing a totalitarian dictatorship in Germany, Hitler also set his sights on conquering Europe. From the very beginning of his regime, Hitler had been expanding German military forces, brazenly violating the provisions of the Treaty of Versailles, which a defeated Germany had signed after the end of the First World War. Britain, France and the League of Nations condemned Hitler's actions, but failed to do anything to stop him. In the USSR, Soviet leaders were also anxiously watching the growth of the military prowess of Hitler.

But for Sasha all these things did not matter – theatre and acting classes became the focal point of his life. These were his world now. From early morning to late evening he attended classes and rehearsals, hardly having time to eat. The routine of the theatrical actor was tougher than he thought, yet Sasha still devoted himself to it fully. He was however becoming concerned that he had no free time to get a job and earn money. The grant that he was receiving was very meagre and was not enough for him to pay his parents back for the ticket. But such was the cost of his dream and he had to make sacrifices.

Rehearsals continued almost until midnight and Sasha was exhausted by the end of the day. On one warm autumn day, he met twenty-three-year-old Pavel, who studied in the same institute. At the entrance of the school, where students gathered after classes to have a smoke, Pavel introduced himself to Sasha. After a short friendly conversation, Pavel invited him to explore the city on foot.

Sasha had not seen much of Moscow and readily accepted Pavel's invitation. They went to Red Square and rode the recently opened metro together. Sasha thoroughly enjoyed the city as well as the company of Pavel, who turned out to be a good listener and before long endeared himself to Sasha. Sasha confided to Pavel his dreams of becoming an actor and touring the USSR and possibly seeing the world. And Pavel was listening to him carefully and was nodding in response.

After that day they began to see each other more often. They would stroll around Moscow after classes until late, even though both had to be up early for classes and rehearsals. During one of their walks down the central Arbat Street, a pedestrian stretch flanked by shopping boutiques in the historical centre of Moscow, Pavel started a conversation, which struck Sasha as unusual at first. Sasha later recalled its details:

he [Pavel] told me that a female actor can get a job in the theatre if the director fancies her, and a male actor can get a job if some old actress or a man who cohabits with other men fancies him too ... Then he told me that he knows one famous actor... he told me he could introduce me to him. He also said that this actor helps him financially.[3]

Their conversation slowly veered towards the topic of same-sex love between men, and Pavel ambiguously hinted that he liked to engage in relations like these as well. Then he unexpectedly asked Sasha whether he was also like that. Pavel later recalled this moment: "I asked him if he was into sodomy and he did not want to admit it at first, but then he said yes."[4] Having verified that Sasha was like him, Pavel offered to take him to see the places where people like themselves could meet.

Sasha nodded and they continued walking, soon reaching and entering a dark park, with only lamp-posts providing a little light. Some couples sat on benches while others strolled past. The park was flanked by roads and opulent tenement blocks on each side and there were many trees. At the entrance to the park there stood a monument to the Russian chemist Temiryazev, and there was also a small building – a public toilet, an underground one.

Suddenly a man appeared. He hesitated at the entrance, carefully looking to the right and then to the left. It seemed to Sasha as if he were either waiting for someone or making sure that nobody was watching him. The man disappeared into the toilet.

Pavel explained to Sasha that this was one of the places where men like themselves could meet for sex. He also mentioned that they could meet men like that in other places nearby such as Nikitsky Boulevard, Trubnaya Square, a bar on Arbat Street and in Moscow's bathhouses.[5]

What Pavel was showing to Sasha was the remnants of the homosexual subculture which had long existed in Moscow. Indeed, although during tsarist times sodomy was a crime, there were many ways in which Russian homosexual men found and had sexual relations with each other.

As early as the 1800s, privileged merchants and other members of the upper class, who often had wives, went to commercial bathhouses, where many young attendants were available for sex. These attendants were peasant workers, who came to Moscow in search of opportunities. Some of them provided sex services for an additional fee, others because they derived pleasure from such sex. Rich merchants also solicited sex from waiters in restaurants, who could also either charge a fee or have sex because such relations brought them pleasure.[6]

Starting from around the 1870s, homosexual relations and sex in large Russian cities became more widespread. Such relations were no longer limited to interactions between members of the upper class and peasants. Homosexual city dwellers were slowly learning how to meet others like themselves in parks and public toilets, where they displayed themselves and showed their willingness to meet other men like them. After 1917, the homosexual scene in large Soviet cities underwent some changes. The economic crisis which ensued, along with the Bolsheviks' desire to cleanse restaurants and bathhouses of illicit sexual activity drove homosexuals to parks and especially public toilets.[7]

Despite the Stalin-era atmosphere of mutual surveillance, suspicion and fear, men who wanted other men still managed to live out their lives. Pavel, for example, preferred to meet new partners in the toilets. There was one on Trubnaya Square which he particularly liked. In this toilet, there were no doors in the cubicles, so everybody could watch each other. It helped facilitate acquaintances, but at the same time it was impossible to proceed if one wanted privacy. And yet Pavel had managed to meet many other men like himself in this toilet.

During the following weeks Sasha and Pavel took strolls and met acquaintances like these many times. One day, they had sex at Pavel's apartment and, although they became more intimate, both had no desire whatsoever to be more closely committed. After sex, they would have a smoke and talk about the theatre and their theatrical routines, discussing their classmates and wondering who was like them and who was not.

Their relationship continued for almost a year. In the summer of 1939, Pavel graduated from the theatre school and had to leave Moscow for Khabarovsk, where he would have to work in the local theatre for two years. Education was free in the USSR, but with one caveat – after graduation the person would be assigned to a particular position anywhere in the Soviet Union, usually for three years. Refusal to do that would certainly warrant a criminal prosecution.

Pavel's departure did not sadden Sasha; instead he was eager to explore places and meet men by himself. He grew bolder – not only did he go to public toilets by himself, but he also approached fellow students and tried to solicit sex from them. That was a risky move, but Sasha enjoyed the adrenaline and he also found it hard to resist some of the good-looking students around him. He was also convinced that there were many other men like him in the university so the risk was, he felt, minimal.

There was a student, Ivan, who entered the university the same year as Sasha and whom Sasha fancied. Sasha made the first move – just as Pavel had done to him once, Sasha introduced himself to Ivan and offered his friendship. Having conversations with Ivan about the theatre, he occasionally attempted to steer the topic of the conversation towards homosexual relationships between men to test Ivan's reaction. They usually had these conversations during the breaks at the university as well as at Sasha's flat. One day, Sasha confessed to Ivan that he preferred men and that they attracted him more than women. Ivan pretended that he did not understand what his friend was trying to tell him on this occasion and their friendship continued as usual.[8]

One day, however, Sasha made another bold step – when both of them were in the university's toilet Sasha asked Ivan to have sex. Ivan latter recalled this incident thus:

> One day I went into the toilet of the music school. Sasha came in with me
> and directly invited me to have sexual intercourse with him. I was supposed
> to play the role of the woman, and Sasha the role of the man. His offer
> took me by surprise and I refused to engage in such sexual intercourse.[9]

Sasha's bold ways led him to try the same tactic with other students, and soon rumours about his sexual tastes began to circulate in the university.[10] Rumours in the late 1930s could easily land someone in jail, but Sasha was unaware of this. Sometimes he couldn't control his homosexual impulses, which he had had to suppress for such a long time.

Sasha managed to meet other men in the years from 1938 to 1941, in which time he had accumulated many acquaintances, whose names he wrote down in his small notebook. Sasha's burgeoning homosexual life was unfolding during an extraordinary time, amid repressions and night-time disappearances at home and growing tensions abroad. In 1938, Hitler, whose power and influence had grown significantly, invaded and annexed Austria. Stalin clearly saw Hitler as a growing threat, and, hoping to buy some time before Germany's inevitable attack on the USSR, began negotiations with the Nazis. In August 1939, Stalin signed a non-aggression pact with Germany.

In September 1939, Hitler invaded Poland, initiating what was to become the Second World War. Following Germany's attack on Poland, France and Britain declared war on Hitler. This, however, did not stop him invading Belgium, the Netherlands, Luxembourg and France in 1940. Defeating France and having conquered a large swathe of Western Europe, Hitler was now ready for Germany's expansion to the east, covertly preparing an attack on the USSR.

In February 1941, several months before the beginning of Hitler's attack on the USSR, someone denounced Sasha. Denunciations and arrests out of the blue were not a rarity in the USSR under Stalin. The NKVD officers stormed into Sasha's flat in the centre of Moscow, rummaged through his apartment and turned everything upside down. They came across his small notebook with telephone numbers and street addresses. Realizing that they had a narrow window of opportunity, they immediately checked these addresses and found men with whom Sasha had had sex. Sasha was delivered to the NKVD building, where his mug shots and fingerprints were taken.

At first Sasha was reluctant to confess to his crime even though the investigator initially tried to be friendly with him. But the investigator soon lost patience and adopted a more threatening approach to the interview. Sasha succumbed to pressure and testified against other men, revealing their names. The investigators found and interrogated all these men within a short period of time.

Under Stalin, to secure a person's conviction, a self-incriminatory confession was sufficient. In fact, a great number of criminal cases which the NKVD opened during the Great Terror were based on such confessions, which NKVD officers beat out of the accused. There was no need for a careful and impartial investigation. The basis for Sasha's case was made up of his own confessions and confessions of other men, some of whom were asked to testify as his victims. These materials were transferred to a court.

The Great Terror unleashed by Stalin meant that conventional Soviet justice was severely compromised, because the government was more focused on accusing, repressing and executing people than on troubling itself with proper investigative procedures. However, conventional courts still existed, and maintained some semblance of justice.

Stalin, who remained committed to instilling fear and obtaining complete obedience from his people, was also concerned about the USSR's international reputation and believed that the operation of conventional justice made the USSR seem like a "normal state".[11] Sasha's case was also heard in a seemingly "normal" court session: there was a judge, the accused, the eyewitnesses, the prosecutor and the advocate in the courtroom. Sasha's friend Pavel was also detained in Khabarovsk and delivered to Moscow to stand trial.

Under Stalin, as well as throughout the whole existence of the USSR, advocates had little power to overturn a prosecution. As extra-judicial terror was becoming the new normal, advocates were needed merely for the semblance of a judicial process. The notorious prosecutor general of the USSR, Andrei Vyshinskii, who himself handed down numerous death sentences to innocent people, constantly criticized Soviet advocates for their desire to defend the interests of the client to the detriment of the Soviet state. According to him, the advocates' job was to defend their clients, but they should not oppose the interests of the state. Advocates, who feared losing their jobs and ending up on trial themselves, had little desire to oppose the arguments of the prosecutor.

In one high-profile show trial, which took place in November to December of 1930, known in history as the Industrial Party Trial, advocates demonstrated the "perfect" behaviour of Soviet advocates, which the state expected from them. The presiding judge was Andrei Vyshinskii himself and the defendants were a group of notable Soviet economists and engineers, who were accused on trumped-up charges of state treason. Instead of presenting the prosecutor with evidence of their clients' innocence, one of the advocates merely congratulated him on his historical accusatorial speech and meekly noted that physical liquidation of his client, on which the prosecution insisted, was unnecessary. In this way, the advocate's behaviour was perfect – he did not challenge the prosecution, although he sought to mitigate his client's sentence.[12]

Sasha and other men accused of sodomy could expect even less from their advocates who were not only reluctant to jeopardize their position but significantly uninformed about the legal practice around the sodomy law. The crime of sodomy was a new phenomenon and there was no guidance or instructions on how to defend such clients, so they had to rely on their own understanding of these cases. There was considerable confusion among advocates and judges as to what constituted sodomy and, in some cases, those who were established to have had only oral sex were convicted under the law of sodomy.

On 22 June 1941, Hitler's army launched an attack on the USSR. Five days later, on 27 June 1941, Sasha stood trial. In court Sasha admitted his guilt only partially. He said:

> I have never had any desire for sodomy and I have always tried to snatch this dirt out of me … I just wanted to strike up acquaintances among the actors. I wanted to get a job in the theatre and that is why I started doing this. I wanted to tell my mother or a doctor, but I was too afraid to tell anybody about that. I was too ashamed … I was scared that I would get arrested.[13]

Sasha argued that he engaged in sodomy with Pavel out of monetary considerations:

> He told me that he could introduce me to an actor who was helping him financially. For example, he paid for his birthday celebrations. Then Pavel came to my house and began to persuade me to have sexual intercourse. My financial situation was poor and I agreed. I played a passive role and

then he asked me to play an active role but I failed ... Then he paid several times for me at a café. Then he invited me to a bar on Trubnaya Square, but I refused.[14]

Pavel, however, admitted his guilt completely, revealing that he had learned of Sasha's inclinations from his former lover Andrei. Once Sasha appeared at the theatre institute, Andrei had pointed him out to Pavel, confidently saying that Sasha was like them. Pavel also confessed in court that he started having an attraction to men at the age of twenty-one. Before this age, he did not feel confident about acting on his desires, but then he finally surrendered himself to them.

Other men with whom Pavel and Sasha had sex were also present at the court hearing. Some of them were classified as victims, but some of them also received prison sentences. One of them was Mikhail Brusnikin, a thirty-year-old man, whom Pavel met thus:

I met Brusnikin on Trubnaya Square in the toilet. He looked at me and I looked at him. We both smiled and went out of the toilet. He invited me to his place and I went. In his flat, we drank wine and then had sexual intercourse. I played a passive role.[15]

Brusnikin also tried to justify himself in court blaming his sexual attraction for men on the alcohol:

All the acts of sodomy that I committed, I did them all when I was drunk. I drink, because I feel lonely and that makes me feel depressed so I find solace in wine. I had a wife as well – I lived with her from 1929 to 1939, but to be honest, with big intervals in between. I am still attracted to women, but when I drink wine, men attract me more. Maybe it is because I am schizophrenic. You see, when I am sober, the acts of sodomy seem disgusting to me.[16]

The court sentenced Sasha to six years' imprisonment. Other men also received similar sentences. Sasha's dream of becoming an actor was not destined to become true.

4

A Soviet celebrity leads a double life and lives in quiet suffering

Moscow, 1940

Vadim Kozin was probably the most popular Soviet singer of the 1930s. Although he mostly performed on stage, the advent of recorded music, radio and gramophones quickly helped his fame spread across the country and made him a household name. As with the early Frank Sinatra, at his concerts people screamed excitedly and cried out for joy when he appeared on stage. They held out their hands in a desperate attempt to touch him and very often during and after concerts police had to hold back the crowds from the concert halls. Kozin had all the love of the Soviet people and he revelled in it.

Although Kozin's songs enjoyed immense popularity, he often drew criticism from high-ranking party officials for being too sentimental and lacking real socialist spirit. Party officials believed that a true socialist singer would want to sing about Soviet workers and glorify their selfless labour for the sake of the Motherland. Kozin's music was very different – it was about romantic feelings, the subtle nuances of human existence and life, joy and pain, hope and suffering.[1] Kozin always appeared on stage in an elegant brown suit with a sparkling diamond in his buttonhole and a silk handkerchief in his hand. He was loved and admired by a great many Soviet people – workers, collective farmers, civil servants and even Red Army soldiers and their commanders, who were sick of the official propagandistic songs.

Spoilt by fame and the unconditional love of his adoring public, Kozin behaved very often like a petulant diva. He hated microphones and literally declared a war on them. He would perform only on a stage without microphones and demanded that they be removed from the stage before his appearance. If the concert organizers failed to comply with this requirement, Kozin might simply refuse to appear on stage despite the waiting audience. At one concert, the organizers dared to ignore Kozin's request and left the microphone on stage. Kozin, unaware at first, started singing until half-way through the song, when he spotted the microphone a few metres away. With an angry glance backstage, and to everyone's astonishment, he cut short his song and stormed off the stage. Bewildered concert organizers rushed to the microphone and swiftly removed it. A few minutes later, Kozin reappeared on stage, smiling and ready to sing again.[2]

Kozin was also notorious for cancelling his concerts at short notice and on a whim, disappointing his fans and putting concert organizers in the awkward position of having to explain what had happened. The singer also charged exorbitant fees for his concerts from the theatres which staged his events, and he had a list of strict requirements they had to fulfil in preparation for his arrival. Much like a temperamental opera diva or pop singer wanting to test their power, he demanded for example that his dressing room be laid with carpets and adorned with bouquets of flowers.

Most people were unaware that Kozin's difficult character and instability were the result of his constant emotional turmoil and a deep sense of unhappiness. Despite all the love and adulation he enjoyed, Kozin felt inadequate in Soviet society and extremely vulnerable. The main reason for this was his hidden emotional and physical attraction to handsome men, which he'd felt since childhood. When Kozin first became aware of these feelings, he was frightened and confused. After unsuccessfully trying to subdue his desire, by his mid-twenties he finally gave in and allowed himself the freedom to experiment. His first sexual experience with another man occurred during one of his first tours around the USSR, which Kozin described thus:

> In our group there was an acrobatic trio: a husband, a wife and her husband's brother, a young interesting man of twenty-six, a little older than me. He was very pale, seemed aloof, he liked spending time on his own and never

smoked. And since I did not smoke either, I had to share the same room with him for the entirety of our six-month trip. One night, a month into our concert trip, we stayed at a hotel – in a room where there was only one wide bed with a couch. He ordered me to go into his bed. "Tell me, how do you like it? I know you like me and I like you too. But what kind of person are you, tell me frankly, and I will tell you what kind of person I am. How have you been living so far?" I told him everything with frankness. He hugged me tightly, kissed me and said: "Sleep tonight and tomorrow we will talk some more."[3]

Over several days he explained to me all the "intricacies", but no matter how hard he tried to make me play an active [that is, insertive] role, I always failed. Several times I played a passive role for him, but I derived no pleasure from it and told him that frankly I didn't want him to do that to me any more. It gave me pleasure just to lie next to him and then masturbate myself while he was asleep. One night he caught me doing this and started kissing me. "Now I see that you like something. I am the same, sometimes I like to fantasize about men and masturbate." After this conversation we continued to share the bed, but there were no more physical touches between us.[4]

As Kozin's career began to blossom and he started performing in Moscow, the number of his fans grew exponentially. They lay in wait for him at the stage door after concerts, screaming wildly and rushing towards him with flowers and pieces of paper for an autograph. Both men and women declared their love for him and desired him. And sometimes Kozin made a veiled invitation to handsome men to his hotel room after the concert. But due to his shame and self-restraint, he never managed to live out his sexual fantasies:

Although I fancy young men and in my fantasies I play a passive role with them, in reality, when being next to them, I can only masturbate myself. Sometimes sitting and having a conversation with a man is already enough. When he leaves, I fantasize about him and masturbate as well … A man can lie or sleep next to me and I won't touch him – I will just derive pleasure from his presence.[5]

By the age of thirty, Kozin had come to terms with his desire and resigned himself to the fact that this was something he would have to live with:

I realized that I was an abnormal and deficient person. My approaches to men were bolder and I knew that at worst they would scold me as a psychopath ... but as far as women were concerned, the remnants of my male self could not bear the feeling of shame for my deficiency ... I became embittered.[6] During the height of my popularity in Moscow, before the war, I was surrounded by crowds of young people. I often sat with them in restaurants, paid for everybody's dinner and then retreated to my hotel room. I didn't need any of them, I thought, let them celebrate my youth and have fun. 100 or 200 rubles was nothing for me [the average monthly salary of a Soviet worker], because I earned up to 125,000 rubles a month! That is probably why rumours circulated that I was corrupting the youth.[7]

Although the secret police were aware of Kozin's sexual trysts with his fans – after all, the luxurious Hotel Metropol, at the heart of Moscow, where Kozin resided, was heavily bugged – they didn't touch him. Until one day. In December 1944, shortly after Stalin's birthday and a few months before Nazi Germany's defeat in the Second World War, the chief of the NKVD, Lavrentii Beria, summoned Kozin to his residence for a conversation about his songs.

A close associate of Stalin, Beria was as feared as Stalin himself. For many decades he had orchestrated the bloodiest purges and with the stroke of a pen sent thousands of Soviet citizens to the GULAG, torture and execution. Even Red Army commanders feared him – they called being purged "having a coffee with Beria". Apart from being a wicked murderer, Beria also had a penchant for debauchery – just like his predecessors in the job. He preyed on young women, snatched by his bodyguards from the streets and delivered to a town house where Beria raped them. "Scream or don't, I don't care," he would say to his numerous victims, "think and behave accordingly". After being raped, the women would receive a bouquet of flowers from Beria's bodyguard – a sign that the sex had been "consensual". Those who dared to try to resist were thrown in jail.[8]

Beria of course knew about Kozin's homosexuality, and as a heterosexual rapist he took the moral high ground, despising Kozin for it. The singer's mannerisms also annoyed and disgusted him, but during the meeting with Kozin he didn't show it.

"So, Vadim, tell me, what do you sing these days?" Beria asked.

Vadim hummed the tune of his only song which glorified the Soviet state.

"And that's all?" Beria asked in surprise. He expected Kozin to have more political songs in his repertoire.

"Yes," Kozin answered somewhat indifferently.

"Well … you need to prepare a song for him," Beria said, gesturing towards the portrait of Stalin on the wall. "He will be very pleased."

"I am a lyrical singer and I am not going to sing anything else."

Beria smiled.

"Are you sure?" The question sounded like a threat.

"Yes."

"Are you one hundred per cent sure?" Beria asked more seriously.

"Yes, I am not going to."

"All right, you can leave. Let's pretend this conversation never happened."[9]

A few weeks later, the NKVD signed an order for Kozin's arrest. In February 1945, at the age of forty-two, Kozin was sentenced to eight years' imprisonment for counter-revolutionary agitation in wartime, depraved acts with minors and sodomy. He was sent to the Magadan labour camp, one of the deadliest and most feared of Stalin's GULAG complexes, where isolation from the rest of the world, polar temperatures and dire living conditions contributed to high death rates among prisoners.[10]

But Kozin's exceptional talent and fame saved him from death. Aleksandra Gridasova, the wife of one of Magadan GULAG chiefs, Ivan Nikishov, ran the camp's cultural activities and took jailed artists and singers under her patronage. With Gridasova's assistance, Kozin was allowed to perform in Magadan's Musical-Dramatic Theatre and his concerts enjoyed immense popularity among the locals. But even though Kozin continued to perform, he was still a GULAG prisoner and his life was at the mercy of Magadan GULAG commandants.

One night Kozin performed at a closed concert for Magadan's police officers and GULAG chiefs. The audience were already liquored up by the time the concert started. The curtains parted, revealing Kozin leaning against the piano and surrounded by bouquets of flowers. The audience froze for a moment and then burst into applause. Then someone in the crowd shouted: "Hooray to Kozin!" Others in the audience picked it up and started screaming "Hooray!" "Hooray!"

Suddenly General Nikishov rose drunkenly from his VIP box, and, trying to steady himself, screamed furiously "Who are you shouting 'Hooray' to?" The audience instantly fell silent and looked in his direction.

"Who are you shouting 'Hooray' to? That faggot?" he shouted, pointing at a terrified Kozin. "You can only shout 'Hooray' for our government! Remove the idiot from the audience! And you!" – he threw an angry look in the direction of Kozin – "Off the stage!"

"Who? Me?" asked Kozin feebly.

"Yes, you! Straight to the punishment cell!" Nikishov barked.

Kozin rushed off the stage to the dressing room and Aleksandra Gridasova rushed after him.

"Vadim Alekseevich, don't worry – no punishment cell – I will sort everything out!", she said, trying to calm him down. She immediately made a phone call to someone and Kozin was taken to an infirmary in the camp, where he spent the subsequent month pretending to be ill. Once everyone had begun to forget about this incident, Kozin returned to the stage – although the humiliating experience lingered in his memory for a long time.[11]

Kozin was released in 1950 but, instead of returning to Moscow, he chose to work as an artist and a librarian in the camp's cultural facilities. After Stalin's death in 1953, Kozin gradually returned to performing. In 1955, at the age of fifty-two, together with the Magadan troupe, Kozin began touring the region.

By this time, Kozin was no longer at odds with his desire. He had accepted it and learnt how to live with it. Even so he was annoyed with the members of his troupe, all of whom were aware of his sexual orientation and badmouthed him behind his back. In 1955, Kozin expressed his indignation in his diary:

> The weather is getting on my nerves ... And the same has to be said for the low level of culture of our artistes. I am constantly trying to understand why. The point of all their conversations, in the end, leads to bawdiness,

double-entendres, coarse jokes. Not just the men, but the women too enjoy this "subject". Despite what they consider to be "my profound moral downfall" it would never enter my head to say such things in company; me, a man of 50, I honestly get quite nauseated listening to their conversations. And these people – the men and the women – believe they are not violating any norms of public morality! To hell with such morality and ethics! It's real, sanctimonious, hypocrisy, of the type that leads to the decline and degeneration of the personality. No, I've got to keep myself apart from them, have fewer points of contact with them.[12]

The acceptance of his desire helped Kozin develop a certain homosexual awareness and understanding that he was a victim of the state's oppression. In his diary, Kozin described an incident which befell him in the military town of Svirsk in August 1955:

Backstage a young man addressed me, Kuvshinov Fedor Grigorevich – a member of the amateur drama group of the Bokhansky district house of culture. He says he won third place in a Russian song contest in Irkutsk. He looks about 29, speaks with a womanish voice, his language is a bit mentally immature, or more truthfully, half-masculine and half-feminine. He walked up to me and naively asked me in a childish voice, "Can I join your brigade of artistes?" "What do you know how to do?" "I can sing Russian songs, but my luck is bad, there was a lucky fellow, he got hired by Cheremovsky theater, he gets 350 rubles there. If only that would happen to me, how happy I would be…"

Kozin also expressed hatred towards the Soviet regime and its homophobia as well as the existing perceptions in society that sexual deviations could be corrected if the person possessing them only engaged in active labour:

I closed my eyes and listened to this peasant-woman's voice and intonation … what could I say to this 30-year-old unmarried man who didn't understand his situation and wanted to escape from misery into the world of art? This innocent stepchild of nature, guilty of nothing whatsoever. He was afraid of IT, but he had to adhere to one or the other sex, and here, in this god-forsaken hole, he became what I saw before me. A man lacking in culture is twice as unfortunate in this situation. He suffers from persecution, mockery, and he resembles a hen that crows like a cockerel. Surely [s]he is not to blame? Some experts pronounce ex cathedra that all these problems can be solved by working up a decent sweat! Moronic, self-satisfied chatterers, for whom the sufferings of such unfortunates are alien and incomprehensible, they are in an appalling situation, persecuted and punished, and for what? For a joke and mistake of nature. It drives me to distraction, this moronic slogan: labor is the most radical medicine! The idiots! I'd like to see these fat chatterers with their "scientific theories" be forced to work up a decent sweat and then see whether they are in any fit state to make it on top of a dame![13]

Kozin even tried to console himself that his homosexuality was a sign not of his degeneration, as society was telling him, but of his being a highly talented person:

However strange it may seem, this almost unnatural combination of genius with a multiplicity of vices and faults that offend all the norms of morality and behavior invented by people themselves, has existed, exists, and will exist for all time. Such is human nature. Deviations from the norm are the lot of highly gifted people. Genius always comes hand in hand with abnormality. Abnormality always expresses itself in very diverse ways in every talented and gifted person... Tchaikovsky's perversion, persecuted by the law, did not however prevent him from musical works of genius, filled with the kind of emotional content of which Rimsky-Korsakov was incapable; for he was less abnormal. And Gogol? Leonardo da Vinci? Chopin? What can one say ...?[14]

By the age of fifty Kozin had finally managed to overcome the shame that had always crippled him and finally come to the self-realization that he was capable of loving other men and having feelings for them as well:

I am out of my mind because of a man ... How I would love, for even just a moment, to look into the depths of those eyes. Why did they cross my path? Again those green eyes. As though I had him with me in my arms. Why did it happen like this? ... He took the place of everything. Who this man is, no one will ever find out. But I fell in love, like a schoolboy, like a love-struck girl ... How many years have passed, and now I see his fateful green eyes again, almost thirty years later. Again a tempest shatters my heart, like the start of spring, with the lilacs in blossom, and you are standing before a lush bouquet and touch it with my lips, to kiss its blossoms tirelessly, to drink the nectar, as it was thirty years ago. I will only let one man read these insane lines. Our life is ordered in a completely different way, and it is impossible to live the way one wishes to. Although in the life I would like to lead, there is nothing of the supernatural. There is good, genuine friendship, and complete trust in each other, forged with a feeling of such power that it overwhelms even passion and love. A firm handshake after the display of a drop of tenderness and friendship, and life becomes something else entirely. I am in floods of tears as I write these lines, for surely my dream will never come to pass and I will never touch the bouquet of youth and strength? If only life could be different, what a cult of personality he would garner. The man with the green eyes.[15]

Despite greater self-acceptance and peace of mind, which Kozin finally reached by middle age, another misfortune awaited him. In October 1959, Kozin was giving a concert in Khabarovsk. One night, at the entrance of the Far East hotel, where Kozin was staying, he was greeted by a young, handsome man who seemed to appear out of nowhere. The man called himself Grisha; he said that he had been robbed and was wondering if Kozin could give him some money for a ticket back home. Kozin invited Grisha to his hotel room and handed him 50 rubles. Grisha seemed to be wanting something else so Kozin ordered food to the room and they had dinner. Then after drinking some wine, they lay on the bed.

What happened next only confirmed Kozin's suspicions that Grisha was a homosexual and, so it seemed, desired sexual intimacy with Kozin. What Kozin didn't suspect was that Grisha was a KGB informant, instructed to seduce and entrap him. After a couple of hours, plain-clothed KGB officers stormed into the room to find Grisha naked with Kozin in bed. Kozin realized that it was all a KGB trap.[16]

The KGB confiscated his diary and opened a new criminal case against him. Although Kozin spent only a few months in prison this time, he took the hint and abandoned any hope of returning to the stage. This second criminal case also shattered him emotionally – he couldn't overcome this second humiliation. He lived in Magadan until his death in 1994. After his release he was permitted to give only local concerts, and journalists were banned from mentioning his name in the press.[17] Like Oscar Wilde, imprisoned in Reading Gaol in the UK for his love for other men, the talented and extraordinary Vadim Kozin had been broken.

A visit to a bathhouse ends in a nightmare

Vologda, 1949

Although after defeating Nazi Germany in the war the USSR became one of the world's superpowers, the cost of the victory over the Germans was too high.[1] The war wrought utter devastation on the country, taking tens of millions of Soviet citizens' lives. Many of those who survived were injured or disabled for life. Many were emaciated due to pervasive insanitary conditions, chronic malnutrition and years of fierce fighting with the enemy. The war resulted in a severe disparity of men and women: in some rural areas there were only 28 men for every 100 women for the age category between eighteen and forty-nine. The unprecedented demographic crisis urged Stalin and his associates to come up with measures designed to remedy the situation. These included urging people to get married, using a system of incentives and penalties, and to raise families with many children.[2]

The living conditions of the vast majority of Soviet people were also appalling. Many people lived in overcrowded dormitories, barracks and communal flats. Most of them had little privacy for essential household activities such as bathing or washing clothes. Even in cities like Moscow most residential buildings had no indoor running water and sewerage, let alone central heating, so that residents were forced to mount primitive toilet facilities in their courtyards or in the streets. To keep themselves warm many people used wood-burning stoves.[3] Not surprisingly, opportunities for sex in such horrible conditions were slim for everyone.

Red closet

On 14 July 1949, forty-nine-year-old Grigorii Kravtsov walked out of a hotel in the city of Vologda, where he was staying for the duration of his concert trip with his theatre troupe and musicians from Leningrad. It was the last day of their stay in Vologda – Kravtsov's band had already played all their scheduled concerts in town, so he finally had some time to himself. He decided to go to the local bathhouse, or *banya* as they are called in Russia.[4]

Bathhouses were popular among Soviet people, especially given the lack of bathing facilities at many homes. Almost every Soviet city, no matter how big or small, had at least one public bathhouse, open for the paid use of visitors from afternoon to late evening. The layout of Soviet bathhouses was almost identical: there was a dressing and a sitting room, where visitors could undress and hang their clothes on hooks. Then, entirely naked, they would proceed to a tiled washing-room, where they would wash themselves using hand-held wash basins or under hot and cold water spigots. There was also a steam room in the bathhouse.[5]

Grigorii had already been in Vologda on many occasions and this bathhouse had been a favourite place of his – perfect for winding down after a hectic concert schedule. The bathhouse was located in one of the tall brick buildings adjacent to the local factory, whose employees were frequent visitors.

On this summer day Grigorii was lucky – there were no queues at the front and, in fact, it seemed there were few visitors. Having undressed in the locker room, Grigorii went straight into the steam room. There were some men there – but the steam was so thick that Grigorii could hardly see their faces. He closed his eyes for a moment, feeling the heat go through his body, and several moments later he went into the washing chamber.

In the corner of the chamber, Grigorii glimpsed a couple of young men – one was lying with his face down, while the other was soaping his back. Their loud voices echoed off the walls. Grigorii looked around the room in search of someone who could also assist him with washing and glimpsed a young man, who appeared to have just entered the chamber

as well. Their eyes met and in a few moments the man offered Grigorii
a back rub – men often soaped each other's backs in the bathhouse and
this often served as a basis for bonding and friendships. The young man
introduced himself as Vasilii and after washing, they decided to have
some beer and a chat outside the bathhouse. Soviet authorities condemned
and tried to discourage regular heavy drinking, but it was an entrenched
habit for many Soviet people, especially men. It provided them with a
respite from the hard life of postwar reconstruction and helped forge new
friendships too.[6]

There were many reasons why Grigorii was fond of going to the bathhouse. Obviously, washing and sitting in the steam room was good for
health and Grigorii genuinely enjoyed it – just like many other Soviet
people. But there was another, no less important reason: visits to *banyas*
provided men like Girgorii with a legitimate excuse to linger in the company
of naked men and strike up new acquaintances. Since *banyas* required
paid entry, they were safer than public toilets, parks, bus stations or
approaching strangers in the street. The complete nudity of visitors also
allowed Grigorii to spot men like himself immediately.

Grigorii and Vasilii left the bathhouse and headed to the nearest kiosk
for a beer. Beer finished, Grigorii was ready to go back to the hotel when
suddenly Vasilii offered to buy a bottle of vodka and go to a cabin on a
steamboat, docked nearby, where he worked. Grigorii readily accepted
the invitation.

Later that day, Grigorii woke up lying in the grass, wet through and
oblivious to what was going on. Straining his eyes, he saw a police officer,
standing over him and shaking him awake. Although he did not immediately come back to his senses, he realized he was in trouble. Grigorii
mumbled something. Sweat was running down his back and his face. His
throat was hot and he felt thirsty. The police officer picked him up,
handcuffed him and tumbled him into the back seat of his car.

At first Grigorii thought that he was being taken to a soberator, a place
where the police gathered drunks, gave them time to sleep it off and then
released them the following day. But once he found himself in the police

station, he knew he was in real trouble. Officers brought him into a dimly lit room with a small barred window and seated him in front of an investigator with a stern face. The investigator motioned police officers to step out of the room and then produced a piece of paper and pen from the drawer of his desk, pushing them across the table towards Grigorii. Later, Grigorii recalled in court:

> I regained consciousness next to the pier, in the grass, where a policeman shook me awake … I was lying all wet from head to toes … I was barefoot and could not recall anything. They took me to the police station in this terrible state and they charged me with sodomy there … Oshurkov [Vasilii] had allegedly testified that I had raped him. All this, of course, came as a complete surprise to me.[7]

Grigorii was shocked. Confession? Rape? What was he talking about? He strained his memory to recall what had happened. His head was throbbing – the room around him was spinning around and he felt like fainting for a moment. His wrists were aching from the handcuffs. Then, slowly, it started coming back to him. Bathhouse. The young man, Vasilii. Oshurkov. The steamboat. Vodka. Kissing and the rest. Grigorii denied all the accusations and refused to confess anything.

The interrogation seemed to last for ever. Grigorii categorically refused to plead guilty, trying to convince the investigator that he had been too drunk to have sexual intercourse with Vasilii:

> I categorically denied the charges against me. First, sexual intercourse could not take place because of my heart problems and the state I was in – drunk to the point of losing consciousness. Secondly, I am a family man, the father of three adult children, I lead a normal sexual life and do not suffer from any sexual deviations. I immediately started demanding forensic medical examination … but my requests were denied. I was told that Oshurkov had already undergone a medical examination and there is a medical certificate confirming that a sexual act between us has taken place.[8]

After several unsuccessful attempts to press Grigorii into self-incrimination, the investigators threw him into a detention cell, where he awaited trial.

Vasilii had been found drunk on the steamboat on the same day. The police escorted him to the station. He was handcuffed, and placed in a chair facing the same investigator. Vasilii recalled later:

> On the day I committed the so-called "crime", I was taken off the steamboat in a completely drunken state. Without allowing me to sober up, they immediately began interrogating me ... Inspector Gryaznykh forced me to confess to the crime, promising that (if I admitted to it) I would be reinstated at work.[9]

It did not take long for the investigator to press Vasilii Oshurkov into "confessing" – the young man had never dealt with the police before and he was willing to do anything to get himself out of trouble. He wrote an elaborate testimony detailing how he met Grigorii and what happened between them in the steamboat cabin. He also asserted that Grigorii had raped him. The investigator was content – he placed the report in his folder and ordered the other policeman to remove the handcuffs.

The court on Grigorii Kravtsov's case convened on 20 August 1949 behind closed doors like so many other cases involving sex crimes. There was a prosecutor, a young doctor, Tamara Feofanova, from the clinic who examined Vasilii, a secretary, the judge, the defendant, Grigorii Kravtsov, and the witness, Vasilii Oshurkov. As instructed by the investigator, Vasilii repeated his testimony in court, mentioning that Dr Feofanova had examined him and established that his claims were true.

Grigorii, who sat behind bars on the bench, stared at Vasilii in disbelief. He was convinced that he would not testify against him, but now he was determined to defend himself as desperately as he could. The next person to give testimony was Feofanova herself – a woman in her mid-twenties, who apparently had just begun her career as a doctor. She testified to the court that she indeed had examined Vasilii Oshurkov, but she did not say whether she had produced any specific conclusion. Grigorii recalled what happened at the court session:

> At the court session Oshurkov repeated his testimony, although without conviction and somewhat evasively. When I asked a young lady, the doctor [Feofanova], at the court sessions, whether she could confirm the fact that

sexual intercourse had taken place, she replied that she could not. She said she could only confirm that she had performed an external examination on Oshurkov and registered his complaints.[10]

A few moments later the judge announced a break and retreated into a discussion room. Once the judge disappeared from view, Feofanova rose from the bench. Blushing, she addressed the room:

> Why ... why did they draw me into that ...? I am not a forensic expert and I am not an expert in criminal cases. I am not competent in these cases at all. I had been refusing to give the medical conclusion and I recommended that the investigator consult forensic experts, who deal with such things ... and not me. But the investigator Gryaznykh insisted that I provide the medical conclusion about Oshurkov's medical examination. And now, I am put in a position, where I have to confirm my conclusions in writing.[11]

When the court session resumed, Kravtsov repeated Feofanova's words to the judge, but the man in the robe remained silent. He also reiterated his demands to be allowed to be examined by a forensic expert and not just a doctor from a local clinic.

The court declined his demands and explained that the materials of the case had been referred to a well-qualified forensic expert, who had already concluded that Kravtsov was capable of committing a sex act. An excerpt from the expert's report was read in court:

> As stated in the textbook by Professor Popov, a person who is slightly intoxicated is capable of performing sexual intercourse, while if heavily intoxicated the person is not. However, as can be seen from the case in question and the testimony of the victim himself, it is possible to assume that such an act took place.[12]

Kravtsov stood in his cage wide-eyed. How could they rely on a medical report if no medical examination had actually taken place? Kravtsov realized that the investigators were going to convict him at any cost and nothing was going to stop them. He sat down on the bench and buried his face in his hands.

Other witnesses continued giving testimony – these were the man and woman whom Kravtsov saw on the day of his interrogation. They turned out to be the captain of the steamer and a cook. Both of them denied that they had seen Oshurkov and Kravtsov in the act of having sex and said that they could not confirm that this had happened. The judge asked them many times if they had seen anything – but they said they had not.[13]

The court session was drawing to an end, and the judge disappeared into the discussion room. A few moments later he emerged to give the final verdict. Holding a thick folder, he pronounced Grigorii Kravtsov guilty of sodomy and sentenced him to four years' imprisonment. In a surprising turn of events, the judge pronounced Vasilii Oshurkov guilty as well and, despite promises of immunity given by the investigator, sentenced him to three years in prison.[14] Oshurkov, shocked and terrified, was handcuffed and taken into custody immediately after the verdict's announcement.

Although consensual sodomy continued to be a crime in the 1940s and 1950s, it was almost impossible for investigators to furnish evidence in such cases, unless the suspects were caught *in flagrante delicto*. If this was not the case, then investigators had to come up with other effective methods. Investigators like Gryaznykh, who led the case of Kravtsov and Oshurkov, found the one that worked for him. If both men were suspected of sodomy, then he pressed one suspect into testifying against the other, promising him immunity from prosecution, before eventually convicting both.

Soviet investigators indeed lacked scientific guidance on how to deal with consensual sodomy. Most manuals on forensic medicine from the Stalin era contained no clear instructions on how to investigate such cases. One popular manual on forensic medicine, authored by a prominent expert, Nikolai Popov, went so far as to admit that forensic experts could be of little help to investigators, since there were usually no identifiable traces of sodomy on the suspects' bodies.[15]

Just like the many other Soviet convicts who believed they had been treated unfairly by the court, Kravtsov and Oshurkov tried to appeal against the verdict the same year. Kravtsov wrote various lengthy letters to the Supreme Court of the USSR hoping to have his sentence overturned.

In this letter he drew the attention of the judges to the confession that Dr Feofanova made in his presence, while the judge was absent:

> It is quite clear that a young doctor, who is not versed in forensic medical science, could not provide a correct and objective conclusion and was influenced by the investigator. And from this, it follows that the conclusion given by such a doctor who is not a specialist does not deserve attention and trust and therefore cannot serve as evidence of the crime imputed to me ... The medical conclusion was compiled on the basis of the words and complaints of the drunk Oshurkov, who was escorted to the hospital, rather than on the basis of special laboratory studies.[16]

He then also commented on the behaviour of Oshurkov, who gave conflicting testimonies in court regarding what had happened between them:

> Oshurkov is significantly stronger than me and moreover on that day he was less drunk than me. Therefore, and naturally, I could not use violence against him. This fact refutes his false statement given during the preliminary investigation that I raped him. As a matter of fact, during the preliminary investigation Oshurkov said that I had raped him, and at the trial he said that he agreed to an act of sodomy. That is, initially he played the role of the victim, but then he started talking about our mutual consent, not assuming that both would be prosecuted. He probably believed that in case of mutual consent none of us would be prosecuted.[17]

Kravtsov then referred to the testimonies of the eyewitnesses, who, as he said, did not see anything and so their testimonies were useless.

The Supreme Court upheld the court's decision and Oshurkov's conviction remained unchanged. This was hardly surprising: in the late 1940s Soviet authorities unleashed a ferocious campaign against acquittals which led to their sharp decrease.[18] Likewise, after the war, Soviet authorities began to pay more attention to the quality of the preparation of criminal cases, paying particularly close attention to the returns of criminal cases for supplementary investigation and the fate of the accused.[19] Criminal cases which failed to produce a conviction were considered "failures in court". Such "failures" badly reflected on the reputation and professional profile of investigators, who tried to avoid them at all costs – even if the arguments for supplementary investigation seemed justified and unavoidable.[20]

This is why investigator Gryaznykh was so determined to make sure Kravtsov's case led to his and Oshurkov's conviction. He was well aware that, if the case was to fall apart, then his superiors would most certainly accuse him of "defective work" and his name would feature in all sorts of damning reports and official documents. But there was another, no less strong motivation on the part of Gryaznykh to convict both men – he despised homosexuals, or "pederasts" as he called them. To him, convicting such people was a matter of professional duty and honour – by putting them away he cleansed society of depravity, which they propagated.

Although the treatment of Soviet homosexuals could sometimes be very brutal it was not unique in this regard. For example, the police in Nazi Germany handled homosexuals in a similar way. Nazi police officers generally assumed that those accused of being homosexual were guilty. In order to extract confessions from homosexual suspects, the German police threw them in detention cells and kept them there for weeks. Homosexual suspects in Nazi Germany endured curses, threats, endless questioning and beating at the hands of police investigators, and were eventually forced to confess their "crimes".[21] Similarly in the US of the 1950s, many homosexual men and women when captured by the police would plead guilty even when the police had insufficient evidence to secure convictions.[22]

6

Soviet homosexuals travel to Siberia for "medical" treatment

Irkutsk, Siberia, 1952

Igor Stepanovich Sumbaev was a very successful psychiatrist whose fame went beyond the remote city of Irkutsk, lost somewhere in Siberia. In 1925, at the age of twenty-five, he graduated from the faculty of medicine of the Saratov State University and then went to Vienna, where he studied psychoanalysis under the celebrated Sigmund Freud. Freud's ideas had an important bearing on his views of human psychology and, even later when Freud's ideas were banned, Sumbaev still continued to espouse them.

That Sumbaev went to study under Freud was not so extraordinary. Pre-revolutionary Russia was one of the first countries to readily embrace Freud's theories of psychoanalysis. His books were published in Russia as early as 1904 and many Russian medical students, doctors and psychologists went to Europe to obtain training and broaden their horizons, resulting in the rising popularity of psychoanalysis across the country.[1]

The situation began to change after the revolution. By the end of the 1920s Freud's work came under criticism from Soviet authorities, who deplored and condemned its "bourgeois" nature. During the arrests and repressions of the 1930s, research into psychoanalysis and Freud's works in the USSR were completely banned.[2] The reason for the ban was simple – psychoanalysis and its tenets were completely at odds with the Soviet totalitarian regime. Stalin wished to instil in Soviet people unanimous total adherence to his rule as well as total intolerance towards the slightest deviations from the societal norms he established. Psychoanalysis, in contrast, would encourage Soviet people to become introspective in trying to understand themselves, while Stalin wanted people to idealize and worship his persona.

Many Soviet psychiatrists dabbling in psychoanalysis had now to abandon their pursuits for the sake of their own safety, but not Sumbaev, who continued to engage in it clandestinely. His dangerous interests did not preclude him from excelling in his professional career – in 1939 he was appointed head of the psychiatric clinic of the Siberian Medical Institute in Irkutsk. The clinic was a far cry from larger modern hospitals which could be found in big cities. In fact, it was merely a house made of logs with several rooms. But Sumbaev liked it the way it was and believed that one day it would become a major psychiatric hospital.

Apart from psychoanalysis and the workings of the human subconsciousness, there was another subject, no less problematic and controversial in the USSR, that fascinated Sumbaev. This subject was homosexuality. Sumbaev's first acquaintance with homosexuals occurred on 22 January 1932, when nineteen-year-old Petr turned up to his clinic. Petr came to the office with his stepfather, and both were embarrassed and initially refused to talk about the situation explicitly. Both were so upset that they could not even use any words to describe Petr's unmentionable "illness". Petr was seemingly ashamed of the presence of his father and, having gathered what was going on, Sumbaev asked his stepfather to leave them alone. Then Petr burst into tears, telling Sumbaev that he did not want to live and that he contemplated suicide.[3]

Sumbaev calmed the young man down and assured him that nothing he was going to say would go beyond the walls of the room. The young man pulled himself together and revealed why he was so anguished, confessing that he was attracted to men. After the conversation Sumbaev carefully noted down the patient's history:

> From the age of twelve he felt attraction to men rather than women, but at that time he did not yet realize that such an attraction was abnormal. Only at the age of fifteen did he clearly discern the essence of his illness. Usually sexual attraction emerged at the sight of men, including strangers. In this case, the patient immediately had to distance himself from men, feeling afraid of betraying his abnormal attraction in some way or even

disgracing himself ... He feels no sexual attraction to women, although he likes some of them as comrades. Until now, nobody has noted his perversion. In 1927, having learned that treatment for homosexuality was futile, he tried to commit suicide by hanging himself. The patient notes that he is always in a bad mood because of his perversion and he often cries when he is alone.[4]

Sumbaev assured the young man that he could help him, but the process of recovery was going to take some time. He also explained to him the method of treatment, which was called "free drawing". Petr had to prepare a series of drawings without any planning. Then, looking at his drawings, Petr would have to speak about whatever came into his head, while Sumbaev would try to understand his internal conflicts and feelings reflected in the drawings.[5]

Petr produced 155 drawings over the course of three months, and Sumbaev sat down with him to discuss them. From Petr's drawings, Sumbaev learnt that his patient did have a desire for women, but a subconscious one. In his article "On Psychotherapy for Homosexuality" (1936), Sumbaev wrote about this case:

After the patient understood this psychological mechanism, for the first time in his life, his attraction to men became weaker and then he developed sexual feelings for one of his female acquaintances. Since the patient had to move with his parents to Crimea, we had to finish treatment ahead of time. Nevertheless, he assured me that sexually he felt quite normal. Although his fate remains unknown, taking into account all the circumstances of his case, we can conclude that the results of the treatment had been achieved.[6]

Little by little Sumbaev's reputation grew by word of mouth. His article in the Soviet scientific journal also contributed to his reputation as a doctor specializing in treating homosexuality. Patients came to him from all over the Soviet Union, through referral and recommendations of their friends and doctors. They revered Sumbaev and hoped that his expertise would immediately help them get rid of their homosexuality. When they came to him they struggled to communicate what was happening to them – they were embarrassed, confused and scared. Many men had never heard of the word "homosexuality" and referred to it as a "vice" and even "sin".

But Sumbaev understood what they meant and equipped them with the words to describe their state. He carefully and compassionately listened to them, educated them on the issue and gave them a hope for recovery.

When Stalin outlawed homosexuality in 1934, Sumbaev did not learn about it at once – he became aware of it only several years later. Stalin and his cronies adopted the sodomy law in silence, which meant that many simply had no knowledge of this important development, especially those living in remote Russian cities like Irkutsk. Even when he learnt that homosexuality was now considered a crime, Sumbaev continued to view it as a treatable illness, receiving patients in hic clinic but with extra caution. He never had a shortage of patients with homosexuality and, in fact, many men were so desperate to become heterosexuals that they decided to stay permanently in Irkutsk in order to be treated and supervised by Sumbaev for the rest of their lives.

Sumbaev was also mentoring young psychiatrists, who came to him to undertake internships. If he trusted them, he taught them the basics of psychoanalysis and even his methods of treating homosexuality. Two of his trainees, Nikolai Ivanov and Aron Belkin, would achieve great prominence in the field of Soviet sexopathology.

In 1951, a twenty-four-year-old graduate of Gorkii Medical Institute, Aron Belkin, arrived at Sumbaev's clinic in Irkutsk to commence his medical internship. When Belkin first met Sumbaev he was a little startled by his mentor's appearance – a plump bald professor, with thick glasses and a rather sullen look. But soon Sumbaev endeared himself to Belkin. Belkin showed signs of promise, and Sumbaev soon revealed to him the dissident nature of his medical practice. What Belkin learnt from Sumbaev was a shattering reversal of everything he had been taught at the university. One striking discovery was that Sigmund Freud's teaching on psychoanalysis could be successful in treating patients with neurosis. Spoon-fed on the idea that Sigmund Freud was just an apologist for the bourgeois ideology and that his ideas and teachings were flawed, Belkin was astonished.

But what struck Belkin even more was that his mentor was dealing with men who were attracted to other men, or in medical terms "homosexuals". Belkin had heard about these people before; from his teenage years he remembered that such people evoked disgust. If a boy wanted to insult another he would call him a "homo" or "pederast" – and that was the strongest insult ever. Belkin had never personally had to deal with genuine homosexuals – or anybody rumoured to be engaging in homosexual relations. Although nobody openly talked about it, there was a tacit social consensus that such people were depraved individuals.[7]

In the late 1940s, when Belkin studied at the Gorkii Medical University, a professor gave a short lecture on "sexual perversions", pointing out that homosexuality was one of the most common and dangerous ones.[8] This professor did not wish to go into too much detail; instead students had to read up on the topic as part of their homework. One of the very few textbooks on psychiatry which discussed the issue of homosexuality and which Belkin managed to find argued that all male homosexuals had "female-like hair growth", "soft skin", "female-like breasts and waist" and a "high-pitched voice". The textbook also argued that male homosexuals wore corsets and powdered their faces.[9] Such descriptions of homosexuals lingered in Belkin's memory and instilled in him a strong aversion to them, which even the most severe and disturbing psychiatric conditions he had read about had failed to do. Sometimes he even wondered: what if one of his friends confessed to him that he had erotic feelings towards men? Would he continue his friendship with such a person? He always found himself thinking that he would not.[10]

But the homosexual men who received treatment in Sumbaev's clinic were so different from what he had read in books and how he imagined them to be. They had nothing to do with those caricature descriptions of "a typical homosexual" which he had read about in university textbooks. And Sumbaev treated homosexual patients with all seriousness. Belkin even expressed his astonishment at that in his memoirs several decades later: "I was astonished when upon my arrival in Irkutsk I learned that 'homos', as I disrespectfully called them to myself, made up a large proportion of the patients of my mentors – Sumbaev and Ivanov."[11]

Having got used to the idea that homosexuals were not distasteful freaks, Belkin observed the work of Sumbaev and Ivanov. Both loved conducting group psychotherapy, gathering all of their patients in a circle

– homosexuals, neurotics and other patients with psychiatric disorders. Although patients did not disclose their conditions to one another, they were all engaging in the group. Belkin had never been allowed to deal with homosexual patients, but he learnt a lot.

Although Belkin managed to overcome his initial aversion to homosexuals, there was one feeling that lingered in him still – fear. Belkin was apprehensive of being punished for not denouncing Sumbaev's homosexual patients to the police and therefore being accused of covering up for them. In the USSR of the early 1950s, denunciations and repressions were still common and if Sumbaev had ill-wishers they could easily have accused him of gathering a den of pederasts in his clinic and taken this information to the police. But it seemed that either Sumbaev had no ill-wishers, or he indeed was successful in keeping his practice a secret.

So in his conversations with doctors from other clinics, Belkin preferred to remain tight-lipped about the types of patients he encountered in Sumbaev's clinic. He told no one that he dealt with homosexuals. One day Belkin came across an article in the local newspaper *East Siberian Truth*, which reported that a group of lecturers and their students at a local university had been discovered to have homosexual relations. A public shaming campaign unfolded: the lecturers were stripped of their posts and students were expelled. The author of the article hysterically demanded a show trial to discourage others from engaging in such relations. Belkin again thought back to what he and his mentors were doing in the clinic – if the author of the article knew that these "criminals" were being treated as patients, there would have been a massive scandal.[12]

Sumbaev's practice and attitude towards homosexuals were very different from what his colleagues believed at that time. Most psychiatrists of the 1950s continued to believe that homosexuals were criminals, treating them with contempt rather than compassion. One textbook, *Psychiatry* (1957), by Soviet psychiatrist Izmail Sluchevskii, branded all homosexuals psychopaths, saying: "When [the homosexual] man comes home, he puts on a female dress and in this dress, does all the housework. Sometimes these psychopaths are even married, because homosexuals may display bisexuality, that is, have sexual intercourse with women and simultaneously display homosexual tendencies."[13]

The internship with Sumbaev significantly shaped Belkin and contributed to his successful career as one of the most renowned experts on the issue of gender reassignment, which unfolded during the subsequent decades. And in the 1970s, when Belkin had already established his own psychiatric practice, a man turned up in his office. Belkin could not believe his eyes and at first thought that this person had mistaken him for someone else. The person was a very famous Soviet performer, a household name and idol for millions of people. He came to Belkin's office not of his own accord – apparently the police had caught him in the act of sodomy and now Belkin, a psychiatrist and a specialist in sexual perversions, was to decide his fate by a mere stroke of pen in his medical report. If the medical report confirmed the artist's homosexuality, then he would go to jail; if not then it would be a strong reason to acquit him. Belkin was not told about the details of the case; his only task was to determine if the performer was a homosexual.

Belkin felt slightly uncomfortable. It is not every day that a famous Soviet performer comes to your office, and, more than that, it is not every day that you have to be responsible for someone's life, especially someone as important as this person. It was clear to Belkin that the Soviet performer was distressed, but he showed a willingness to answer everything Belkin asked him. Despite the fact that Belkin was the authority in the room and the performer's fate was in his hands, he just did not have the heart to delve into the details of his life, which, Belkin clearly realized, would hurt him. So they sat in the office for several hours, talking about art and life. The performer was very verbose and he willingly engaged in the conversation; he asked Belkin if he had already seen him on stage and what was his opinion about his performances. Struck by the performer's unusual way of thinking and his erudition, Belkin concluded the long conversation:

"May I be of help to you – do you have any problems that require psychiatric intervention?"

"Not, really. I don't think so," the performer said and shrugged.

"That is good then. Our appointment is over."

They shook hands and the performer left. Once the actor had left, Belkin sat down at his desk, pulled out a medical report form from the drawer, took his pen and carefully choosing every word he gave a description of the patient's state. At the end of the report he wrote: "The patient displays no homoerotic desires". Belkin hesitated for a moment – was he making a false declaration? Then in a split second he realized that he had nothing to worry about. The actor indeed had displayed no homoerotic desires during their conversation, so what Belkin was writing was entirely truthful.

Belkin did not know who would then read this report and what bearing it would have on the actor's fate, yet judging by the performer's continuing career and acclaim he deduced that the actor had dodged a bullet.[14]

Part II

Under Khrushchev

7

Stalin's heirs deal with homosexuality in the GULAG 1953–1959

When it started to get dark on 1 March 1953, the guards at Stalin's country residence not far from Moscow began to worry: he still had not emerged from his room and was unusually silent. Having summoned their courage, one of the guards and a maid ventured into the room to meet with a shocking scene: Stalin was lying on the floor of his bedroom, conscious but making incoherent noises. He had also wet himself. Members of the Politburo – Stalin's main associates – quickly arrived but were told the leader was in an "unpresentable state" and was asleep. Not realizing how serious the situation was, they left. Doctors were not summoned until the following day. Only several days later, on 4 March, did radio stations broadcast reports about Stalin's illness, and the next day, 5 March, he died. A massive stroke was thought to be the cause of his death.[1]

Stalin's body, embalmed and uniformed, was placed in the Hall of Columns of the House of Unions, a historical building in one of Moscow's central districts, where Lenin's funeral had taken place. The body lay in a casket on a high pedestal adorned by a sea of flowers, which seemed to have come from all over the Soviet Union. Many thousands of people, brainwashed by Soviet propaganda and spoon-fed with the idea that Stalin was the absolute authority and divinity, the only hope of the USSR, lined up to bid their farewell to the dictator, whom they had both feared and worshipped. The Soviet press published photos of grieving crowds and letters from Soviet citizens mourning the leader's death, while radio broadcasters solemnly beseeched the nation to stay unified in the face of their great loss.

During the funeral on 9 March 1953, huge crowds thronged on to the streets of Moscow, so tightly packed that hundreds of people were crushed and died. Troops were soon summoned to the capital to maintain order. Stalin's former associates, in black and brown coats, carried Stalin's casket on their shoulders from the House of Unions to the Mausoleum, a building on Red Square where Lenin's body lay. Each of these associates now wondered how they might secure a place in the country's new leadership and most importantly how they would emerge victorious in the inevitable brutal struggle for succession.

The main candidates for inheriting Stalin's throne were the former chief of secret police and notorious rapist of young women, Lavrentii Beria; Georgy Malenkov, a veteran of the civil war and Stalin's protégé; and First Secretary of the Moscow Regional Committee Nikita Khrushchev, who at that time seemed the least likely candidate. These three divided the power among themselves, pronouncing their adherence to collective leadership, while in reality each candidate sought to undermine the others.

Apart from the struggle for power, Stalin's heirs faced a number of other urgent problems. One of them was the GULAG – a vast network of concentration camps scattered across the USSR's coldest and most inhospitable regions, where millions of Soviet people, including criminals, political prisoners, women and children were imprisoned. All were housed in primitive and overcrowded barracks, starved and forced to work. The dire living conditions in the GULAG and hard labour left inmates susceptible to deadly diseases, often leading to their swift physical deterioration and death.

By the early 1950s, the whole GULAG system was in deep crisis. Prisoners refused to work and were becoming increasingly rebellious. GULAG directors struggled to manage the growing the number of prisoners. The time was ripe for change and a reform of the whole GULAG system.

Shortly after Stalin's death, Lavrentii Beria, who now ran the Ministry of Internal Affairs, in a move to secure a leading position among the candidates for the throne, granted amnesty to a million prisoners. Fearful of Beria's growing grip on power, Khrushchev plotted against him with the support of Malenkov and a number of high-ranking generals. In June 1953, Beria was arrested, stripped of his posts and by the end of the year had been shot.[2] Khrushchev and Malenkov, the remaining candidates for Stalin's throne, continued reforming the GULAG.

As prisoners began to be released from the GULAG, the Soviet leadership was now wondering how to ensure their swift and effective reintegration into society. GULAG directors were instructed to teach prisoners new skills and indoctrinate them politically in order to prepare them for release. It was also important to make sure that former prisoners did not bring their prison habits and lifestyles into society. GULAG officials were especially concerned about homosexuality, fearing that prisoners' release would lead to the spread of same-sex relations in wider society.

On 27 January 1956, Sergei Yegorovich Yegorov, the head of the GULAG, signed a decree, which was circulated among all labour camps and colonies across the country:

> The Central Administration of prison camps and colonies ... has information about increased instances (among both male and female prisoners) of sodomy, lesbian love and other types of sexual perversion, including rape and syphilis resulting from this. Considering that this state of affairs is abnormal and that it is likely to have serious consequences, I request that you study this phenomenon on the ground and in detail and then submit an elaborate report.[3]

Soon reports from regional directors of GULAG colonies started dropping on Yegorov's desk with proposals to introduce additional sanctions for prisoners engaging in homosexual sex, establish night surveillance over the prisoners' beds, gather prisoners for public lectures on the harm of sexual perversions and even criminalize lesbian relationships among prisoners.[4]

GULAG directors also reported another problem – widespread homosexual rape among men. Older prisoners raped young newcomers, making them "passive pederasts". Any prisoner could rape or abuse such "passive pederasts" following which these unfortunate young men would occupy the lowest rung of the prison hierarchy. Commenting on the existence of such a hierarchy, GULAG directors wrote: "recidivist criminals, who, because of their long stints in camps and prisons, without families, indulging in casual sex, acquired the vice in the form of sodomy … their partners, or rather victims, are young inmates whom recidivist criminals under the threat of punishment rape and convert into passive pederasts".[5]

Although many GULAG doctors had much challenging work on their hands, GULAG directors often undervalued their work, scolding them for the high rates of illness in the camps and blaming them for their inability to address other long-standing issues.[6] The GULAG directors typically didn't care about the health of prisoners as they regarded them merely as a workforce who could increase the productivity of the GULAG. But now that the GULAG leaders were emphasizing the need to prepare prisoners for release, the directors were forced to admit their need for medical expertise and change their attitudes towards GULAG doctors.

And GULAG doctors were willing to participate in the efforts to combat homosexuality. Compared to their usual tasks – operating bathhouses and controlling epidemics among prisoners – the research on homosexuality promised to be an interesting change. Dr Krasuskii from a psychiatric hospital of the Yaroslavl' corrective labour colony wrote a whole treatise on the topic, titled "On the Issue of the Study of Perverse Forms of Sexual Relations among Women Prisoners", 68 pages with his own observations and recommendations as to what should be done with lesbians.[7]

Krasuskii first learnt about lesbianism in the course of his conversations with women prisoners who came for a gynaecological consultation in the prison infirmary. During the consultation, women sometimes confessed to him that they had a female partner with whom they had romantic and sexual relations. Krasuskii carefully listened to these women and then advised them to discontinue homosexual relations due to the harm to their health.[8] Indeed, according to his own observations, the women who engaged in lesbianism were lethargic, prone to losing their appetite and vulnerable to genital illnesses.[9] Many lesbians faced condemnation from other prisoners and had to live in constant worry of being found out, which negatively affected their mental health.[10] But what worried Krasuskii most was that homosexual relations between women were very strong and quite often resembled a heterosexual marriage. Women in such relationships courted each other, wrote love poems and were utterly loyal to their partners.[11]

One of Krasuskii's female patients, Larisa, confessed that, when the camp authorities threw her partner in a punishment cell in an attempt to separate them, she just patiently waited for her lover outside until her release. Other women, who faced pressure from camp authorities for maintaining romantic relationships with other women, protested by refusing to work and disobeying orders.[12] Krasuskii also wrote in his treatise:

> Some women prisoners get accustomed to same-sex forms of cohabitation to such an extent that they seek to retain them after their release from the camp – in some cases, this leads to family dissolution and perverse forms of same-sex cohabitation go beyond places of confinement.[13]

Krasuskii was convinced that there were several ways to make women end these relationships:

> It is interesting that pregnancy and child-rearing, evoking the women's biologically inherent aspiration to become a mother, even after lasting perverted forms of cohabitation with women before pregnancy, decisively eliminate these abnormal forms of sexual relations.[14]

As an example, Krasuskii mentioned a female patient called Galina Mirovaya, who maintained sexual relations with other female prisoners until she had sexual intercourse with a man and became pregnant:

> It is interesting that after her release, the prisoner Mirovaya wrote a letter to the head of the camp subdivision, in which she expressed condemnation of her behaviour during her stint, writing that now she was leading a normal life and would continue to do so from now on.[15]

Krasuskii also had other proposals – he suggested publicly reprimanding and shaming lesbian couples in front of other prisoners:

> It is precisely the fact that they have to confront not just the camp administration but their own comrades, who call a spade a spade so that there is no point in denying the guilt, that in some cases even makes them stop maintaining perverse forms of sexual relations.

Other proposals for eradicating lesbianism in the GULAG included broadcasting talks on the prison radio by prisoners who had previously engaged in sexual perversion but had stopped doing so. Such prisoners were supposed to encourage other prisoners to follow suit. Wall newspapers, according to Krasuskii, with articles on the pernicious influence of lesbianism on the colony regime, could also be effective.[16]

Krasuskii's pamphlet was approved by the GULAG leadership and was circulated throughout all camps and colonies for internal use. But GULAG directors on the ground were simply uninterested in combating homosexuality. Not all of them believed that homosexual relations were harmful and some camp directors simply preferred to turn a blind eye to them. Although the GULAG leadership constantly emphasized the need to combat homosexual relations in the GULAG and did acknowledge the problem on paper, in reality they did very little.

On 13 May 1959, a conference for GULAG directors convened in Moscow to share their experiences of dealing with prisoners. The head of the Karaganda GULAG, Colonel Chekin, intended to use this conference as an opportunity to seek advice from his colleagues on the problem that he struggled to resolve. He prepared a report, in which he was intending to speak frankly about the increasing prevalence of lesbian relationships in his camp:

> The problem on which I would like to dwell is the struggle with lesbianism that has become widespread in our camp. Because of jealousy, women create a scene, fight, knife one another and commit a range of crimes, drawing the younger women into this and corrupting them. This also prevents other inmates from serving their sentences in peace. We need to step up repressions. From the talks with women convicts, engaging in this activity – engaging very actively, talks with medical staff and other GULAG operatives, we have concluded that stable lesbians need to be isolated and put into facilities … which may be called 'isolation wards', whose harsh incarceration conditions would serve as a deterrent. We are contemplating creating such facilities in the whole [Kazakh SSR] republic, if financial considerations do not thwart our plans.[17]

When he showed his speech to his colleagues to see their reaction, they advised him to delete the whole section and avoid mentioning the issue at the conference. After some thought and several discussions with his colleagues Chekin decided to delete it, despite the effort that he had put into it. Indeed, by the late 1950s the MVD leadership was very keen to hear that all criminal activity in the GULAG – and they regarded lesbianism as such – had been liquidated and Chekin understood that very well. But of course, homosexual activity in the GULAG remained and was just ignored.

By 1962, Khrushchev had significantly reduced the GULAG, breaking it up into a network of light-regime "colony settlements" and improving prisoners' living conditions and medical services.[18] However, homophobia within the system of the Soviet penitentiary and the brutal prison hierarchy, based on the submission and rape of prisoners by more experienced and respected prisoners, remained.

The anxieties about homosexual contagion spreading from the GULAG into Soviet society were mirrored by somewhat similar sentiments in the US, where fears about an insidious homosexual threat to society also grew. The Cold War, a period of tension and distrust between the US and the USSR, which began in the late 1940s, only aggravated the fears of the American public about a growing homosexual threat. In 1947, the State Department, concerned about issues of internal security, unleashed campaigns to rid the department of communists and homosexuals, both seen as threats to national security. In 1950, before a congressional committee, Deputy Undersecretary John Peurifoy further shocked the American public by announcing that ninety-one homosexuals previously employed by government departments had been forced out. Instead of taking this statement as evidence that American security services had done a good job, many in America became convinced that the entire government must be infiltrated with "sexual perverts".[19]

This widespread panic and sudden labelling of American lesbians and homosexuals as security risks afforded local police forces the freedom to harass them. Police arrested men in bars, parks, public toilets and at beaches, while lesbians were tracked down in bars and arrested. Newspapers frequently published the names, addresses and even places of employment of men and women caught in anti-homosexual raids.[20]

In the US, as in other countries, the public attacks on homosexuals ironically expedited the articulation of a homosexual identity, and made many people aware that homosexuals existed in large numbers throughout American society. The public panic about the "homosexual threat" also encouraged homosexuals to organize and mount resistance to societal homophobia.[21] In the USSR, meanwhile, the government's anxieties about homosexuality spreading out from the GULAG had a far more modest significance for Soviet homosexuals. Certainly, homosexuality became a more common topic of discussion in Soviet medical circles, but these discussions rarely went beyond these circles and thus had little effect on the perception of homosexuality in society at large. For most Soviets, homosexuality remained an unmentionable subject.

8

In which a murder occurs
Leningrad Province, 1955

Private Mikhail Yermolaev was tired and exhausted. It was November 1955 and the cold weather was unbearable – it was very unusual even for the notoriously cold Russian winter.[1] He and his comrades – other soldiers in their early twenties – slowly trudged through the thick snow against the harsh wind. By the end of the day they had finally reached their destination – the village of Rakhia, a small settlement near Leningrad on their way to the military base. The soldiers were all hungry and needed shelter for the night. And maybe to have some fun.

When one of the soldiers invited his comrades to a party with lots of pretty girls in Rakhia's Barrack 18, they erupted with a cheer. It had been a long while since any of them had enjoyed the company of women. That night Barrack 18 was indeed hosting a party, with music from a gramophone, vodka and many pretty young women eager to meet young soldiers, viewing them as prospective husbands. Finding one in the USSR after the war was after all an uphill task.

At the party, Yermolaev drank and ate his fill. His exhausted body had not fully processed the alcohol he got through and he quickly became drunk. He went outside for a smoke. Suddenly everything started to spin around, he stumbled forward, grabbed a lamp-post for support and vomited. Then again. Then he slumped over and vomited again. He nearly passed out and was unsure how long he spent outside when he heard a soft voice behind his back. The voice belonged to a middle-aged stocky man with a balding head and a wide friendly smile.[2]

Red closet

The man introduced himself as Alyosha (the familiar form of his name Aleksei) and then helped Yermolaev up, putting his arm on his shoulder and helping him hobble to another wooden hut. This hut was a bathhouse, where Aleksei worked as a stoker and also lived, occupying a tiny room next to the showering chamber.

Aleksei gently placed him on his bed and after a few moments Yermolaev fell asleep, with Aleksei lying next to him. In the middle of the night, Yermolaev woke up – it felt like someone was fumbling with his belt trying to pull his pants down. Bleary and still dizzy, he strained his eyes to peer through the gloom. It was Aleksei, the stranger who had brought him to this room. Later Yermolaev recalled:

> I woke up and heard Alyosha say, "Get on top of me." At that very moment my belt was undone, my trousers and underpants were down, and my penis was exposed. Then he pulled me toward him and said, "Give it to me, give it to me in the ass." I got on top of him, for Alyosha was on his stomach with his back to me, but I was revolted so I didn't use him, even though my penis was erect. I went back to sleep ... After a little while Alyosha came to me again, first turning me over on my stomach. He got on top of me and tried to use me in the ass, but he didn't manage it because I wouldn't let him. He was only wearing his underpants, and I could feel his erection. He didn't say anything. I just turned away and went back to sleep.[3]

Aleksei did not insist and left his attempts to initiate sex with the private. They both fell asleep again. Several hours later, Yermolaev finally woke up. It was still dark. Next to him lay Aleksei, whose chest rose and fell with the steady rhythm of sleep. Yermolaev cleared his throat and sat up in bed, reaching for his boots. He scribbled his address on a piece of paper and left it on the bed next to the sleeping Aleksei. The door squeaked open and Yermolaev stepped outside. He walked across to the barrack, which had hosted the party the previous night, where his comrades were standing smoking.

"How did you sleep?" one of his army buddies asked, gesturing with his head in the direction of Aleksei's barrack. "They say he is a man and a woman."

"Yes, of course – he is a queer," he said and then switched the topic uncomfortably, reminding his comrades that they were late for the train. Everyone nodded in agreement. The soldiers finished smoking, stamped on the butts and started making their way to the railway station.[4]

Aleksei Kiselev never really knew why he was attracted to men, nor did he try to fathom his desire. What he knew was that this desire made his life more difficult and it was something that he had to hide. In Rakhia, where he lived, Kiselev had a reputation, but again he was not bothered about it. Many people in the village gossiped that he loved soldiers and behaved like a woman, concurring that he was an "oddball".[5] In the 1950s, the shame and silence around the issue of homosexuality ran deep and people talked about it in euphemisms.

Kiselev had always had a penchant for men in uniform and fortunately for him soldiers often stayed overnight in Rakhia to carouse with the women from Barrack 18. These women were all in their early twenties and worked in Rakhia as cleaners for the local peat-cutting trust. The barracks, where they lived and hosted parties, had the reputation of a place where men could have sex in return for small gifts for the women and was a favourite place of soldiers whose way to the base lay through Rakhia.[6] Kiselev was often present at these parties, where he struck up acquaintances with the soldiers and invited them to his home. And even though most soldiers remained indifferent to his attentions, some of them responded.

The women from the barracks did not mind having Kiselev around because he often brought his gramophone with him, which made their parties more entertaining. They were also aware that Kiselev fancied soldiers, so they never considered him to be sexually threatening, changing their clothes in his presence and gossiping about men.

On a cold January night of 1955, Aleksei dropped by Barrack 18, where yet another party was in full swing. Inside there was the usual sight: a gathering of girls and soldiers around a big wooden table, soldiers, smoke, food and bottles of vodka. Kiselev played music on his gramophone and then he sat down at the table. He was immediately offered a glass of vodka, which he downed in one. He then looked around – many faces were familiar to him, as some soldiers frequented this place and had set foot in the village previously. At the far end of the table sat a young, handsome, broad-shouldered man with sharply defined cheekbones and red hair, who immediately caught Kiselev's eye and whom he had never seen before. Unlike other tipsy soldiers busy with the women, this man appeared to be sober. With a serious face, he was silently observing what was happening in the barrack and it seemed that he was not enjoying the party at all.

Kiselev downed another glass of vodka and then looked towards Olga Gurova, who already knew what was on Kiselev's mind. He was going to ask her to introduce him to the silent soldier at the back of the table. She had been used to such requests from Kiselev and found it very amusing to watch him striking up acquaintances with unsuspecting soldiers. The introductions were made – the soldier introduced himself as David Morozov and they shook hands.

Kiselev looked into Morozov's eyes and asked if they could become friends. Morozov's handshake was strong, and his touch excited Kiselev so he held Morozov's hand a little longer and flashed him a smile. Clearly this made his new acquaintance feel uncomfortable, so Kiselev told Morozov that he had a sister, and that Morozov should come to Rakhia again to visit them.[7] When Kiselev left the party, other soldiers warned Morozov that Kiselev did not really have a sister, did not love women and entered into sexual relations only with men.[8]

On that night, Morozov did not visit Kiselev's bathhouse and in the morning he left Rakhia with the other soldiers. But on his way to the base, Morozov could not stop thinking about the strange man he'd met the night before; there was something in Kiselev that intrigued and attracted him. Morozov was uncertain if it was his demeanour, his voice or his stare. Other soldiers who had seen Morozov shaking hands with Kiselev had warned him that the man liked to "seduce" soldiers and advised him to steer clear, but despite that, during his subsequent visits to the barracks, Morozov exchanged friendly conversations with Kiselev. Every time Kiselev met Morozov, he would ask him to stay the night in his room in the bathhouse. Over the nine subsequent months Morozov visited Barrack

18 several times. In November, during his visit, he told Kiselev that he was about to be demobilized and that he had married a woman, who lived not too far from Rakhia. The news disappointed Kiselev; he still invited Morozov to listen to his gramophone in his room, but to no avail. But on 13 December, when Morozov and Kiselev met in Barrack 18 again, Morozov unexpectedly accepted the invitation.

That night Morozov was sober as usual, despite the numerous attempts by his fellow soldiers and Kiselev himself to give him vodka. They left the party very early and went into the bathhouse, to Kiselev's tiny room, where he fried some potatoes and played music on the gramophone. During this time Morozov was silently lying on Kiselev's bed, occasionally going out for a smoke and whistling along to the music. After dinner, during which little was said, Morozov pulled off his boots and shirt and lay down on the bed. Kiselev undressed as well, putting out the kerosene light and lying down next to Morozov. Morozov appeared to have fallen asleep instantly, but Kiselev was awash with thoughts. Was Morozov just like him after all? Why did he come to spend the night with him if he was now married and his wife lived less than a kilometre away from Rakhia?

After about half an hour Kiselev decided to take his chance. Morozov did not make a sound, but appeared to be asleep. Kiselev threw out his arm trying to reach for Morozov's crotch, but Morozov gently pushed his hand away. Kiselev then lifted his body and tried to get on top of Morozov whose eyes shot open and whose face now contorted with rage. Morozov pushed Kiselev away again, groaned something and turned over.

Kiselev looked hungrily at Morozov's body, and his heart began to beat faster. Morozov was absolutely sober and Kiselev had always made sure that those who went to his house were under the influence of alcohol. Otherwise, making a move on a sober soldier could lead to unexpected embarrassment and other unpleasant situations. For a few moments, the voice of reason in Kiselev took over and he resisted the urge to lean towards Morozov. But then it struck him: if this man was not here for what Kiselev desired, why did not he go back to his wife, who lived so close? Why had he decided to come to Kiselev, a man he hardly knew and who so unambiguously hinted at the possibility of sexual intimacy between them? He had definitely come here for something, even if he was unable to bring himself to do it.

Morozov was lying on his side facing the wall. Kiselev decided to wait. If nothing happened, it was probably because Morozov was sober and could not do what he really wanted to do. Kiselev waited for almost an hour – and then again tried to make a move on Morozov. This time Morozov was livid – he was still not asleep.

Then a terrible sequence of events unfolded. Morozov rose and hit Kiselev several times in the stomach, knocking him to the floor. He pulled off his belt and wrapped it around Kiselev's neck and with one violent move pulled it tight. Kiselev, still not aware of what was happening, tried to remove the belt but received several more blows from Morozov. Morozov held the belt tight around his neck until Kiselev stopped moving and his face became blue. Morozov then hanged the body by his belt on the clothes hook and, taking the gramophone with him, left.[9]

The next day, 14 December, Galina Loginova, who worked in the bathhouse during the daytime, discovered Kiselev's hanging body and immediately called the police. Having found no signs of foul play or forced entry in the room, the police concluded that Kiselev had committed suicide and closed their investigation.[10]

Four years later, however, in 1959, during one of the police routine raids, they apprehended Morozov and found stolen goods at his place along with Kiselev's gramophone, which was soon identified by one of the women who had sold it to Kiselev. Morozov promptly confessed to murdering Kiselev and related everything that had happened on the night he stayed at his room in the bathhouse. He alleged that Kiselev was trying to embrace him and touch his penis and that these unwanted sexual advances forced him to defend himself and ultimately strangle Kiselev.[11]

The investigators were not convinced by Morozov's assurances that he was not seeking intimacy with Kiselev, finding it difficult to believe that there had been no sexual liaisons between the two over the course of nine months since their first encounter and on the night of the murder. Investigators also found out that Kiselev wrote letters to Morozov while he was serving in the army. Finally, investigators deemed it suspicious that Morozov, instead of going home to his wife, chose to stay in the company of a man with a questionable reputation, as he was known to all the villagers.

From their conversations with the village residents and those who knew Kiselev personally, investigators realized that Kiselev's homosexuality was an open secret in Rakhia, but when speaking of Kiselev they preferred to refer to his sexuality using euphemisms such as his being "strange" or "an oddball". Nikolai Voronin, a metalworker who had known Kiselev for five years, confessed: "In conversation Kiselev constantly referred to himself as a woman ... I was aware that Kiselev loved soldiers, and he often spent time with them."[12] Laundress Loginova mentioned another characteristic of the deceased: "While I was working in the bathhouse I noticed that Kiselev never washed in the bathhouse when it was serving men, and I know that he never even washed with the other male bathhouse employees but always tried to wash alone."[13] Witness Mikhailova added that "Aleksei himself sometimes said that he had had a lieutenant over to stay, and then he would laugh, and I never knew if he was serious or not".[14] Bystrova, a stoker, made a nervous comment that Kiselev told her that "he found some soldiers very beautiful", but she briefly added: "but why he said this I don't know".[15] The manager of the bathhouse, Irina Vaganova, when interrogated by the police about Kiselev, also felt nervous: "Kiselev ... was a very nervous person. Kiselev made friends with soldiers. I even criticized him for this, for the fact that he invited them to come and stay with him."[16]

Although Morozov argued in court that he was only protecting himself against Kiselev's sexual advancements, the judge ruled the following:

> The court had found that the personal relationship with the commission of sodomy had existed for some time between Kiselev and Morozov and this fact has been substantiated by medical forensic examination and therefore there was nothing unexpected or perturbing in Kiselev's approaches."[17]

At the end of the trial Morozov was convicted for murder, theft and sodomy.

Red closet

Aleksei Kiselev's queer life in the village of Rakhia in the 1950s, as well as the fact that many in the village were aware of his "oddness" but did not dare name it "homosexuality", was not unique to the USSR. Similar scenarios occurred in the rural areas of other countries, far from large cities. During the same period, in the American state of Mississippi, homosexual men were neither wholly isolated nor invisible. Mississippi at that time was the nation's poorest state, with the least educated people, and yet many Mississippians were aware of the homosexuality of their friends and relatives, although they avoided discussing it overtly.[18] Despite the tacit acceptance of Kiselev's homosexuality by his fellow villagers, which allowed him to lead a quiet homosexual life in his tiny village, his encounter with Morozov, an outsider who was uncertain and insecure about his sexuality, was to be his downfall.

9

Soviet jurists push for the decriminalization of sodomy

Moscow, 1959

Following Lavrentii Beria's arrest in June 1953, Khrushchev began to accumulate power. In 1955 he expelled Malenkov from high leadership positions and became the undisputed party leader. In 1956, in a closed session of the XXth Congress of the Soviet Communist Party, Khrushchev gathered party leaders and delivered his shocking "secret speech", telling party delegates that Stalin, who had hitherto been glorified, was not a divine father but a self-obsessed, cowardly tyrant, who had killed millions of Soviet people. Khrushchev accused Stalin of the arbitrary arrests of high-ranking officials, his failure to prepare for Nazi invasion, mass deportations of Soviet people and many other grave crimes. He underscored that it was all because of Stalin's "cult of personality" and his violations of "socialist legality". Khrushchev's speech threw Soviet officials into shock, confusion and turmoil. Some delegates could not bear the report and had heart attacks; others shot themselves later. Khrushchev's secret speech and his repudiation of Stalin's terror regime inaugurated a new period, which went down in history as "the Thaw".

During the Thaw, the Soviet society underwent significant transformations. Khrushchev rehabilitated political prisoners, allowed the press to have limited freedom and opened up the country to the rest of the world. Foreigners came to the USSR to participate in festivals, while some Soviet citizens could travel overseas. Khrushchev also unleashed a construction campaign, trying to solve the problem of housing. New housing blocks began to spring up in cities, and many Soviet citizens, who thus far had lived in communal flats and barracks, now finally had the physical privacy of their own apartment.

Khrushchev also initiated changes in laws and jurisprudence and in the ways justice operated. In particular, he denounced the extreme legal terror and ruthless repressions of the Stalin era, and facilitated the formation of a professional and much less arbitrary system of criminal justice, based on strong adherence to law. He deprived the secret police force of its powers to conduct investigations without external supervision by other organs. Criminological research, which had been proscribed under Stalin due to the widespread arbitrary terror, made a comeback in specialized university curricula and research institutions.[1] Criminologists taught investigators and police officers how to investigate criminal cases professionally, stressing the importance of finding enough evidence of crime to secure a conviction. Overall, even though the Soviet system of law remained fully totalitarian, the Soviet citizen under Khrushchev was far more protected against police terror and false charges and much less likely to receive a visit from the secret police at night.

Khrushchev also set out to change Stalin-era criminal codes in order to bring them in line with the partial liberalization of society. In each Soviet republic, special Legislative Commissions, comprising distinguished Soviet jurists and legal scholars, were created and their members decided which republican laws would remain in force and which would be abolished.

On 23 July 1959, a subcommittee of the Legislative Commission of the Russian Soviet Federative Socialist Republic, chaired by forty-three-year-old Boris Nikiforov, a member of the Moscow City Bar Association, proposed changes to the law on sodomy. Nikiforov proposed to reduce the maximum sentence for consensual sodomy from five to three years, and nobody objected to it, so changes were made.[2] Nikiforov himself supported such a move – as a lawyer he knew first-hand how difficult and painful the enforcement of the first article, penalizing consensual sodomy, was. Indeed, if two adults engaged in consensual homosexual sex, what would be the grounds for initiating a criminal case? How would investigators be able to deal with such crimes in practice? The rationale for having such a useless piece of legislation was simply beyond Nikiforov's comprehension.

Nikiforov was not the only one who understood the tricky nature of Part 1 of Article 154-a, criminalizing consensual sodomy. Other criminologists also openly expressed their concerns about the virtual impossibility of identifying the defendant in such crimes. The authors of the manual *Investigation of Sex Crimes*, published in 1958, wrote for example:

> Both subjects carry criminal responsibility for consensual sodomy and because of this they seek to conceal the committed crime and tend to give no testimony that may help to solve the crime. Eyewitnesses can rarely be found. That is why, when investigating such cases one has to deal with circumstantial evidence.[3]

Forensic experts, who often bore the brunt of examining those suspected in sodomy cases, also struggled. There was nothing they could find on the suspects' bodies in such cases and there was no sound advice they could give to investigators who faced such cases. Just like the ban on consensual homosexuality itself, their advice on how to seek forensic evidence in such cases made no sense. For example, one of the chief forensic experts in the USSR, Mikhail Avdeev, described in his manual *Forensic Medicine* (1951) the type of reasoning forensic experts and investigators should adhere to when dealing with cases of consensual sodomy. He did so by giving the example of a real criminal case, which dealt with a Soviet citizen, Vasilii Vinogradov, apprehended on charges of sodomy. Investigators found out that in the period from 1937 to 1941 Vinogradov had lived with a woman, with whom he had normal sexual intercourse once a week. During this time he also met other men, with whom he had sexual intercourse as both active and passive partner. Investigators sent Vinogradov for a forensic examination to secure scientific evidence for his conviction. Having examined Vinogradov's body, forensic experts came to a conclusion that he was likely to have committed sodomy – only because he was healthy:

> During the examination of Vinogradov, we have not found any signs of venereal disease on his body. His external genitals are developed normally and they have no congenital or unhealthy alterations that would prevent

him from performing sexual intercourse as an active partner. Vinogradov does not deny that he experiences penile erections. Likewise, no physical disabilities that would serve as an obstacle to having sexual intercourse as a passive partner were found on his body. There are also no clear traces of passive sodomy.[4]

Far from being convincing, such findings suggested that anybody who had good erections could be found guilty of sodomy as an active partner. Similarly, if a man had no physical characteristics that prevented him from being sexually penetrated then this man could be accused of being a passive partner, which only testified to the absurdity and the possible abuses of the law. Nikiforov was aware of all these problems and he genuinely believed that the removal of such an ambiguous piece of legislation would be a welcome move, and even more so in line with the resurging principles of socialist legality in Soviet justice.

Yet Nikiforov also realised that advocating openly for the repeal of such a controversial law, despite its absurdity, could be dangerous. It would definitely raise a few eyebrows and could even cost him his career. Despite the general relaxation of the political climate under Khrushchev, sex still remained a taboo subject, let alone homosexuality. Nikiforov's numerous colleagues – party officials and legal scholars – held very conservative views on such matters and could have unpredictable reactions to such a proposal to remove criminal penalties for consensual sodomy. Defending homosexuals would immediately invite the question of whether their defender was a homosexual himself, with all the corresponding consequences.

Although Nikiforov expected objections from his colleagues, his proposal was met with none. In fact, nobody said anything – it seemed that everybody was uncomfortable with the topic and just wanted to move to the next piece of legislation. The changes recommended by Nikiforov's commission were not final – the next step would be approval by the republic's Legislative Commission, whose decision would be definitive.

One month later, on 27 August 1959, the RSFSR Legislative Commission convened. This time, instead of Nikiforov, the commission was chaired by Aleksei Gertsenzon, a distinguished professor from the Institute of Soviet Law, who had extensive legal experience under his belt and who had published numerous articles on criminal sociology. The commission consisted of other renowned scholars, and Nikiforov was one of these. After a tedious discussion of other laws on the agenda, the commission moved to the sodomy law.

"Now, sodomy," announced Gertsenzon, looking across the table at the other members of the commission. "Any suggestions regarding the first part?"

Nikiforov swallowed and raised his hand. This was the moment and the chance when he could voice his concerns about the law, but still saying everything that he thought was not as easy as he thought it would be.

"The first part of the law is totally incomprehensible," he said drily.

"The first part can be abolished," said another scholar. Nikiforov looked in the direction of the voice. It was Comrade Stepichev, who surprisingly supported Nikiforov's initiative. Nikiforov had known he was not the only one against the law, and he was pleasantly proved right. He even thought that he could have worked up the courage to suggest removing the first part of the law himself, but didn't mind not being responsible for this decision. Nikiforov nodded and looked across the table at Gertsenzon.

"There are suggestions to abolish the first part. I am opening this up to a vote. Does anyone support the abolition of the first part?" Gertsenzon glanced around the table.

Nikiforov was almost convinced that his initiative would not be objected to, as was the case during the discussion in the commission that he had chaired a month ago, but his hope crashed when he heard the opinion of his other colleague:

"We can't abolish this norm. On what grounds do you want to do that?" asked Comrade Korotkov, sitting at the other side of the table with a stern look on his face.

"Well, then, are we going to open a discussion or not? Who is in favour of opening the discussion of the article?" Gertsenzon said.

Nikiforov and Stepichev raised their hands. Seeing that the remaining twelve members of the commission were reluctant to discuss the law and feeling a certain discomfort himself, Gertsenzon said:

"We are not going to discuss it, then. The article stays, then."

Gertsenzon glanced at the draft of Nikiforov's commission, which proposed reducing the existing penalties for consensual sodomy. "Let me see, what are the suggestions regarding the essence of the article? Here the punishment is to be reduced compared to the previous penalty. Deprivation of liberty for up to three years or exile up to three years. So, comrades, are we approving the first part of the Article?"

Silence hung in the hall again. Nikiforov expected that someone would suggest reviewing his penalties, but nobody objected to it.

"We are approving it. The second part: any suggestions? No. The whole article is approved," Gertsenzon concluded with a sigh of relief.[5]

Although he had failed to push through the elimination of the article on consensual sodomy Nikiforov was content that at least he managed to make the punishment for consensual sodomy less severe – from five to three years. A year later, when the criminal codes were finally adopted, Nikiforov received a copy of the RSFSR Criminal Code. Flipping through the pages, Nikiforov was glad that many laws had been modified and brought in line with the state's thrust towards socialist legality. Yet, when he reached the page with the sodomy law – in the new Criminal Code it received a new number, 121 – he was shocked.

Article 121. Part – 1.
Sexual intercourse between a male and a male (sodomy) is punishable by deprivation of freedom for a term of up to five years.

The changes which his commission had initiated, which were then approved by Gertsenzon's commission, had been ignored completely. The law remained the same as it had been under Stalin, retaining the maximum penalty of five years' incarceration for consensual sodomy. Someone in the Party apparently did not like the changes that had been proposed by legal experts so had just crossed them out, apparently as an afterthought. That person clearly wanted to keep the penalties for consensual sodomy in place.

In other Soviet republics, where similar legislative commissions were convened, different proposals regarding sodomy law emerged. The Legislative Commission of the Soviet Republic of Latvia, which gathered on 24

March 1960, received a proposal from local police to criminalize lesbianism, saying: "in practice one may encounter cases of satisfaction of sexual desire between the persons of the same sex, which do not fall under the definition of 'sodomy', yet these activities also pose a danger to society".[6] This proposal was considered by Latvian legal scholars and then sent for an evaluation to Moscow, but was subsequently declined. To Moscow legal academics and authorities, lesbianism did not seem to be dangerous. Although in 1959 legal scholars failed to decriminalize consensual sodomy, more attempts to do so would come in the following decades.

While in the USSR the attempt of Soviet scholars to remove consensual homosexual acts proved to be unsuccessful, in other countries positive political changes in the direction of gay liberation were slowly taking place. In the US, in the early 1950s, a national gay rights organization called the Mattachine Society appeared. Founded by the ex-communist activist Harry Hay in Los Angeles, by 1953, the society already had two thousand members. The organization urged homosexuals to adjust to a "pattern of behaviour that is acceptable to society in general and compatible with [the] recognized institutions ... of home, church, and state" and "aid established and recognized scientists, clinics, research organizations and institutions ... studying sex variation problems", using them as the agents of social change.[7] During the 1950s, various national gay rights organizations began to spring up across West Germany and France.[8] In 1957, the Departmental Committee on Homosexual Offences and Prostitution known as the Wolfenden Committee in England produced a report with recommendations to decriminalize consensual homosexual acts between two men. However, this recommendation became law only in 1967.[9] Even in socialist countries, positive changes were occurring. In Czechoslovakia, for example, in the 1950s, prominent sexologists argued that homosexuality was a medical problem and therefore should not be prosecuted. In 1961, Czechoslovakian authorities heard these arguments and decriminalized consensual homosexual acts between two male adults.[10]

Soviet psychiatrists try to cure lesbianism

Karaganda, 1960

In 1960, Abram Sviadoshch, a young ambitious psychiatrist from the town of Karaganda, about three thousand kilometres from Moscow, decided to conduct medical research on homosexuals. Sviadoshch had always been interested in issues of sexology and especially homosexuality and in the Department of Psychiatry of the Karaganda Medical University, where he worked, he was the only psychiatrist who pursued such unusual topics. This was hardly surprising: after Stalin's ascent to power, sexological research in the USSR disappeared almost entirely and authorities believed that sex was not a matter worth studying.

According to Soviet authorities of the Stalin era, if people needed to learn what sex was, they would have to learn from their own experience or turn to *The Great Soviet Encyclopaedia* (1940) and its entry on "sex life", which would instruct them to rechannel their sexual energy into something productive:

> The system of upbringing of children and adolescents in the USSR is based on cultivation of ardent love for the Motherland, comradeliness, love of labour, respect for the woman as a comrade in labour. A mass of creative impulses is created, diverting the youth's attention from excessive sexual pursuits and rechannelling its energy to joyful labour and healthy recreation, combined with physical culture.[1]

After Stalin's death in 1953, against a backdrop of partial relaxation of censorship and rigid ideological controls, some Soviet doctors began to return to hitherto proscribed sexological research. They focused on the issues of male impotence and female infertility, but some of them, like Abram Sviadoshch, became interested in a more exotic topic – homosexuality. Sviadoshch became fascinated with the issue after reading *Sexual Behaviour in the Human Male*, a study by the American sexologist Alfred Kinsey, published in 1948. Kinsey's treatise revealed a shocking truth: 37 per cent of American men had had a sexual contact to the point of orgasm with another man at some point in their lives.[2] While these findings created a stir in the West, Soviet psychiatrists remained largely indifferent to them, not wishing to engage in bourgeois studies on sex, let alone homosexuality, a punishable crime and a taboo subject in the USSR. The majority of Soviet psychiatrists also simply did not read or speak English.

Unlike the majority of his colleagues, Sviadoshch did not wish to be insulated from Western psychiatric research, trying to stay informed about its most recent trends and developments. Although Kinsey's work was not officially published in the USSR, Sviadoshch managed to smuggle it into the USSR and had it translated into Russian.

Kinsey's discoveries fascinated and troubled Sviadoshch and prompted him to conceive and conduct research on a similar scale in Soviet conditions. Sviadoshch was very keen to test Kinsey's findings about male homosexual behaviour in Soviet society and find out whether the same proportion of Soviet men had engaged in homosexual behaviour. But he clearly understood that, unlike his American counterpart, he would have to clear his project with the party bosses, who would most likely accuse him of sexual debauchery and criticize his pursuits.

It was also clear to Sviadoshch that, while male homosexuality was officially a criminal offence in the USSR, researching the issue or even finding candidates for participation would be out of the question. Such scandalous research could even jeopardize his own career. Party bosses and most of his colleagues believed homosexuality to be a shameful and disgusting perversion, which did not merit scientific examination, so the project would inevitably be fraught with risks and many problems.

Compared to male homosexuality, lesbianism seemed like a far more researchable topic, especially since police treated lesbianism as either a non-issue or something that doctors had to take charge of – so such research would not raise as many eyebrows as research on male homo-sexuality. Likewise, Sviadoshch was aware of the growing interest in the scientific expertise on lesbianism in the GULAG, where authorities tried to eradicate same-sex relations between women prisoners. Although Sviadoshch never worked in the GULAG himself, Karaganda was adjacent to one of the largest GULAG labour camps, whose doctors maintained professional ties with the Karaganda Medical University and knew Svia-doshch personally. They often told him about their problems with lesbians and their bosses' desire to resolve this problem.

Sviadoshch engaged one of his young interns, an aspiring psychiatrist – a shy and timid woman named Elizaveta Derevinskaia. Since the topic of the project was female homosexuality, Sviadoshch felt that a female researcher would be more able to empathize with other women and have more insights into their issues. Besides, the women participating in the study could feel more comfortable with gynaecological manipulations and interventions performed by a female doctor.

Finding participants for this project was not difficult – Sviadoshch's professional acquaintances in the Karaganda GULAG found several dozen lesbian women in the camp for him to examine.[3] Sviadoshch also invited female patients from his own medical practice, who in the course of their treatment for psychiatric problems confessed their sexual desire for other women. In total, in the period from 1954 to 1964, Sviadoshch and Der-evinskaia managed to examine ninety-six lesbians at the psychiatric clinic of the Karaganda Medical University.[4]

Although the appearance of the majority of women at first startled Derevinskaia – their muscly arms, tattoos and manly way of speaking seemed unpleasant and shocking to her – she soon got used to their looks and even grew sympathetic to them and their stories. She carefully wrote them down and typed them up. The story of Kristina, a robust woman with an athletic body aged thirty-five, produced a particularly memorable impression on Derevinskaia:

> She once had a casual sexual encounter with a man, but she is reluctant to speak about it. She never felt attracted to the people of the opposite sex, nor did she feel pleasure from intimacy with men … She often passed off

as a man and even received a passport which indicated that she was a man named Andrei Petrovich. She also registered a marriage with a woman.

In her non-sexual life, she does not do women's work, but only men's work such as chopping wood and repairing shoes. She demands attention to herself, but with her wife she displays affection and tenderness … and often gives her presents.[5]

In the hospital, she is calm, sociable, but shy to undress in front of other females. She looks at the young women and compliments them. She claims that she is no longer able to fall in love with others, as she is madly in love with her wife.[6]

Derevinskaia had never realized that it was possible for a woman to dress like a man and even have her female name changed to a male one on her passport. It was also inconceivable for her to imagine two women living together as a married couple.

Three years after the interview, Derevinskaia and Sviadoshch visited Kristina's home, where she lived with her female partner. The couple reported that they were happy. Kristina proudly told Derevinskaia that she was working as a janitor and that they even intended to move in with her wife's relatives, with whom they had friendly relations.[7]

In her notes Derevinskaia classified the women whom she interviewed into two categories: those who played the role of the man – so-called "active" lesbians – and those who played the role of the woman – "passive" lesbians. "Active" lesbians appeared to have very distinct male characteristics – a male skeleton, narrow hips, well-developed muscles, a deep voice and male-like pubic hair growth.[8] During sexual intercourse, they undressed their "passive" partners, carried them to bed in their arms and actively caressed them.[9] "Active" lesbians demanded total obedience from their "passive" partners. The final decision was always theirs. "Active" lesbians always managed and kept the money in the household, including money earned by their passive partners. "Active" lesbians despised work that was considered female, preferring instead to do men's work – chopping wood, repairing fences and roads. They were also very jealous of both men and women and they tried not to leave their "wives" on their own. If their "wives" were undergoing treatment in a hospital, they frequently visited them, bringing bouquets of flowers and parcels with food.

In contrast, those lesbians whom Derevinskaia described as "passive" appeared to be more feminine and soft. Many of them had long braided hair and a feminine gait. Many of them loved it when their "husbands" carried them in their arms. They washed clothes, cleaned the rooms and set the table when their "husbands" came home. They even readily endured beatings and abuse from their "active" partners. All "passive" lesbians donned only women's dresses, loved to wear rings, earrings and bracelets.[10] Many of them had lived heterosexual lives in the past and even had children, but generally talked about them in an unaffectionate way and often did not even know where their children were.[11]

It was active lesbians who sometimes made Derevinskaia feel ill at ease. Not only did their appearance make her feel uncomfortable, but their actions as well. One woman, Masha, openly flirted with and courted Tatiana, one of Derevinskaia's female assistants. She even wrote love letters to her. During one of the interviews with Derevinskaia Masha confessed that she was starting to have an erotic attraction to Tatiana and demanded to see her more often. Derevinskaia said no to Masha's advances and decided to discharge her from hospital and discontinue interviews with her.

But Masha was adamant: two months after being discharged, she even came to see Sviadoshch to tell him that she loved Tatiana and missed her. She also complained that Tatiana never wrote her letters since she had been discharged. Having realized that Sviadoshch would not let her see Tatiana again, one night Masha imitated a suicide attempt – she pretended to have drunk mercury from a thermometer – so the doctors at the hospital had to admit her to the clinic where Tatiana worked. Realizing that Masha could again resume her attempts to chase Tatiana, doctors decided to transfer Masha to a different psychiatric hospital.[12]

Derevinskaia collected data and biographies from her patients from 1954 to 1960. Sviadoshch was very happy with Derevinskaia's work – she was now far more experienced and less shy about talking and dealing with lesbian women. By the 1960s, Derevinskaia had managed to nurture relations with many of the lesbian women during her career and now felt comfortable in their company. However, Sviadoshch's ambition was not just to collect the descriptions of these women's biographies but actually to try to cure them of their homosexuality. He was well aware of the attempts of Western doctors to do that and he asked Derevinskaia to study these attempts thoroughly.

He also understood that he would need to be very careful about approaching women in his care and asking them whether they wanted to receive treatment for their homosexuality. Many women seemed comfortable with their sexuality, and were unlikely to welcome his invitation to receive treatment. But some of them loathed their sexual desire for women and wished to lead heterosexual lives. This is what Derevinskaia noted down about the women who expressed a desire to be cured:

> She says she is not able to leave her [female] partner, although she would like to do it and she understands that her relationship is unnatural. She asks [me] to rid her of her orientation.[13]

Although most Western doctors by the 1960s had come to the conclusion that homosexuality was incurable, Sviadoshch disagreed. He also knew that many homosexuals did not consider their state a disease and therefore they declined medical treatment if such was offered to them.[14] That Western doctors gave up on curing homosexuality could be explained, according to Sviadoshch, by their erroneous methods. He opposed castrating male homosexuals – not only did such a method fail to turn homosexual into heterosexual desire, but it also completely ruined patients' libido, causing irreversible changes in their endocrine system and dealing a devastating blow to their psyche. He was also aware of unsuccessful treatments with electroconvulsive shocks delivered to homosexuals in one of the clinics in Los Angeles. Removal of the thalamus and electroconvulsive shock treatment in various countries were other barbaric practices of capitalist doctors that Sviadoshch rejected outright.[15]

What Sviadoshch thought would be effective in treating lesbianism was the use of aminazin, an anti-psychotic drug, widely employed in Soviet closed psychiatric hospitals against opponents of the Soviet regime. The drug had many grotesque side-effects, ranging from involuntary facial movements, which could persist even after the drug was discontinued, to intensifying medical conditions that already afflicted the patient. Forcibly confined in psychiatric clinics, opponents of the Soviet regime received injections of high doses of the drug as punishment for daring to oppose Soviet authorities. Their torturers also hoped that the dissenters would recant their political views under the effects of the drug.[16]

Aminazin was also routinely used by Soviet psychiatrists for treatment of schizophrenia, paranoia and manic depression. Sviadoshch used this drug for the treatment of neurosis and psychosis as well. He noted that even in small doses aminazin deadened patients' libido without causing any other serious side-effects. This observation led him to believe that this drug could be used to reduce the strength of homosexual desire in lesbians under his care.[17]

Only nine women – five "active" and four "passive" – consented to undergo medical treatment, and all of them were sceptical about the outcome.[18] Sviadoshch administered 50 mg of aminazin and then gradually increased the dose to 150 mg. During treatment, he and Derevinskaia measured the women's blood pressure, pulse and body temperature. During the first two hours of treatment all women became pale, fatigued and complained of dry mouth.[19] On the fifth day of medical therapy, they also reported a marked decrease in libido and some complained of its complete disappearance. The absence of libido made women depressed – during their interviews with Derevinskaia they looked lost, staring blankly at the walls of the hospital's room, while Derevinskaia was writing down their testimonies:

> "I became somewhat indifferent to everything … I have no desire for anything, I feel no passion, I have no feelings …"
> "I don't recognize myself … I became unfeeling and cold."
> "I was reading a book about love and this would usually stir emotions in me, but now I have no reaction to it whatsoever."
> "Yesterday one of my girlfriends came over, sat next to me and spoke to me tenderly, but I felt like a stone."[20]

Once the drug had completely suppressed the women's libido, Sviadoshch arranged psychotherapeutic sessions: women lay in bed with closed eyes, while Derevinskaia and her assistants repeated hypnotic suggestions. In her dissertation, Derevinskaia described them thus:

> As part of the treatment the women patients are told that homosexual relations are unnatural, abnormal and unacceptable. They are told that such relations will negatively affect women's health and that they have no future; that a homosexual woman will never be able to have a stable family and will never experience the joy of motherhood. We also point out to our patients that homosexuality is an entrenched habit and that we will help them get rid of it if they actively and willingly participate in the treatment process themselves.
>
> The woman patient is then told that she will be given a drug that will reduce her sex drive and will lead to the loss of sexual interest in her female partner and in women in general. After that she is told that she will acquire a sexual desire directed towards men.
>
> Then we tell the patient that she will have feelings for men like all other women do. She will forget about her past unhealthy relationships and such relationships will disgust her. She will be able to hold her head high and she won't be ashamed any more. She will have new opportunities to lead a new happy life, which will give her both moral and physical satisfaction.[21]

Sviadoshch administered aminazin to the women for ten days and then started decreasing the dose to 50 mg. The women reported that they felt that their libido was coming back, but it was still very weak. This, Sviadoshch believed, was the most propitious moment that he as a doctor had to take advantage of. While their desire was still weak and they remained on the drug, Derevinskaia delivered ten more psychotherapy sessions, during which she told women about the prospects of starting a normal heterosexual family and raising children.[22] Then Sviadoshch weaned the women off the drug, continuing to deliver psychotherapy sessions to solidify the women's new-found heterosexual desire.

The treatment produced differing effects on the women. Marina, a woman aged thirty-one, seemed to have improved. At the age of nineteen she had got married, but her husband failed to give her any sexual satisfaction, so she left him five months after their wedding. Living on her own, Marina soon met another young woman, with whom she formed a homosexual bond.[23] Her former husband did not know about their relationship and he begged her to come back. Marina confessed to Derevinskaia that she wanted to come back to him, because she realized that her relationship with another woman was unnatural, but she simply could not tear herself away from her. Marina was administered aminazin and participated in psychotherapeutic sessions. When Derevinskaia weaned her off the drug, Marina assured her that she had started developing interest in her husband again. She told her that she had started having dreams in which other men courted her and had conversations with her. Marina also confessed to Derevinskaia that for the first time her life she felt she wanted to become a mother.

Marina's husband, whom Derevinskaia interviewed as well and who was still unaware that Marina was having a homosexual affair (when asked why she was in hospital, Derevinskaia told him that she was being treated for neurosis), also said that he had never seen his wife being so affectionate to him and happy. Six months later, Derevinskaia again interviewed Marina, who now asserted that she was disgusted by her "past life". She also shared wonderful news with Derevinskaia: she was eight weeks pregnant already and seemed very happy with her husband.[24]

Another woman, Yekaterina, aged thirty-four, was serving a prison sentence at a corrective labour institution. She agreed to undergo medical treatment. Derevinskaia described the results of Yekaterina's treatment thus: "she noted that she became calm and that she was in a good mood … She received a letter from her female partner, but left it unopened. She then sent her a short note asking to leave her alone."[25]

Galina, aged thirty-two, also agreed to undergo treatment. It seemed that while on the drug she indeed lost interest in her girlfriend. Sitting in the chair, with a blank look on her face, Galina confessed to Derevinskaia that treatment of her homosexuality put a significant strain on her relationship with her female partner. Derevinskaia noted her testimonies:

> When her female partner came to visit her in the hospital, Galina was unable to say anything affectionate – she was silent most of the time and just smiled. She felt guilty because of this. She was still friendly with her partner, but she had no sexual desire towards her. When her partner tried to give Galina a hug or caress her, she just pushed her away abruptly …

On the fifth day following Galina's discharge from hospital, she resumed her homosexual relations.[26]

Another woman, Svetlana, aged thirty-seven, felt the unpleasant effects of the drug as well. Just as with other women, she was given psychotherapeutic sessions combined with the administration of aminazin. Svetlana was told that her desire was unnatural, that she was a healthy woman and she had to lead a heterosexual life and feel the joys of motherhood.[27] On the fifth day on the drug, Svetlana noted that her sexual desire had gone away completely and that she had become indifferent to everything around her. Her body temperature rose to almost 38 degrees, so Sviadoshch decided to take her off the drug, until her body temperature stabilised. But Svetlana refused to continue her treatment, and instead started writing letters to her former female lover, whom she had abandoned before checking into hospital. She pleaded for her to come back and soon they resumed their homosexual relations.[28]

The results of Sviadoshch's grand experiment on medically treating female homosexual desire were far from what he had expected. In fact, the gains were very modest. It was clear that aminazin merely eliminated the women's desire and did not affect their sexual orientation. Only three out of nine women who consented to medical treatment reported that they had become heterosexual – all of them were "passive" lesbians. In the case of "active" lesbians treated for homosexuality, all of them reported that their homosexual desire came back.[29] Despite this Sviadoshch was still convinced that treating homosexuality was possible and it was just a matter of time before an effective treatment scheme would be discovered.

On 4 June 1965, after almost ten years of working on the subject, Derevinskaia defended her dissertation at the Karaganda State Medical University. Her work received much praise from other doctors. Despite its ground-breaking potential and innovative research – after all it was the first Soviet attempt to conduct medical treatment of female homosexuality on such a scale – Derevinskaia did not turn her dissertation into a book. She knew that this topic was still very controversial and at the time of her defence, 1965, Soviet society was still rigid in terms of moral norms. Derevinskaia grew tired of this topic, wanting to work in a hospital with patients with general psychiatric conditions.

Her research supervisor, Abram Sviadoshch, was more ambitious. In the early 1970s, he moved to Leningrad, where he wrote and published his bestselling book *Female Sexopathology* (1974).[30] The book had an extensive section on lesbianism, which drew extensively on his former trainee's research. It could be argued that in effect he took advantage of her by using her research in his own publication.

While in the Soviet Union Derevinskaia was attempting to cure lesbians and to devise a cure for them, some of her American counterparts were working to disprove the theory that homosexuals were even sick at all. One of them was Evelyn Hooker, who in 1954, despite the prevailing homophobia and panic about homosexuals in American society, had the courage to challenge the orthodox psychiatric thinking that homosexuals were maladjusted, pathologically sick individuals.

In her research, for example, Hooker denied the popular assumption among psychiatrists that homosexuals were unable to sustain long-term relationships. Hooker argued that homosexuals experienced difficulty sustaining relationships only because of the fear of public exposure and humiliation. The main implication of Hooker's research was that homosexuals needed to be freed from exclusion and stigmatization.[31] Hooker's research created a scientific foundation for the subsequent challenging of the status of homosexuality as a psychiatric aberration. In the USSR, however, no such research existed at that time.

11

A KGB lieutenant goes rogue

Ukrainian SSR, 1963–1964

After the feared chief of Stalin's secret police and rapist of young women Lavrentii Beria was executed along with the members of his entourage in 1953, Khrushchev, as we have seen, set out to reorganize the secret police apparatus in the USSR and bring it under Party control. In 1954, he created the KGB – the Committee for State Security directly accountable to the Party.[1] Although the KGB was still headquartered at the same building on Lubyanka Square, Khrushchev sought to craft a new public image of security police officers – young, highly intellectual and respectable officers dressed in suits in contrast to the brutal and merciless thugs of the Stalin-era NKVD in leather jackets.[2] "Illiterate" and "backward" officers were gradually dismissed from the KGB ranks, giving way to young and tertiary-educated recruits.

Aleksei Petrenko had always dreamt of working for Soviet security organs and in 1952, at the age of twenty-three, he was admitted to serve in their ranks. In September 1956, he was transferred to the Special Department of the KGB in Kharkov to serve as a special agent. There he met his future wife Liudmila, and after getting married they started a family. When their first child was born, they obtained an individual flat in one of the newly built five-storey buildings not far from the city centre.[3]

But despite his rapid career advancement and marriage, Petrenko was unhappy. He and his wife Liudmila always had terrible rows and she often complained to the Party officials that her husband humiliated and beat her. Liudmila also thought that her husband's behaviour was very strange and secretive. He always came home very late, explaining that he had been at the bathhouse. Although they had a bathtub at home he went there at least twice a week. The bathhouse operated until ten o'clock but Petrenko came home at midnight, blaming his lateness on the long queues in the bathhouse and unreliable buses.[4] He was also frequently absent on Sundays and on these occasions he never explained where he had been either. If Liudmila casually enquired where he had been, Petrenko simply swore at her and went to bed. Once he even beat her and dragged her by the hair, spewing out insults.[5]

Through Petrenko's colleagues, some of whom she knew well, Liudmila tried to find out where her husband was spending all this time away from home. When one of them, Artem Glotov, approached Petrenko at Liudmila's instigation and tried to broach the subject, Petrenko drily explained that he worked with people and therefore was constantly busy with work. Glotov just shrugged and nothing else was said between them.[6]

One day, when an enraged Petrenko again beat Liudmila, she called up her father, who immediately reported Petrenko's behaviour to the local Party authorities and his KGB superiors, urging them to intervene. In Khrushchev's Russia it was common for local Party organs to summon spouses for an official meeting to discuss their family rows and reprimand them for their inability to live happily in their marriage – this is how Khrushchev made sure that families did not fall apart. A meeting of this kind was arranged in Petrenko's case with his KGB bosses and local Party officials in attendance. Apart from domestic violence, they were also going to discuss other, more recent instances of Petrenko's misconduct – his failure to return a sum of money which one of his colleagues had lent him and his disappearance from service for five days several weeks earlier. Petrenko, the lover of baths, was in hot water.

On 22 June 1963, he was summoned for a public dressing-down before Party and KGB officials. Taking turns, each Party member rose from their seat to criticize Petrenko for his physical attacks against Liudmila and his failure to pay back his debts. KGB officials also chimed in, accusing him of a graver crime – desertion from service for five days. Petrenko tried to explain himself and show some repentance for his actions. He admitted that his family life was not going in the desired direction, blaming Liudmila's father who obviously wished him ill. Petrenko's attempts to save face and his flimsy excuses regarding his desertion for five days found little sympathy with his superiors and Party members. They unanimously came to an agreement that Petrenko's irresponsible and disgusting behaviour made his retention within the ranks of the KGB impossible and harmful for the organization as a whole. It was decided to expel Petrenko both from the KGB and from the Party ranks, and this decision would come into effect in a few days' time.[7]

The outcome of the meeting devastated Petrenko – his career and personal life were at one fell stroke doomed. He left the Party building and sat on a bench at a bus stop, burying his head in his hands. He had to do something – but what could he do? A bus pulled up, discharging a group of people and suddenly a crazy idea came into Petrenko's head – he would just run away from all of them. From his problems, KGB and Party superiors and most importantly his wretched wife and her father. With this thought, he hopped on the bus, without even asking the driver where the bus was headed. He would go anywhere in order not to see Liudmila and her father again. Their faces blurred in his mind, forming one overwhelming dark cloud, that he struggled to put out of his head. On the bus he closed his eyes and fell asleep.

Petrenko did not even notice that the bus was bound for Zaporozhie, a city three hundred kilometres from Kharkov. Early in the morning of the next day, the bus pulled into Zaporozhie's bus station and all the passengers, including Petrenko, got off. He had visited the city before and was very familiar with the surroundings. After spending the entire night on the road, he needed to freshen himself up, so he resolved to pay a visit to the local bathhouse.

In the bathhouse, he managed to take his mind off his problems and unwind. In the washing chamber a tall man with a thin body and bald head asked Petrenko for a backrub, and then returned the favour. There was not much of a conversation between them. Once the bathing was finished, Petrenko thanked the stranger, got dressed and left the bathhouse.

Although the visit to the bathhouse calmed Petrenko's nerves to some degree, his thoughts were still frantically revolving around the events of the previous day. He needed to find a quiet place, where he could determine his next course of action to save his career and family life. He knew that, even though his bosses were about to fire him from the KGB, his disappearance would still be regarded as desertion as all the paperwork on his dismissal had not yet been put through. Wandering along the streets of Zaporozhie with his briefcase in one hand and deep in thought, Petrenko ended up in one of the city's leafy parks with lush green trees. There were a few benches here and there, standing in the shadows of the trees, and he chose one and sat down.

All of a sudden, he saw the figure of a man approaching from a distance. As the man drew closer, Petrenko recognized a familiar face – this was the man whose back he'd rubbed in the bathhouse an hour ago!

"What a coincidence," he thought to himself.

When the man was a few steps away, their eyes met and for some reason Petrenko felt nervous. A sudden thought flashed through his mind – this man must have been an undercover KGB officer, who had been following him all the way from Kharkov and had now come here with officers to entrap him. Petrenko shifted uneasily on the bench as he looked at the man.

The man introduced himself as Boris Kogan, extending his hand with a friendly smile. After they exchanged greetings, Petrenko moved to the side of the bench, motioning the stranger to take a seat by his side. Still wary of potential entrapment, Petrenko was initially reluctant to speak, until the stranger's amiable manner eased him into a lazy conversation about the weather. Kogan said that he worked as a doctor in the local hospital and that he had just seen his wife and son off to the countryside, where they usually spent the entire summer.

This remark left Petrenko wary of the man's genuine intentions. Was this man trying to invite him to his home? Was this a KGB entrapment, or something else? Petrenko could do with a place to stay as he did not have much money in his wallet to pay for a hotel. He thought for a second and said that he worked as a teacher and was visiting Zaporozhie on business. Petrenko also added that none of the hotels had vacancies and he was at a loss where to stay. Kogan invited Petrenko to stay the night at his flat and Petrenko readily accepted the offer.[8]

Kogan lived in a two-bedroom flat in a five-storey apartment block not far from the park. At home, he cooked dinner for Petrenko and treated him to a bottle of wine. Despite Kogan's hospitality, Petrenko still could not shake the suspicion that all this was an ambush. But as the time went by and nothing suspicious seemed to be happening, his fears gradually subsided. After their dinner, they washed the dishes and settled on the sofa to watch television. It was already dark outside.

Around midnight, Kogan suggested going to bed, explaining that he had to get up early for work the next day. Petrenko did not mind and both proceeded to the bedroom, where Kogan drew the blinds and switched on the floor lamp. He then pulled his shirt and trousers off – Petrenko followed suit. Unexpectedly, Petrenko asked Kogan if he had Vaseline.[9]

Kogan paused for a moment, making a mental note that Petrenko was experienced, and after a few seconds, nodded. Petrenko went to the bathroom for a shower, while Kogan produced a small tube of Vaseline out of the drawer of his desk. Kogan washed himself too and then lay in bed. No questions were asked and no conversation ensued – both knew perfectly well what was going to happen. Under the sheets, Petrenko embraced Kogan and drew him closer, pressing his lips against his.[10]

Despite Petrenko's initial intention to spend only one night at Kogan's flat, their sexual liaison protracted his stay for several days. During the day, Kogan left for work, leaving his guest alone in the flat. Upon his return in the evening, they cooked dinner, watched television and indulged in sex. An emotional bond was forming between the two, but Petrenko still refrained from telling Kogan the truth about himself – about his wife, his desertion and especially his work for the KGB. In fact, Kogan never asked any questions, seeming just to enjoy the company of his newly found lover.

On the third day of his stay in Kogan's flat, Petrenko decided to take a stroll around the city. Meeting Kogan had distracted him from his predicament, but now he needed to think things through and devise a clear plan to regain the respect and trust of his superiors and achieve reinstatement in the Party and the KGB. Consumed by his thoughts, Petrenko ended up in the same leafy park where he'd met Kogan a few days earlier.

In one of the park's corners sat a tiny concrete building – a public toilet, which Petrenko decided to use. Inside, dirty puddles spread across the concrete floor and the pungent aroma of urine hung in the air. The toilet was also uncannily silent. Wincing at the foul smell, Petrenko walked towards the urinals and began unbuttoning his trousers. Suddenly he heard shuffling steps behind his back, indicating that someone else had entered the toilet. Petrenko turned his head to see a stocky man in a raincoat with a briefcase in one hand. The man placed the briefcase on the floor and started fumbling with his belt at the far end of the urinal. The man threw a furtive glance at him, but Petrenko looked away. A few seconds later, when Petrenko glanced back uneasily, he realized that the stranger was still staring at him. Petrenko finished his business and promptly went, leaving the stranger standing at the urinal.

Driven by curiosity, Petrenko decided to watch what the stranger did next. He found a bench facing the toilet and sat there for a while, waiting for the stranger to come out of the toilet. Half an hour had passed but the stranger was still inside – Petrenko wondered if he'd somehow missed his exit. What was he doing there all this time? Petrenko waited for another ten minutes – but the man was still inside. His fascination and curiosity got the better of him and Petrenko walked back into the toilet. Just as he was about to enter, the stranger emerged from the darkness – their eyes met for a moment and their shoulders brushed against each other. Petrenko felt uneasy, so he lingered in the toilet for a minute, then stepped outside. The stranger was nowhere to be seen.[11]

Petrenko returned to the bench, watching the world go by for another half hour, until the man from the toilet reappeared. What happened next resembled Petrenko's first meeting with Kogan. The man politely enquired if Petrenko did not mind his sitting down, and, with an inviting gesture to proceed, Petrenko indicated that he did not. The stranger immediately introduced himself as Kirill Dolgorukov. Petrenko told the stranger his name and they shook hands.

Dolgorukov sat down and put his briefcase on his lap. Then he explained that he actually lived in Nikopol' and was visiting Zaporozhie on a business trip. Dolgorukov later recalled the details of his first encounter with Petrenko:

> Petrenko endeared himself to me and I started telling him about myself in more detail. I told him that I had been married ... Then I told him that during the war I was an army officer and that back then one senior lieutenant cajoled me into sodomy.[12]

Petrenko was listening carefully, surreptitiously checking Dolgorukov's appearance. Then he resorted to his usual story, telling Dolgorukov that he was a teacher visiting on business in Zaporozhie. As their conversation progressed, Petrenko also learnt that, apart from dabbling in homosexual sex, his interlocutor was also a priest and helped to operate a local church in his native town – Nikopol'. Furthermore, he helped to gather money for imprisoned priests to help them through their ordeal.

Dolgorukov did not disguise his contempt for the Soviet regime.[13] This took Petrenko by surprise – it was not every day that he heard such harsh and open criticism of the Soviet authorities. Petrenko listened and watched attentively. Again, for a second he feared that his interlocutor could be a KGB agent, but as Dolgorukov went further into details of his life, spewing ever more hatred towards everything Soviet, Petrenko became convinced that he was not.

Half-way through their conversation, Petrenko hit on a brilliant idea – he could worm himself into Dolgorukov's confidence, find out the names of other priests and then hand them over to the KGB as a dangerous group of state criminals who hated the Soviet Union's power and sought to undermine it. He could even explain that he disappeared on purpose to ensure the success of his 'undercover' operation. After they conversed for about an hour, Dolgorukov invited Petrenko to visit him in Nikopol' and Petrenko promised that he would do so over the following days.[14]

Later the same day, at dinner with Kogan, Petrenko announced to Kogan that he was going to Nikopol' to meet one of his fellow teachers there. The news saddened Kogan as he'd grown fond of Petrenko's company and did not want him to leave. Before Petrenko's departure, Kogan gave him a gift – a postcard with an inscription "To my beloved friend Vladimir, from Boris".[15] Although the inscription on the card made Petrenko feel uncomfortable, as he had not been used to receiving such signs of attention and affection from men, he put the card in his pocket.

After several days of spending time together, Kogan had developed a strong affection for Petrenko. Petrenko's intelligence and somewhat secretive comportment intrigued him even more. Although Kogan lived with a wife and had a child, he longed for a deep connection and an emotional bond with another man. He grew weary of casual encounters with strangers and he knew that constantly bringing men to his apartment while his wife and child were away was risky and could end in trouble. Kogan's tragedy, just like that of many other men like him, was that finding such emotional connection with other same-sex-desiring men in the USSR was extremely difficult, if not impossible. Men whom he met did not wish to fall in love with another man. Indeed, they never allowed themselves to think that love between men was possible. They did not wish to identify themselves with their desire – since society was telling them that it was either a crime, a pathology or a perversion.

Like many other men like him, Kogan relied on an extensive secret network of connections and acquaintances among other same-sex-desiring men in his town to find partners for sex. In the summer of 1962, a year before meeting Petrenko, Kogan had packed his family off to the countryside and gone to the bathhouse. There he met a handsome man named Filipp Pronin, who was bathing there with his little son. Kogan and Pronin rubbed each other's backs and had a conversation, from which it became clear to Kogan that Pronin was like him.[16] After bathing they went outside to have a chat, but since Pronin was with a child he could not accept Kogan's invitation to his flat. Several months later Kogan happened upon Pronin in the street and again they had a friendly conversation. Pronin mentioned on this occasion that he was friends with Gennadii Litrovnik, the chief doctor of the city's Children's Hospital Number Four.[17]

In winter of the same year, Kogan undertook an internship in the Children's Hospital Number Four with a group of other doctors. While he was standing in the hospital's cloakroom and checking in his coat, a doctor in a white gown came up to him, silently extended a crumpled piece of paper and then walked away. Baffled, Kogan unfolded the piece of paper, which was an invitation to Litrovnik's office after hours.[18] Kogan followed the instructions and after five o'clock he found himself standing in the required room, which turned out to be the office of the hospital's chief doctor – Gennadii Litrovnik. Litrovnik gestured Kogan to take a seat in the chair across from his table.

Litrovnik explained that he had seen Kogan in town a couple of times and that his friend, a certain Filipp, also told him about him.[19] The name Filipp did not ring a bell with Kogan at first, but then he flashed back to his encounter with Pronin in the bathhouse earlier that year and their conversation about his new acquaintance – the chief doctor of a children's hospital. Kogan realized that Pronin must have mentioned him to Litrovnik and probably had told him about his sexual interests in men. Scribbling his address on a piece of paper, Litrovnik invited Kogan to his flat.

Although Litrovnik was not married, he had a two-bedroom apartment, something that many Soviet families could only dream about in the 1960s. At home Litrovnik threw off his mask of the stern superior and seemed to become more at ease. Kogan and Litrovnik had dinner, conversing about unrelated matters and work – since both were doctors they indeed had many things to talk about. Yet once they started drinking wine their conversation shifted to more interesting matters.

On the face of it, Litrovnik was an exemplary member of Soviet society – he was a member of the Party and ran the city's children's hospital. But his lifestyle, which remained unknown to his subordinates, was a shattering reversal of his decent public image. He had been engaging in sex with men since he was twenty and he had many male acquaintances across the whole republic of Ukraine, who served him sexually in the hope of obtaining favours in return. In the middle of the conversation Litrovnik nonchalantly unbuttoned his trousers and, to Kogan's astonishment, pulled out his penis, firmly motioning Kogan to give him oral sex.[20] Kogan recoiled and winced at the exposed penis of his interlocutor, whom he found unattractive and whose manner struck him as condescending. Seeing that Kogan was not impressed, Litrovnik sighed disappointedly and pulled his pants back up. For a moment they sat in silence, but then both resumed their conversation as if nothing had happened. Kogan was telling Litrovnik about his life, while Litrovnik listened with a bored expression on his face. It astonished Kogan that Litrovnik was living a single life and did not even try to find a wife to fend off possible gossip among the staff of his clinic. Kogan later recalled the incident:

> I asked him why he was not married. He replied that he was not attracted to women and he would never marry. I told him that he needed to quit his "habit", pull himself together, but he told me that it was impossible. To my comment that he could be found out, he said that in that case he would commit suicide.[21]

After that Kogan heard nothing from Litrovnik, until one day he ran into him at one of the bus stops. It was raining heavily, buses were pulling up, with people getting on and off, hastily folding and unfolding their umbrellas. Kogan and Litrovnik stood in the pouring rain, waiting for their respective buses, when all of a sudden, Litrovnik's eyes shot in the direction of a young man in glasses who was trying to use a newspaper sheet as a shield against the rain. As the young man disappeared into the crowd on the bus, Litrovnik nonchalantly said that the young man had once given him oral sex.

Kogan shivered and looked about – could somebody have heard them? The rain was drumming against the roof of the bus stop – so probably not. Still, Kogan shuddered at the idea that somebody could have overheard their conversation.

When Kogan met Petrenko, he immediately forgot about all his past acquaintances. He even hoped that somehow they would manage to sustain their relationship, but Petrenko's news about needing to go to Nikopol' upset Kogan.

Nikopol', where Dolgorukov lived, was a small town, situated two hours away by bus from Zaporozhie. Once Petrenko arrived, it did not take him long to find Dolgorukov's flat. Seeing Petrenko in the doorway, Dolgurukov threw himself into his arms as if they were long-term acquaintances who had not seen each other for ages. Such a reaction took Petrenko aback and even made him a little embarrassed. Helping his guest to take off his jacket, Dolgorukov whispered to Petrenko not to worry about the presence of his father at home.

There was only one room in Dolgorukov's tiny flat, which he shared with his old father. They slept on separate beds with a single bed against each wall, with a distance of about one metre in between. There was one more person living in Dolgorukov's flat – his aunt, who slept on a couch in the tiny kitchen. Such an arrangement was not unusual in the Soviet Union – many flats remained in multiple occupancy and, despite the mass housing construction launched by Khrushchev, there was still a shortage of flats in the USSR. Dolgorukov's father and aunt always thought it was strange that Dolgorukov brought unknown men home and slept with them in the same bed, but it never occurred to them that they were his son's lovers. After all there was no free space in their flat and no place where they could put a guest, so having them share Dolgorukov's bed seemed reasonable.

On the first night, when Dolgorukov made space for Petrenko in his bed, he nodded in the direction of his father, who lay in the other bed. A few moments later, when his father started snoring, Dolgorukov pulled off his pants and with his buttocks exposed, turned his back to Petrenko. As Dolgorukov explained later, he wanted Petrenko to take the active role first in an attempt to demonstrate hospitality.[22]

The next day Dolgorukov took Petrenko to the local bathhouse, where they had sex several times in the steam room.[23] At night, when Dolgorukov's father fell asleep, they had sex too. During these first few days of his stay, Petrenko's initial plans to entrap Dolgorukov seemed to lose their relevance as he rejoiced in sexual ecstasy. He even scolded himself for being so brazen and fearless about having sex in public places and in the presence of Dolgorukov's father.

As he spent more and more time in Dolgorukov's company, Petrenko learnt about his wide range of acquaintances – other men who liked men. Petrenko had an immediate and impulsive desire to meet all these men and do the things that he had already done with Kogan and Dolgorukov, but then he put a stop to this train of thought. Time was against him and he urgently needed to come up with a plan for getting his life back and escaping punishment for desertion. He knew that he was playing a dangerous game: the more absent he was and the more he let himself indulge in his desire, the harsher the punishment and retribution would be. It had been more than two weeks since he'd left Kharkov and he would need to have something to show for his absence. There was also another problem – if he was to proceed with his plan, how could he make sure that Dolgorukov held his tongue about their sexual adventures when the police caught him? A fear of being brought to reckoning for his own actions loomed large in his mind.

About two weeks into his stay, Petrenko learnt more unsavoury details about the life of Dolgorukov, who, as it turned out, made friendships with young boys living in the neighbouring apartment blocks with the intent to importune or seduce them. One of these boys was fourteen-year-old Kostya Korablev, whose address Dolgorukov willingly shared with Petrenko. A few days later, Petrenko went to Kostya's flat, where he met his parents and broke the news to them about their son being the victim of sexual harassment.

Sitting in a tiny kitchen opposite Kostya's astonished parents, Petrenko informed them that a certain Kirill Dolgorukov was trying to sexually harass their son. But, he also hastily assured them, the KGB had the situation under control, and were aware that Dolgorukov was a member of a dangerous secret gang of homosexuals operating in the Soviet Republic of Ukraine. According to Petrenko, this gang seduced young people and tried to involve them in other illicit, mainly religious activities. Petrenko explained that in order to secure enough evidence for Dolgorukov's conviction, he needed to spend some time in their flat and would take Kostya out for a chat one day.[24]

Kostya's parents agreed and Petrenko stayed several nights at the Korablevs' flat and soon became acquainted with their son Kostya. Now a new plan came to him, which deviated, naturally, from his original intention to use Dolgorukov and his friends only as a target for the KGB. One day, as he took Kostya for a walk, Petrenko told him that he knew about his liaison with Dolgorukov. He then flashed his KGB card and said that Dolgorukov was a dangerous criminal who was preying on children and that the KGB needed Kostya's help in capturing him. Petrenko even promised Kostya that he would be able to take part in the KGB's secret operations against other homosexuals. Kostya was excited and willingly agreed to help Petrenko, who informed Kostya that their "secret operation" to entrap Dolgorukov would start immediately. Later Kostya recalled:

> Petrenko brought me to Chekistov Street and led me to a public toilet. On our way there he told me that the doctor was short and bald; he then told me that when the doctor entered the toilet, he [Petrenko] would give me a sign and I would have to follow the doctor into the toilet and make him invite me to his flat. I would have to go to his flat and when the doctor started molesting me, I was to throw something out of the window as a signal. Petrenko was to run for help, to walk in on us and to demand money from the doctor. We did not manage to do that, because the doctor would not come to the toilet.[25]

After this first unsuccessful operation, Kostya suggested visiting a local priest whom he knew and who, according to him, also corrupted young boys. Kostya's enthusiasm delighted Petrenko. Soon they found themselves standing in front of the porch of a five-storey apartment block, similar to the one Dolgorukov inhabited. This priest lived on the ground floor and before knocking on his door Petrenko gave Kostya new instructions: he should greet the priest and then tell him that one of Kostya's friends had fallen seriously ill because he had been molested by him. Then, Petrenko instructed, Kostya would have to demand money for his friend's "treatment".

Kostya nodded and went into the porch. Petrenko stood outside listening, and ready to come to Kostya's rescue if something went awry.

Kostya tapped on the priest's door and soon heard approaching steps. A tall, stocky man with a beard appeared in the doorway, frowning at Kostya. Kostya repeated what he had been instructed to say but the priest did not seem to understand what the boy wanted from him. Petrenko, who stood a few steps away, decided to intervene.

To the priest's shock, Petrenko emerged from behind Kostya, reached into his pocket and produced a KGB card. The priest, nervous now, motioned Petrenko into the apartment, while Kostya waited outside. Inside the flat Petrenko explained that the KGB was conducting a secret operation aimed at capturing homosexuals in the cities of the Soviet Ukrainian republic.

According to the information that Petrenko claimed to have gathered, the priest, who introduced himself as Vasilii, along with other adult homosexuals, met young boys in streets, befriended and then molested them. As a result, one of them, Denis, whom Kostya had mentioned, had become seriously ill and needed specialist treatment. Petrenko threatened to charge Vasilii with homosexual offences if he did not pay 150 rubles for the boy's medical treatment. Although Vasilii vehemently denied all allegations at first, he eventually agreed to help Denis, explaining that he felt sorry for him and genuinely wished to help the boy.[26]

Petrenko was content with his own quick thinking and ingenuity. Using his KGB card and Kostya as bait could not only help him entrap Dolgorukov and his friends but also improve his financial situation. Although one month had elapsed since his desertion, Petrenko was in no hurry to go back to Kharkov. He wanted to make the most of his situation, extorting as much money as he could and having sex with as many men as he could. He promised to himself that once he came back to Kharkov he would forgo his homosexual lifestyle and commit himself entirely to his family. He would start over, a new life! So he spent the whole of July staying at the Dolgorukovs' and the Korablevs' flats, occasionally updating Kostya's parents on the course of his "operation". Dolgorukov meanwhile, unsuspecting of Petrenko's actual intentions to entrap him, introduced him to various male friends, facilitating sexual relations between them and Petrenko. Dolgorukov liked Petrenko, he felt that there was some bonding between them, but he also did not mind him meeting and sleeping with other men.

By the end of July Petrenko had finally satiated his hunger for men and hastily began to orchestrate his secret plan of entrapping Dolgorukov and his friends on charges of creating a network of clandestine religious groups, corrupting young men. Petrenko also had to make sure that his own sexual liaisons with these men remained a secret for ever. He had to cover his tracks somehow – but how could he possibly do that? In the end, Petrenko decided that, if Dolgorukov and his friends ever dared to tell the investigators about their relations, he would be able to disprove them somehow. He did not know how – what occupied his mind now were the practical arrangements necessary for Dolgorukov's entrapment.

Kostya introduced Petrenko to his older friends Artem, Anton and Yura; all were seventeen years old and all of them regaled Petrenko with tales of Dolgorukov's sexual advances. In early August, Petrenko gathered the boys not far from Dolgorukov's house and warned them not to say anything to their parents. He explained that Dolgorukov was a criminal who had been under the KGB's watchful eye for a long time and that it was now the time to capture him red-handed.

Petrenko instructed the boys to approach Dolgorukov in the street and, by suggesting the possibility of sexual intercourse between them, lead him to a secluded spot in the bushes next to the stadium. There the boys were to start unlacing their shoes to encourage Dolgorukov to also undress. Then they would have to snatch Dolgorukov's pants and quickly bring them to the police, explaining that Dolgorukov had lured them into the bushes and tried to rape them. Petrenko promised to follow the boys closely and to help if they needed him.[27]

Enthusiastic about the exciting opportunity to take revenge on Dolgorukov, the boys headed to Dolgorukov's apartment block. Petrenko, who carefully followed them, knew that Dolgorukov would be at home that morning and he was just about to go to the park to look for men.

Petrenko instructed the boys to wait for Dolgorukov in front of the porch and went away to watch from a distance.

Dolgorukov emerged a few moments later and he could not hide his surprise at seeing all the boys together. Before he even managed to utter a greeting, Artem, smiling, took him by the hand and led him in the direction of the stadium.

Intrigued and grinning, Dolgorukov followed the boys. Petrenko, walking closely behind, was pleasantly surprised to see that the boys were quick on the uptake – they acted very convincingly and did everything as he had instructed them. They led Dolgorukov into the bushes behind the city's stadium and unlaced their shoes, pretending they were going to take them off. They also gestured towards his clothes, signalling their willingness to see him naked. Unsuspecting, Dolgorukov took the bait: he readily pulled off his trousers, expecting that the boys would follow suit. But instead, to his shock, he received a heavy blow into the stomach from Artem, who snatched his pants and ran away.

"Queer! Pederast!" the boys screamed in unison, running away from Dolgorukov, doubled over on the ground because of the sharp pain. "We are going to the police now!"[28]

Having finally recovered from the shock and the sharp pain in his stomach, and trying to cover his crotch with both hands, Dolgorukov made his way to the stadium building and reported the incident. The stadium's officials promptly called the police. There was no need to look for the boys – they had showed up at the police station themselves, holding up Dolgorukov's pants and screaming that Dolgorukov had tried to rape them. They also claimed that they were working for a KGB agent, who was following behind them. The police officers smelled a rat immediately.

Soon Petrenko was apprehended, handcuffed and taken to the police station. His KGB superiors and wife were immediately notified. A few days later, Petrenko was transferred to Kiev, where the KGB opened a criminal case against him and commenced interrogations. Dolgorukov was transferred to Kiev for interrogation too and when KGB investigators discovered the nature of his relations with Petrenko at first they could not believe it. But during the subsequent interrogations of Dolgorukov and his friends, who had also been detained, it became clear that allegations about Petrenko's homosexuality were truthful.

Major Timko, who was in charge of Petrenko's criminal case, could not hide his disgust towards his former colleague. He could bear the news about Petrenko being a deserter, an extortionist and even a liar, but not a homosexual. Embarrassed, Petrenko vehemently denied all allegations of his involvement in sex with other men, despite the mounting evidence to the contrary.

Petrenko tried to convince Timko of his genuine intention to hand over Dolgorukov on charges of homosexuality.

"But you know that the state security agencies are not interested in homosexuals," Timko argued. "We advise you to relate the true underlying motives of your acquaintance with Dolgorukov and identifying his friends."[29]

To this Petrenko responded: "I am indeed aware that state security agencies do not deal with homosexuals unless such individuals are guilty of other state crimes ... I got acquainted with Dolgorukov merely because I perceived him as a conspirator against the state; according to Dolgorukov he had previously been a member of a clandestine religious organisation ...."[30]

But Timko was not convinced. Dolgorukov testified many times about his and Petrenko's sexual relations as well as the fact that he had personally set Petrenko up with other men to facilitate sexual relations. Investigators also apprehended Kogan, who told them in detail about his and Petrenko's sexual relations, and found the victims of Petrenko's extortions. After extracting sufficient confessions from Dolgorukov and Kogan and their friends, Major Timko handed their cases over to the police for further investigation – Dolgorukov and Kogan subsequently stood trial and were convicted of sodomy.

The investigators suspected that Petrenko had begun to engage in homosexual relations long before his desertion in June and used his position with the KGB as a means of finding such men. Although they failed to establish any clear facts, the testimony of Petrenko's former colleagues suggested that it could have been the case. One of Petrenko's colleagues testified: "Petrenko collects data on homosexuals, that is, he does work that we, as KGB officers, are not supposed to be doing."[31] Another colleague of Petrenko said: "He imposed on me a number of ideas about homosexuals and insisted that we needed to work among them, since, according to him, there could be enemies in their circles – he tried to talk me into giving him freedom of action in these matters."[32] Another one testified: "Having come into contact with materials on homosexuals, Petrenko literally showed a very special interest in them, although by the nature of his work he did not have to deal with homosexuals ... Petrenko believed that among them he would find a spy."[33]

After the interrogations were complete, Major Timko sent Petrenko to Moscow for a month-long psychiatric evaluation at the Serbsky Institute of Forensic Psychiatry, run by the KGB psychiatrists. Timko hoped to discover what compelled Petrenko to seek sexual relations with other men. During the 1960s and 1970s, critics of the Soviet regime were confined to the Serbsky Institute, strapped to a bed for days and forcibly fed highly toxic drugs, causing them severe physical and mental pain. Such "treatment" lasted for months and its main purpose was to render these individuals incapable of continuing their attempts to undermine the Soviet state and to intimidate them.

Petrenko was put under the supervision of the notorious Daniil Lunts, a doctor and KGB colonel, who never donned a white gown as a Soviet doctor did, instead wearing his KGB uniform. At the Serbsky Institute, Lunts worked with political dissidents and was a strong advocate of punitive medicine. For a month, Lunts held conversations with Petrenko, gathering information about his family life and mental health. When Lunts asked Petrenko to comment on his homosexuality, Petrenko refused to say anything. A month later Lunts produced a report in which he described Petrenko's personality and pronounced his diagnosis, concluding that the patient was "sane" and that he did not "suffer from any mental illness".

According to Lunts, Petrenko demonstrated "psychopathic traits of character in the form of a tendency to irritability and excitability, self-centeredness, increased self-esteem, unstable interests and affective instability". As for Petrenko's sexual attraction to men, Lunts produced one terse phrase: "strongly denies a propensity for homosexuality".[34]

On 29 April 1964, the Military Tribunal of the Kiev Garrison sentenced Petrenko to six years in prison.[35]

12

Soviet doctors invent a new medical science and try to cure male homosexuality

Gorkii, 1963–1970

After Stalin's death, sex continued to be an obscure taboo subject, which generated a great deal of discomfort, tension and uneasiness in the overwhelming majority of Soviet people. Although many people did have sex, they rarely talked about it in their bedrooms and even less frequently with a medical professional, even when they experienced sexual problems such as impotence which threatened to ruin their marriages. Most men and women were too embarrassed to seek medical help, choosing to suffer quietly, while their untreated ailments developed further and worsened over time.

The embarrassment and shame around issues of sex made male impotence and female sexual dysfunction almost endemic in the USSR. To make matters worse, the profession of sexologist did not yet exist in the USSR as Soviet authorities believed that sex was an inherently unproblematic and straightforward matter, which required neither medical intervention nor counselling. Most doctors paid little attention to their patients' sexual lives, enquiring about it only in passing during medical appointments:

"And your sex life?" doctors would ask with lowered eyes, embarrassed to ask such a question.

"Normal," the patient would be expected to answer.

The uncomfortable conversation would usually end here. But if the patient unexpectedly decided to take the matter further, seeking advice, the doctor would just say something like: "Don't worry. You don't have cancer or an infection. And what you have, you won't die of. Give it a little time and it will cure itself." The problem, however, often didn't go away and usually got worse.[1]

Women suffered as well as men – and most of them, like Soviet men, silently embraced and accepted their lot. If some of them dared to complain to a doctor about the lack of sexual pleasure in their conjugal life, they would, in the majority of cases, hear a lecture on the seriousness of marriage and be reminded of their duties and responsibilities as wives.[2] A female gynaecologist might be slightly more sympathetic, saying: "Never mind, my dear: we manage to get by somehow and raise lovely children!"[3]

But not everyone was willing to embrace a life of quiet suffering. Some desperate men, suffering from impotence, wrote letters to the President of the Academy of Medical Sciences, Soviet's highest medical authority, pleading for help. One such man wrote:

> I can't call myself a coward, I fought with dignity and have been given state awards several times, but now I can't live, nor do I want to. I grabbed a rope in despair, but quickly came to my senses – this is unworthy of a Soviet man. Therefore, I suggest that you use me for any medical experiments that science needs.[4]

These men did not receive medical treatment as there were very few doctors in the USSR who had profound knowledge on the treatment of sexological problems. Dr Nikolai Ivanov, who, as we have seen, underwent a medical internship under the illustrious professor Igor Sumbaev from Irkutsk, was one of these doctors. In the mid-1950s, Ivanov left his mentor for the city of Gorkii, where he began his medical practice as a psychiatrist in one of the city's hospitals and a lecturer at the Gorkii Medical University.

Ivanov's lectures invariably attracted a large number of students avid for knowledge about sex, a topic which other lecturers preferred to avoid. Speaking in packed auditoriums, Ivanov would find a small pile of crumpled pieces of paper on his desk with students' questions, which they passed to the doctor. Ivanov would read them out loud to the audience and then offer an elaborate answer. Students listened mesmerized – nowhere before had they been able to find such full and compelling clarification on the issues in their questions – either in textbooks or in encyclopaedias. Students' ignorance about simple matters related to sex and their lack of knowledge on how to counsel patients on matters pertaining to their sex life struck Ivanov and drove him to look for ways of filling this gap in students' knowledge.

It wasn't only medical students who displayed a deep ignorance about sexual problems and their medical treatment. Ivanov's colleagues at the hospital also understood very little about how to render help to their male patients who complained of an inability to pleasure their wives or to maintain a steady erection. Urologists, for example, having heard complaints from the patient about "lack of marital happiness", would immediately run a battery of tests on their male patients to see if their penis was functioning properly. Having found no physiological pathology, they would refer their patient to a neurologist, who, after conducting a medical check-up, would send the patient back to the urologist. Sometimes they would refer him to the psychiatrist, who would also find no pathology and send back the patient, now convinced that they must be suffering from some identifiable terrible disease. Ivanov knew that the problem was not the patients' "unique" disease but the doctors' ignorance about anything outside their branch of knowledge as well as a lack of sexological training.[5]

Ivanov was certainly not the only one aware of the sexual disorders that Soviet men and women silently suffered. Other prominent urologists and neurologists were ringing alarm bells about the rising rate of untreated impotence and female sexual dysfunctions in the USSR and their disastrous consequences for Soviet people's family lives. Il'ya Porudominskii, a distinguished professor of urology from Moscow, raised the issue for the first time in the Soviet *Medical Newspaper*, a leading newspaper of the Soviet medical profession. On 29 November 1963, the newspaper published Porudominskii's article "Who Treats Sexual Disorders?", which alerted the medical community to the problem that blighted thousands of Soviet families:

> Male sexual disorder is a severe affliction, which often leads to the loss of ability to perform labour as well as irreparable family tragedies. Both the impossibility of creating a family and family conflicts have a negative bearing

on the physical and psycho-nervous state of the patient ... At the same time, diagnostic and therapeutic care for such patients [in our country] is extremely unsatisfactory. At clinics ... specialized practices should be organized to receive patients with impotence and infertility. And for the co-ordination of research work in this area, it is advisable to hold a special symposium.[6]

When Ivanov read Porudominskii's article, he wrote to the professor, proposing to host a symposium on sexology at Gorkii Medical University. Porudominskii welcomed the idea and shortly afterwards the first Soviet symposium on "sexopathology" – the name of the Soviet sexological science – was held in Gorkii in December 1963. The symposium drew doctors from many corners of the USSR, including psychiatrists, neurologists and urologists, who had already been curious about sexology, a science which they knew existed in some socialist countries but was absent in the USSR.[7]

More symposiums for sexologists followed in the subsequent years and, at last, in 1965 the Soviet Health Ministry inaugurated a Department of Sexopathology within the already existing Moscow Research Institute of Psychiatry.[8] The emergence of the first Soviet institution, albeit a small one, devoted to the problems of sexology was largely the result of lobbying from Porudominskii and Ivanov, who managed to convince the authorities that sexological research was needed to boost declining birth-rates in the country. The Department of Sexopathology occupied just a couple of offices and only a handful of doctors were engaged in its work, but at least now the government acknowledged the importance of such science and newly trained sexologists could do their work without the fear of being accused of indecency or pursuing "shameful" subjects.

Ivanov felt content: although he knew that Soviet sexological research was sparse and weak compared to that of Czechoslovakia and East Germany, the establishment of a Soviet Department of Sexopathology, with yearly symposiums and conferences on the latest trends in sexological treatment, was still better than nothing. He knew that the official establishment of such science and the involvement of greater numbers of Soviet doctors in sexological research would inevitably raise people's awareness about sexual disorders and make them more willing to seek treatment without shame and fear.

There was one particular group of people, Ivanov was convinced, who would especially benefit from the developments in Soviet sexology – homosexual men and women. He knew that many homosexuals were desperately trying to make sense of their feelings and desires, searching for information about their desire in medical encyclopaedias only to find a brief statement that homosexuality was a sexual perversion and a criminal act. They also suffered harassment at the hands of the police and lived in fear of prosecution. Ivanov believed that criminal prosecution of such individuals was pointless as homosexuality was a mental disorder, which should be treated by psychiatrists.

Ivanov expected that, with the development of Soviet sexology, more homosexuals would realize that medicine could help them "regain" their heterosexuality and live a happy family life. Working clandestinely under Sumbaev, Ivanov invented his own methods of treating homosexuality and, soon after the first series of sexological seminars, he published a treatise, *Questions of Psychotherapy of Functional Sexual Disorders* (1966), in which for the first time he presented his method of treating homosexuality to the Soviet public.[9]

Not everyone, however, was amenable to the scheme that Ivanov proposed. Prospective patients had to accept that their desire was a burden and a huge obstacle to their happiness, and they had to demonstrate a strong commitment to the treatment. The patient needed to be determined to get rid of his or her homosexuality. Homosexuals seeking help who had come to terms with their same-sex desires long ago, accepting it as a given, were not amenable to Ivanov's psychotherapy.[10]

Perfect candidates for treatment were homosexuals going through an acute life crisis, caused or aggravated by their sexuality. Some of them, for example, were severely depressed because of a recent rupture with their same-sex partner, or a betrayal by them, creating a receptive environment for the doctor's methods. Some homosexual men confessed that they were in love with their heterosexual friends and were suffering from unrequited love. Ivanov willingly took on such patients, because he believed these life events would give them the strength to reconsider their lifestyle and embark on a path to recovery.[11]

It was also very important for Ivanov to know whether the patient had already acted on their homosexual desires or not. If his patients only indulged in homosexual fantasies, but did not act on them, then they could be helped.[12] If the patient had bisexual tendencies, that is, desired and slept with both men and women, this was also a good sign and such a person could be given psychotherapeutic treatment with a possibility of success.

Ivanov also judged the way his prospective patients behaved and carried themselves during the appointment. Feminine behaviour in men and masculine behaviour in women made the success of treatment unlikely in Ivanov's view, so he advised these "stereotypical" kinds of patients to forgo the idea of treatment.[13]

Ivanov usually commenced treatment by having a conversation with the patient, in the course of which Ivanov learnt about their past and present life. Ivanov warned his patients that if they left their homosexuality untreated then their life would be miserable. Describing this initial stage of the treatment process Ivanov wrote:

> The doctor must convince the patient that his sexual experiences would be more enriching if they had an adequate heterosexual orientation … Homosexual desire does not lead to harmonious relationships and inevitably leads to spiritual emptiness. In addition, the clash of perverse desire with the demands of society can lead to the failure of one's career and contempt from loved ones and can entail legal responsibility.[14]

Then, during subsequent appointments, Ivanov encouraged his male patients to make friends with women and spend more time in their company, instructing his patients to "focus on the positive qualities of the [woman's] personality as a whole, and not to worry about the extent of his desire towards her".[15]

Ivanov accompanied these instructions and reassurances with lectures on how homosexual desire originated, believing that patients equipped with this knowledge about the origins of their desire would respond better to his therapy. To those patients who complained that they still struggled to divert their attention from men to women, Ivanov provided his "formulae of resistance" to male bodies, that is, special phrases and sentences, which the patients were supposed to repeat to themselves whenever they felt that their homosexual desire was getting the better of them. One of these formulae was the sentence: "I am now free of my previous desires, I am indifferent to anything that used to excite me."[16]

Ivanov's patients diligently followed all his recommendations and employed all his psychotherapeutic techniques, and although, by sheer force of will, some of them managed to convince themselves that they had become heterosexual and could even bring themselves to date and marry women, other patients were deeply disappointed by Ivanov's treatment methods and lack of results. Even so, during conversations with Ivanov, they always reported that they had achieved some degree of heterosexual desire and became more confident when communicating with women – trying to make themselves believe that the treatment had indeed produced results or out of fear of disappointing the doctor, fretting that he would hand them over to the police as incorrigible homosexuals. Ivanov, of course, never intended to report any of his patients to the police, and closely guarded their secrets and maintained their confidentiality.

In 1966, Ivanov received a patient named Leonid, a handsome young man in his twenties, who, by his own admission, enjoyed a wide popularity among ladies at the university, but was never truly interested in them. What is more, he believed that he was attracted to men, and this horrified him – he came to this realization during his university years. Leonid was saddened to see that all his male peers were happily getting married, while he was at a loss, not being able to bring himself to love a woman.

Ivanov attentively observed Leonid, who was fidgeting and shifting in the chair uncomfortably. He knew well how his patients felt when they were talking about matters as delicate as these and he always tried his best to put them at ease.

Leonid shuddered – he did not like the word "homosexual". He knew what it meant: a criminal and a psychopath – at least this is what he had read in the few books he managed to find in the city's library. He didn't want to associate himself with the word. He was still hoping that his feelings for men and this dreaded word were unconnected, but deep inside he suspected that there was no other term which could describe his affliction as accurately as this did. He was scared even to pronounce it as it seemed to him that if he acknowledged that he was a homosexual, then indeed he would always be one. The love that dared not speak its name, indeed. Leonid remembered his first encounter with Ivanov thus:

> I realized that I had an anomaly. I was attracted to men. I made numerous attempts to date girls. Through my acquaintances I came to Ivanov. After reassuring me that our conversation would not go beyond the walls of his office, he asked me: "Is it worth breaking nature?" And after I told him that I had had contacts with women, he said that we could try.[17]

Leonid convinced Ivanov that he would be fully committed and the treatment began, but then Ivanov suffered a stroke and had to discontinue the psychotherapy. Being compelled to focus on his own health, Ivanov handed his patients over to his young protégé – Yan Goland, who had been his dedicated trainee since the late 1950s. Like his mentor, Goland took great interest in the psychotherapy of homosexuality and, expanding on his mentor's psychotherapeutic method, created his own. We shall meet several of Goland's patients in later chapters.

Goland's version of psychotherapy for male homosexuality consisted of three key stages. The first stage was aimed at achieving "a sexual-psychological vacuum", a special state of mind, where the patient has lost his homosexual desire, but still has not developed any sexual feelings towards women.

During this stage Goland gave his patients hypnotic suggestions to develop a "calm, cold and indifferent attitude to men". Goland forbade his patients from visiting bathhouses and public toilets in order to avoid encounters with homosexuals, recommending that his patients occupy themselves instead with work or studies. He also gave his patients auto-training techniques, which were supposed to help them reduce the intensity of thoughts about men, encouraging patients to do auto-training every day and especially before going to bed. Goland recorded his patients' feelings after they completed the first stage of psychotherapy:

1. A feeling of liberation, joy and victory over themselves.
2. Indifference, calmness.
3. A feeling of being unwell with elements of confusion.
4. A fear of losing erotic emotions ... and uncertainty about whether they will be able to acquire heterosexual feelings. A feeling of emptiness and being sexless.
5. A rational and pragmatic approach ... A rational assessment of their new state.[18]

Goland construed these reactions as a sign of a successful completion of the first stage and recommended that such patients proceed to the second stage, during which Goland taught his patients how to perceive women aesthetically. Goland believed that at the heart of his patients' pathological desire was their distorted perceptions of women's beauty. Goland explained to his patients that it was important not just to learn to find beauty in women's appearance but also to appreciate her inner world, her kindness, gentleness and her caring attitude.

As part of the second stage Goland would seat his patient in a chair in front of him and deliver a hypnotic suggestion, holding up a woman's portrait by Russian and French artists or a photograph cut out of a magazine. Goland described this stage of treatment thus:

Demonstrating the portraits of women (reproductions of paintings by famous artists and photographs), the doctor draws the patient's attention to their aesthetically perfect, classically beautiful facial features ... The doctor instructs the patient to pay attention to women's faces and describe the most memorable face at the next appointment.[19]

Goland's patients complained that, although they were trying hard to replace their thoughts and fantasies about men with women, sometimes, in the streets or public transport, handsome strangers could stir a new spike of erotic sensations and emotions in them which they found difficult, sometimes impossible, to control. For cases like this Goland provided another coping strategy:

In the event of an unexpected fixation of attention on a man in the street, we recommend that the patient quickly switch his attention to some woman standing nearby, who is aesthetically interesting to him, which helps to immediately extinguish the accidental fixation of attention on a man.[20]

Discussions of women's beauty in the women's portraits and photographs continued until Goland became convinced that his patients were indeed becoming more appreciative of women's beauty.

During the third stage, Goland seated the patient opposite himself and held up more explicit photos of women, featuring partial nudity. According to Goland, it was important not to confront the patient with photos featuring complete nudity as it could evoke disgust on their part. First it had to be pictures of women with bare shoulders, then pictures with their breasts exposed and finally complete nudity. Goland explained:

Further conversations are also accompanied by illustrative materials, but of more explicitly erotic nature ... During these conversations we focus on individual parts of women's body.[21]

Goland took his patients' positive feedback at face value, without questioning its truthfulness. He was more than happy to hear about his patients' progress as it only confirmed the efficacy of his treatment methods and elevated his status as the leading specialist in the treatment of homosexuality. Goland collected his patients' testimonies and cited them in his research papers, which he then presented to his colleagues at conferences. Although many of Goland's patients indeed reported positive outcomes of the treatment, they still felt that the treatment was not working. But seeing how proud Goland was of his therapy and how passionate he was about helping his patients, they did not dare question his methods and just tried to tell Goland what they thought he wanted to hear. Some patients were unsuccessful in convincing themselves that the treatment was working, but still they significantly exaggerated the extent of their progress.

Soon Goland presented the results of his psychotherapy for homosexuality as well as testimonies of his patients in his research paper "Consecutive Three-Step Psychotherapy of Male Homosexuality", which he published in 1972. The paper described the course of the therapy and its early results.[22] The final paragraph of his paper proudly reported:

> A follow-up study … of the ten patients who underwent our psychotherapy demonstrated that the patients successfully carry out a normal heterosexual life and completely got rid of their previous pathological desire.[23]

Goland wished to impress his colleagues with his successes and wanted them to see the fruits of his work with their own eyes. He persuaded some of his former patients, who had been successfully treated for homosexuality, to give their testimonies about their past homosexual life and their present heterosexual life at one of the conferences, in front of other psychiatrists. Understanding that his patients could find such a public appearance uncomfortable, Goland's assistants put heavy make-up on them, wigs and dark glasses to make sure that their identities remained anonymous.[24]

These confessions of Goland's patients deeply shocked experts and psychiatrists, but most of them still remained sceptical of Goland's patients' testimonies. Even so, Goland's fame as the only Soviet psychiatrist qualified to treat homosexuality continued to grow, spreading across the entire USSR.

While Soviet doctors were only slowly attempting to wrest homosexuals out of the police's hands and turn them into patients, doctors in other European nations had already succeeded in pressuring the authorities to decriminalize consensual homosexual acts between males. Following the decriminalization of homosexuality in Czechoslovakia in 1961, in 1967 England and Wales decriminalized most homosexual acts and West Germany did the same in 1969. Even communist countries like East Germany and Bulgaria removed sodomy laws from the books in 1968. Other countries would soon follow suit, but in the Soviet Union, as in Australia for example, progress was far from swift.

Part III

Under Brezhnev

Soviet jurists try to decriminalize consensual homosexuality

Leningrad, 1966

On 14 October 1964, the Soviet leader Nikita Khrushchev, who had presided over the USSR for eleven years, was stripped of his party posts and forced into retirement by the men whom he had hitherto considered his closest comrades. Khrushchev's fellow Party members accused him of violating collective leadership, consolidating power in his own hands and promoting a cult of personality. Fortunately for Khrushchev, he was not executed – nobody even publicly criticized him. He was merely cut off from public life. Overnight, his name was scrubbed from mass media and consigned to oblivion. Such a "smooth" transition of power signalled the increasing maturity of the Soviet society – violence was becoming a thing of the Stalinist past. Indeed, had Khrushchev faced similar charges under Stalin, he would have been shot immediately.

Leonid Brezhnev, one of Khrushchev's most trusted people, succeeded him as the country's political leader. The Brezhnev era, which spanned eighteen years, began with an impressive economic growth, leading to an unprecedented rise in Soviet people's living standards. The mass housing campaign launched by Khrushchev continued during the Brezhnev era, moving millions of Soviet families out of cramped barracks and communal flats into their own separate flats. As a result of the government's efforts to keep prices down, and because of rising wages, ordinary Soviet citizens could now finally afford to buy furniture, fashionable clothes, household appliances and even a car. Despite shortages which afflicted Soviet stores, the Brezhnev era was still a time of a veritable consumer boom, which was especially evident in big cities like Moscow and Leningrad.[1]

However, at the same time Brezhnev backpedalled on the liberal reforms of his predecessor and unleashed the prosecution of Soviet intellectuals who dared to speak critically about the Soviet government. In 1966, the Soviet writers Andrei Sinyavskii and Yuli Daniel endured a show trial in Moscow, facing accusations of anti-Soviet agitation and propaganda for their satirical writings on Soviet life, which they published abroad under pseudonyms. The sentences passed down on the writers were severe: Sinyavskii was sentenced to seven years in a strict-regime labour camp, while Daniel was sentenced to five years' imprisonment.[2]

Along with a clampdown on dissent, Brezhnev hushed up the anti-Stalin campaign in the press, beginning a gradual restoration of Stalin's respectable reputation. In part, he was doing so to gain the support of the old party members who were terrified by Khrushchev's attack on Stalin, which to them represented the loss of the party's ideological control along with a threat to their own power and influence.

Brezhnev's political repressions and odes to Stalin did not, however, discourage Soviet dissidents from protesting. Despite their small numbers and lack of strong political organization, reform-minded people were still a perennial headache for authorities and the KGB. Soviet dissidents leaked written works critical of the Soviet regime to the West, staged protests and ran underground periodicals about violations of human rights in the country and the state of political protests in the country. The KGB did everything they could to crush this movement, harassing, intimidating and forcing dissidents into emigration. Some were even imprisoned or confined to closed mental institutions for compulsory medical treatment.[3]

Abroad, Brezhnev also wanted to show that the USSR had zero tolerance for any capitalist sentiments or calls for democratic reforms in its satellite countries of the Eastern Bloc. When in 1968 the newly elected government of Czechoslovakia led by Alexander Dubček announced plans to democratize the nation and lessen Soviet control over the country's affairs, Brezhnev sent Soviet tanks into the country, crushing Dubček's movement. Many dozens of Slovaks and Czechs were killed and many others were severely wounded. Dubček, who called upon the people not to resist, was removed from the country's leadership and the Soviets restored their political control over the country.[4]

As for Soviet homosexual people, many benefited from the continued construction of housing in the country. New apartment complexes springing up in cities afforded Soviet homosexual people opportunities to congregate and meet each other in private flats, thus avoiding the watchful eye of their neighbours. Although public toilets, railway stations and bathhouses were still widely used for cruising, private apartments were far safer and less likely to attract the attention of the police.

Moscow and Leningrad, the country's largest cities, continued to attract Soviet homosexuals from all corners of the country, promising better living standards and ample professional opportunities unavailable in smaller cities. Moscow was an especially desirable destination and, in order to get a Moscow residence permit, homosexual men and women from other cities, like their heterosexual counterparts, sought to marry someone from the capital.[5]

The political developments of the Brezhnev era also brought about the possibility of a change in Soviet legislation regarding the regulation of homosexual behaviour of Soviet adult men. The development of criminological scholarship and enhanced participation of legal scholars in Soviet policy-making, which began under Khrushchev, continued well into the Brezhnev era. In a bid to improve the quality of investigative work, scholars wrote educational tracts, in which they explained how to lawfully perform interrogations, collect evidence and even shed light on the ambiguous articles of the Soviet Criminal code, which inexperienced investigators could find hard to comprehend. Article 121.1, which penalized consensual homosexual sex between two adult men, was particularly ambiguous – investigators simply did not know how to approach such cases as the consensual nature of relations between the men implied a lack of basis for initiating a criminal case. The tricky nature of the law and difficulties in solving such crimes, which many investigators often complained of, sparked discussion among Soviet scholars about whether such a piece of legislation was needed at all.

In 1965, a jurist from the Saratov Legal University, Mikhail Khlyntsov, published a manual, *Investigation of Sex Crimes*, which focused specifically on sex crimes and explained to investigators how to collect evidence, interrogate suspects and find criminals when investigating them. Despite the ambiguity of the Article 121.1, Khlyntsov sought to justify its retention in the Soviet Criminal Code:

> This crime is especially dangerous because it encroaches on the moral foundations of our society and demoralizes the psyche of its members. The propensity for sodomy in certain individuals can be explained by ... their lack of fulfilment with normal means of satisfying sexual desire and the pursuit of new sensations which attests to their debauchery and their contempt for moral norms.[6]

> As our practice shows, if sodomy is committed on a voluntary basis, then homosexuals do not limit themselves to one encounter and continue to meet in the aftermath. Some of them develop a certain kind of affection for each other, which eventually turns into a long-term unnatural relationship. As a rule, this inclination for sodomy turns into a habit, and the person who engages in it becomes a habitual pederast.[7]

Prosecuting such people under Article 121.1, Khlyntsov lamented, was a tall order as there were often no witnesses and the main suspects were reluctant to co-operate with investigators because both of them faced imprisonment.[8] If investigators did not manage to catch homosexuals in the act of their crime, then Khlyntsov recommended that investigators should gain information on their "moral profile", by interrogating the suspects' social circles and finding out information about their inclinations and hobbies. The suspects' neighbours in the apartment block were also useful sources of intelligence as they could point out suspicious traits of suspects' behaviour, proving their inclinations to sodomy.

Khlyntsov also recommended that investigators should interrogate the suspects' wives. Homosexual men in the USSR, as in other parts of the world, married women for many reasons, including a desire to disguise their sexuality and conform to society's expectations. If suspects' wives reported that their husbands had tried to incline them to "perversions" such as oral and anal sex, then their testimonies could serve as good evidence of their husbands' inclinations to homosexuality.[9]

Conducting forensic examination of the suspects could also help, but only in a handful of cases. Khlyntsov commented that forensic experts could find very few signs of sodomy on the suspects' bodies and it was almost impossible to identify such signs on the body of "active" homosexuals. "Passive" homosexuals were more likely to present signs of sodomy such as anal tears or even bleeding, but again such evidence could not be taken at face value and had to be considered in conjunction with other evidence.

While Khlyntsov struggled to provide practical advice on how to investigate cases under Article 121.1, other jurists saw no point in doing so and suggested eliminating the Article altogether. Jurists from Moscow, like Aleksei Ignatov, who graduated from the prestigious Moscow State University and lectured at several Moscow universities, made the first attempts to challenge the usefulness of Article 121.1. It was obvious to him that, if sexual relations between the men were consensual, then prosecuting them was pointless. The developments in socialist countries of Eastern Europe, where doctors and jurists managed to achieve the removal of laws prohibiting consensual homosexuality between adults, lent further support to his ideas.

Ignatov believed that the removal of Article 121.1 could actually be of benefit to the country's international reputation as it could be construed as proof of the USSR's ostensible tolerance towards minorities. But, at the same time, he was also cognizant of the obstacles along the way to removing the article from the Criminal Code. The country's political establishment held extremely conservative views about sex and most probably would not appreciate a proposal to legalize sexual acts between men. Party officials were also unlikely to support the decriminalization of sodomy due to fears that the prevalence of homosexual relations in society would further exacerbate the acute demographic situation in the country.

Ignatov was also aware that proposing such bold reforms could have a negative bearing on his professional career since he himself could be accused of being a homosexual. Like many other successful university lecturers, Ignatov had ill-wishers who would be willing to spread rumours about his own propensity to homosexuality not just to get him fired and take his place at the university, but also to have him expelled him from the Party for immoral behaviour and barred from future employment.

Still, he simply could not turn a blind eye to the fact that many judges punished men for any type of homosexual behaviour. Under Article 121, only sodomy, or anal intercourse, was illegal – other forms of homosexual behaviour such as kissing or oral sex were not mentioned and therefore could not be deemed illegal. Nevertheless, many courts ignored this definition or simply did not wish to adhere to the strict interpretation of the law, prosecuting men for oral sex and sexual touching.

Ignatov raised this issue in his monograph *Liability for Crimes against Morality* (1966), condemning this practice and calling on judges and investigators to draw a clear line between those who engaged in oral and in anal sex, arguing that only the latter should be prosecuted under the existing legislation:

> We cannot approve of the tendency of some courts to expand the notion of sodomy, placing any satisfaction of sexual passion between men within this category. If two men commit consensual depraved acts between one another [without engaging in anal intercourse], thereby satisfying their sexual desire, they should not be subjected to a criminal penalty, since the Soviet criminal code does not view such actions as a crime.[10]

Many Soviet people would still disagree with Ignatov, believing that anything other than "traditional" vaginal sex was a perversion and therefore, had to be punished, or at least condemned. For many people oral and anal sex, even between a man and woman, were reprehensible acts per se, so Ignatov's call that men who engaged in such practices should be deemed innocent would find little sympathy with homophobic judges and investigators.

As we will see in Chapters 18 and 23, Ignatov continued his attempt to advocate for the decriminalization of consensual homosexual acts between males during the 1970s and 1980s. But Ignatov was not the only jurist who challenged Article 121.1. In the 1960s, Pavel Osipov, a young doctoral student from Leningrad University, was also of the opinion that Article 121.1 should be removed from the Soviet legal code. In his dissertation boldly titled "Sex Crimes", he wrote:

> First of all, the desire to satisfy sexual need in a homosexual way may be congenital in nature, that is, conditioned by the biological peculiarities of an organism ... As a result, for people endowed with this anomaly, homosexuality is a natural means of sexual fulfilment. That is why the widespread contention, according to which sodomy is always a result of moral depravity, cannot be regarded as valid.[11]

Osipov also gave a nod to the emerging sexological research in the USSR, which framed homosexuality chiefly as a medical problem:

> One may ask what goal the legislator pursued when criminalizing non-forcible homosexuality, if at issue here are the people with a biologically distorted sexual instinct. There is no doubt that with the help of criminal law it is impossible to rectify this biological anomaly and encourage the individuals in question to satisfy their sexual need in a heterosexual way.
>
> In the Soviet legal literature there has never been an attempt to justify criminal liability for consensual sodomy, and the only argument which is usually offered against it – the [resulting] individual's depravity and his violation of communist morality – cannot be regarded as sufficient.[12]

Osipov also stated that it was pointless to impose heterosexuality on homosexual people, since they could still engage in homosexual behaviour in the privacy of their flats undisturbed by the police. If housing shortages of the Stalin era made domestic spaces precarious and inconvenient places for sex, Brezhnev-era mass housing construction and the increasing accessibility of private flats made such encounters more possible for homosexuals. Osipov urged the police to acknowledge this fact and bring the obsolete legislation in line with reality:

> Taking into consideration the exceptionally intimate nature of actions directed at the satisfaction of sexual desire and hampering the effective control over behaviour of the subjects involved, the legislative ban on homosexuality cannot be effective in preventing undesirable forms of sexual desire satisfaction from arising, nor can it stimulate people to behave properly.[13]

Yakov Yakovlev, a legal scholar from the Soviet Republic of Tajikistan, also argued that male homosexuality should not be treated as a crime. In his article "Liability for Sodomy According to the Soviet Penal Law" (1968) he admitted that homosexual relations indeed violated socialist morality, but preferred to fight them with sex education, rather than police oppression:

> We also believe that this liability should be abolished due to the following considerations. It goes without saying that homosexual relations go against our socialist morality and we should fight them even in those cases, when they do not violate the sexual freedom ... of adults ... Yet, the fight against homosexuality in the absence of aggravating circumstances should be conducted not through criminal repression, but through proper sex education in the family and school as well as application of the measures of medical character to those homosexuals, whose sexual perversions are caused by pathological alterations in their body.[14]

Although these views were expressed by renowned academics, their voices and opinions in the 1960s were still too weak to be taken into consideration by authorities and even less so to initiate legal changes.

In the US during the same period of the 1960s, the idea that private, consensual adult homosexual relations should be decriminalized was winning support among prominent jurists and attorneys.[15] American newspapers also reported on the decriminalization of most homosexual acts in England and Wales, either endorsing Britain's progress towards decriminalization or adopting a neutral stance when reporting on it.[16] American legal professionals argued that private consensual homosexual acts posed no danger to either the person or their property. Like their Soviet counterparts, American jurists pointed out that sodomy laws were difficult and even impossible to enforce, especially when it came to private consensual sex between two men.[17] But despite such overwhelming support on the part of American legal professionals for the repeal of sodomy laws, their views were still taking time to become law.[18]

14

A couple try to save their marriage
Gorkii, 1968

Nadezhda was furious and just couldn't stand it any more.[1] By 1968 her marriage with Andrei was falling apart and it seemed as if he couldn't care less. Shortly after their wedding, it had become clear to her that there was little love between them and she soon realized that their marriage was a grave mistake. They struggled even to have a friendly conversation, and most of the time they spent together Andrei treated Nadezhda like a housewife. There were no kisses, embraces or affection, let alone sexual intimacy. During the first months of their conjugal life, Nadezhda attributed this to Andrei's shyness and modesty but soon she grew impatient. Whenever she attempted to initiate sex, Andrei pushed her away and when she insisted he lost his temper.[2]

When they went to discotheques at Gorkii's dance hall on Sundays, Andrei never danced with Nadezhda. Very often he just left her there alone and went off to have a beer at a nearby café with his buddies, none of whom, Nadezhda always noted, were other married men with faces bloated from drinking, but handsome young men.

Two months into her marriage she struck on the idea that Andrei was having an affair with another woman. She even attempted to extract confessions from him, starting fights, but Andrei firmly denied everything. Soon Nadezhda abandoned this idea: after all how could he possibly have another woman? They lived in a tiny town and, if he did have one, Nadezhda would soon have heard about it.[3]

In fact, deep inside, Nadezhda suspected that it was very unlikely that Andrei would be cheating on her with another woman. It seemed as if he was more interested in friendships with young men, and sometimes she even conjured up certain images in her mind, but then pushed those thoughts away. Then again, seeing all the men around him, and only men, her mind would return to her suspicions which she again tried to dispel.

Four months into their family life, exasperated and weary of the constant fighting, Nadezhda confronted Andrei, asking whether he really loved her. It happened in bed, after another unsuccessful attempt on her part to initiate sex. Andrei's face contorted with rage; he leapt out of bed, and stormed out of the room into the tiny kitchen, where he vowed to spend the night. Nadezhda described this incident thus: "I realized that he had stopped loving me. And did he ever even love me at all? I tried once to talk to him – four months into our marital life. He cut me off, warning me that he wouldn't tolerate any more such conversations."[4]

After working a day shift at the town's chemical plant, Andrei went to the local theatre, where he worked a second job as the director's assistant. He spent most evenings there, coming home very late to evade Nadezhda. One night, consumed by her dark thoughts about Andrei's infidelity, Nadezhda decided to pay him a surprise visit at work in the theatre. What she saw shocked her deeply, and froze her to the spot. Behind the stage, among the set decorations in the dark, Andrei lay embracing another man, kissing him long and hard on the mouth. Both seemed to be drunk.

Nadezhda stood stunned and frozen, while a thousand conflicting thoughts raced through her mind. She felt both offended and humiliated. Andrei reappeared with his coat and, grabbing Nadezhda by the elbow, hustled her out of the theatre. They walked home in silence and did not speak for several days. Andrei preferred to ignore the incident and gloss over it, but Nadezhda could not calm down, terrifying questions repeating themselves over and over. What was happening with her husband? Was anything wrong with her? Was she so horrible a wife that Andrei preferred the company of other men? Whom could she turn to for help?

At first, she was at a loss as to what to do, but then she decided to turn to medical literature in the local library in the hope that it would shed some light on her quandary. Leafing through the *Great Soviet Encyclopaedia* she stumbled upon one entry which precisely described what was happening with Andrei. The entry was titled "homosexuality" and it read: "A sexual perversion, consisting in an unnatural attraction to persons of the same sex. There is a criminal punishment for sodomy in the USSR."

Rereading the entry in horror and shock, Nadezhda tried to get her breath back. She suspected that Andrei had some medical condition, but she hadn't suspected, even in her angriest moments, that it could also be a crime. Nadezhda was devastated – her husband Andrei was a criminal! What was she going to do? Her first urge was to report him to the police, but she quickly rejected the idea – although Andrei had treated her poorly, she still loved him and she wanted to help him.

She decided to confront her husband that very day. She knew her interrogation would aggravate him and trigger another huge argument, but she didn't care at this stage – things had gone too far and she needed clarity. In the evening, when Andrei silently got into their bed and was about to switch their bedside light off, Nadezhda started the unpleasant conversation. She later recalled this episode thus: "And one day, after reading some literature, I asked him directly whether he was a homosexual. He replied affirmatively. That drove me mad. I forbade him to talk with boys and I told him if I saw him again with them – I would report him to the police".[5]

Andrei didn't take his wife's threats seriously and despite her warnings he continued to meet other men. On one occasion at a party, Nadezhda spotted him in the embrace of another young man, whom he was also kissing. She didn't demand explanations this time despite being angry and frustrated. She consoled herself that, even though her love for Andrei was not reciprocated and he brazenly cheated on her, at least their faulty marriage gave them the right to live in their flat. If they got divorced, the government would probably take the flat back and she would be forced to go back and live in a crowded dormitory.

But soon she lost her patience – one evening she came home to catch Andrei having sex with another young man in their bed! Andrei tried to explain that he and the young man were just friends, but Nadezhda wouldn't let him deceive her again. Nadezhda described this episode thus: "Once I came home from work and I found him with a nineteen-year-old guy. He told me that the guy had nothing to do with him ... He [Andrei] also said he had become impotent."

Andrei's confession that he became impotent sounded like a cry for help and it deeply moved Nadezhda. Andrei was ill and he needed help, and Nadezhda, who still had deep feelings for Andrei, wanted to help him and save their marriage. She immediately offered to find a doctor, and Andrei, to her surprise, agreed. From her friend, who worked as a nurse in the local hospital, Nadezhda learnt about Yan Goland, a young and promising expert in sexual problems, who lived and received patients in the nearby city of Gorkii, as we learnt in Chapter 12.

Nadezhda took the bus to Gorkii and soon she found herself sitting in a chair opposite a tall and broad-shouldered doctor with a wide smile – Yan Goland. There was something magical and eccentric about him – when Nadezhda heard his last name she could not stop thinking about Woland, a character from Bulgakov's controversial novel about good and evil, *The Master and Margarita*. Goland certainly had a mysterious aura. He spoke with an air of authority and his strong booming voice rang with knowledge and confidence. Nadezhda felt that he could help her husband and described her problem, while Goland made notes and nodded understandingly.

Goland listened to Nadezhda's story, after which he asked her to bring Andrei for an appointment. He also promised her that everything they would be talking about would be completely confidential. Soon Andrei sat in Goland's office too. Goland asked Andrei to share his story.

Although Andrei had not intended to disclose everything, planning to avoid embarrassing details and explain his problem only in very broad terms, Goland managed to put his mind at ease. Andrei told Goland absolutely everything about his attraction to men and how difficult it was for him to live with Nadezhda. Somehow this giant in a white gown gave Andrei confidence that maybe his life could indeed be rectified with a medical intervention, so maybe Nadezhda's nagging him to seek medical help was not in vain. After all, leading a double life and having to live in constant fear exhausted Andrei. Goland assured him that his homosexuality could be corrected with psychotherapy but only on the condition that he did psychotherapeutic exercises with conscientious regularity and most importantly cut off all his affectionate liaisons with other men. Andrei promised Goland to follow all his recommendations.

To begin with, Goland instructed Andrei to produce an autobiography with a special focus on his sexual fantasies, emotions and liaisons, detailing when and how he first felt his desire for men and how it manifested itself. At first, Andrei felt uneasy. What if someone found his notes and read them? he thought. What if Goland decided to hand him over to the police and use these notes as evidence of his homosexuality? After all, sodomy was a crime and producing such a detailed account of one's homosexual trysts could bring many undesirable consequences. When he raised his concerns with Goland, the doctor allayed his fears and asked him to omit all personal details from his autobiography. Goland also hastened to assure Andrei that he had no intention of handing him over to the police and that, by providing medical help to homosexuals, he himself ran a certain risk of getting in trouble.

Andrei had written autobiographies before – like many other Soviet citizens he had to write one when he was applying to study at the university, but the autobiography that Goland asked him to write was a difficult one. The main difficulty was naming and describing his desires and emotions towards men – never in his life had he attempted to articulate or reflect on his homosexual urges, or written about them. When he struggled to commit his feelings and emotions to paper, he often consulted with Goland, who equipped him with the correct words and helpful medical terms. It was in the process of writing his autobiography that Andrei finally learnt the name of his medical condition – homosexuality. Now he knew that he did not have to beat himself up over his desire, as it was not his fault – he was just sick. And he was doing the right thing – he sought help and this was surely going to help him. Soon Andrei's autobiography was complete:

> I began to feel attracted to girls in secondary school and I always sought reciprocity from them. But from the age of thirteen I also began to fall in love with the boys. I usually loved the two: a girl and a boy, but while I loved girls like a boy, I wanted to be a girl for the boys I loved.
>
> At the same time I never thought about my strange feelings as I believed that attraction to a man was a normal feeling ... Moreover, back then I had a natural attraction to girls.
>
> But my interest in girls gradually ceased during my life at the university. I explained to myself: I just can't find the ideal of female beauty and intelligence among the girls around me. I went to discotheques, but I avoided the company of girls. I attended a drama club and sometimes during rehearsals even hugged and kissed girls, but all these actions were theatrical and had no genuine intention behind them.
>
> During my second year of university, I became alienated from girls, an invisible wall arose between me and them and I began to feel like an actor in my own life. In order to demonstrate to everyone that I am a real man just like every other man, I forced myself to meet new women, I persuaded them to have intimacy. During my sexual encounters with them, I conjured a man in my imagination...
>
> The sight of naked young men in the showers on the beach thrilled me and caused an erection. Once in the shower pavilions, a young man standing in the adjacent shower cabin noticed my erection and suggested masturbating each other. We agreed on a meeting. On the day of the meeting I went to a flat, where I was met by three more homosexuals. I had sex with each of them taking turns.
>
> Up until my graduation, I frequented meeting places of homosexuals and I had regular encounters with them. Most often, I played a passive role in sexual intercourse. But at the same time, I maintained a heterosexual relationship.
>
> In 1965, after graduating from university, I arrived in the city of K. It was a small city where everyone worked at a chemical plant and knew each other personally. At first I was afraid to show my true side to anybody in the town. Soon, my workmates started to wonder why I was still not married. Living in a small town like this, where everyone was friends with one another, made me careful and made me disguise myself in every possible way as a heterosexual.

My workmates started to introduce me to girls and I even began to have hopes that I would be able to have a family life. In the local club house, I met a homosexual, who advised me to get married and thereby shield myself from all the unnecessary questions.

Then I started courting a young lady, who was also part of our drama club and we got married in 1966. With great difficulty I tried to satisfy my wife, but our sexual intercourse never worked out. Even imagining other men during intercourse did not help. So I continued maintaining homosexual contacts.

After a year of marriage, my wife decided that I was impotent and offered to seek treatment. At first I tried to deny that and continued to maintain homosexual contacts nevertheless. Once, after a family party, my wife noticed that I was very cheerful in the company of young men, whom I had invited and was kissing there with great pleasure. After that, I confessed to her that I was a homosexual, explaining that sex between us would not work.[6]

Goland collected Andrei's handwritten notes and typed them up with a view to using them for the treatment of his future patients, for whom Andrei's success story would be a source of inspiration and a positive example. Goland also needed to show his colleagues the written evidence of the efficacy of his treatment methods for homosexuality.

Goland introduced Andrei to all his psychotherapeutic methods, delivered sessions of hypnosis to him and held up pictures of naked women before Andrei, urging him to develop appreciation of the women's beauty. Goland also gave his usual instructions on how to divert his attention from handsome men on public transport and asked Andrei to pay attention to pretty girls and study their beauty. Establishing a deep friendship with his wife was also strongly advised. Andrei followed his recommendations conscientiously but after several weeks his enthusiasm was already on the wane. He felt that his sexual desire for men never seemed to diminish, no matter how hard he tried to make himself believe that Goland's techniques were working.

Andrei soon came to the bitter realization that, however determined Goland was to help him eradicate his homosexuality and however committed he was to treatment, there was no magic bullet for his condition and he was unlikely to become "cured". After several sessions of psychotherapy,

Andrei grew tired and impatient. He just wanted these pointless sessions to be over. But he also feared that, if the results of the treatment failed to satisfy Nadezhda, she could indeed report him to the police as she was on the brink of emotional breakdown and seemed capable of anything.

Andrei also had misgivings about Goland's promises to keep his privacy and not to give him away to the police. Although Goland indeed reassured him that this would never happen, deep inside Andrei fretted that his failure to demonstrate improvement in his sex life with his wife could upset Goland, make him angry and compel him to hand Andrei over to the police as some untreatable pervert. If it ever came to that, Goland would have plenty of evidence on his hands – Nadezhda's testimonies, his own written autobiography with all the tantalizing details. Andrei shuddered to think what all this could lead to.

So now he was thinking hard how he could extricate himself from this situation and how he could end this medical project without upsetting Goland and Nadezhda. He vowed to himself that he would do everything to improve his nose-diving relationship with Nadezhda and resist meeting other men at least until after the treatment was over. He would have to make himself fall in love with her and demonstrate to the doctor that the treatment was working.

And soon Nadezhda started noticing positive changes in Andrei's behaviour, which she reported to Goland a few months after the treatment had started. Goland asked Nadezhda to provide a written testimony of the successful treatment, which he made anonymous and typed up for future patients. Describing changes in Andrei's behaviour, Nadezhda wrote:

> He started helping me about the house, beating carpets, doing the shopping. Now he never leaves me alone, he is always with me everywhere. He flirts with me, whenever we are alone. He started thinking about the baby.
>
> Previously he never paid attention to the way I dressed or my hair. Now he buys me fashion magazines and gives me presents. I am always part of his plans now. We travelled to Moscow, Stavropol', Arkhangelsk, whereas before he never thought of taking me anywhere with him. But the most important change in him is that he pays a lot of attention to me and shows great care for me. It may seem like it is not that much, but thinking about our past, I realize that it is a lot. I rarely see him drunk. He has become

more self-confident, because he is not a threat to society as he was before – on the contrary he benefits society as an engineer and a human being.

He started sexual relations with me very unexpectedly. It was after 1968 new year ... After the first time he started showing more affection and day after day I could feel his growing desire. The intervals between intimacies at first lasted three weeks, then two, now one.[7]

Pleased by the feedback and the treatment outcomes, Goland bade farewell to Nadezhda and Andrei, telling them that if they ever needed help they could resort to his services again, absolutely free of charge. Soviet medicine was free, and treating homosexuality for Goland was a hobby and a way to enhance his medical reputation and authority.

For Andrei however there was little contentment. Certainly, he managed to improve his relations with his wife, convincing her that Goland's therapy had rekindled his romantic feelings for her. He even brought himself to have sex with her and it seemed that Nadezhda was finally satisfied. But he still felt a strong sexual attraction to other men.

Andrei knew that he would not be able to keep up the pretence of being in love with Nadezhda for long and he had to come up with a more sustainable way of cohabiting with her. Divorce was out of the question – Nadezhda knew too much and, upset by their separation, she could report Andrei to the police out of spite and desperation. Even if they were to part ways amicably, they would lose the flat as the government allotted housing only for married couples. Andrei dreaded having to live in a dorm or communal flat again.

But it soon dawned on him that making Nadezhda pregnant and having a baby would allow him to shift her attention from sexual pleasure to the well-being of the baby. He figured that maybe they would never need to have sex again and Andrei would not have to worry about this any more. After all, sexual intimacy was for procreation, not for pleasure. That would be a perfect excuse for him to live a life with Nadezhda without sex, while he could meet men on the side. And Andrei's plan proved successful: a year later they had a baby, who now occupied Nadezhda entirely, diverting her attention from her unsatisfactory sex life with Andrei. Meanwhile, Andrei quietly resumed his encounters with men.[8]

In 1969, seeing an increasing number of patients with sexual problems from other towns, Goland conceived the idea of establishing a specialized sexological centre in Gorkii, which could cater specifically to their needs. Indeed, there was a great demand for his services in society where sexual problems and issues had been suppressed and ignored. Goland drew up a proposal, spelling out his idea in detail. He promised that the centre would also concentrate on providing homosexuals with special psychotherapy, which, as he proudly stressed, was not provided in any Soviet clinic. Goland sent his proposal to the head of the Moscow Department of Sexopathology, Pavel Posvianskii, who approved it and forwarded it to higher authorities. But officials in the Health Ministry, who would have the final word on any such decision, rejected Goland's proposal. Despite that, Goland continued his medical practice, providing psychotherapy for sexual disorders and trying to accommodate all his patients.

Meanwhile, while the issue of homosexuality in the USSR was still largely shrouded in silence, with only a few doctors and legal experts daring to talk about it, in the US the attitudes towards homosexuality were changing. Indeed, American legal scholars, despite their support for the repeal of the law, were still struggling to implement their views. But something more important was happening.

During the 1960s, the sheer volume of discourse about male homosexuality and lesbianism in American society and many other countries began to grow exponentially. Gay portrayals multiplied in pornography, literature and the mass media. The whole issue of homosexuality, which had hitherto been a taboo subject, was finally beginning to lose its ability to shock and frighten. The growing public familiarity with the issue now triggered not contempt but a variety of viewpoints.[9] Likewise, the whole political climate of American and Western society in the 1960s was transforming, with the so-called "sexual revolution" and the emergence of many civil rights and feminist groups. And gay activists were now preparing to take advantage of these important social changes for the benefit of gay liberation. By the end of 1965, they were ready to emerge from isolation and step into the mainstream of social and political reform.[10]

Under Brezhnev

On a hot June night in 1969, New York police raided one of the city's gay bars, the Stonewall Inn. During the 1960s, police frequently raided places where the city's gay, lesbian and transgender people gathered, and there had recently been a number of similar raids on other nearby bars in Greenwich Village. On this particular night, the patrons of the Stonewall Inn had had enough and they decided to fight back. The police barricaded themselves inside the bar, while four hundred people rioted outside. The so-called Stonewall riots, which waxed and waned over five days and nights, sparked a nationwide grassroots liberation movement among American gay, lesbian and transgender people. Describing the effects of Stonewall, the American historian John D'Emilio wrote: "A small, thinly spread reform effort suddenly grew into a large, grassroots movement for liberation. The quality of gay life in America was permanently altered as a furtive subculture moved aggressively into the open."[11]

Yan Goland tries to cure a youth of his homosexuality

Orenburg, 1970s

Young people had always been a central preoccupation of Soviet authorities. In order to indoctrinate and impart communist values to younger generations, the Soviet government had as early as the 1920s created various youth organizations.[1] One of them was Vladimir Lenin's All-Union Pioneer Organization, which accepted children and adolescents from the age of nine to fifteen. Although participation in the Pioneer organization was optional, almost all Soviet adolescents were members. Being a Pioneer was a matter of immense pride for every Soviet schoolchild and an important milestone in their life. The Pioneer organization was supposed to assist the government in raising active members of society, whose dreams and aspirations would be directed towards the building of a bright communist future.

Despite this, starting from the 1950s Soviet youth began to fall increasingly short of the government's expectations. After Stalin's death and the ensuing Khrushchev-era liberalization of Soviet society, more foreigners began to visit the USSR. They brought Western culture – pop music, newspapers and magazines – with them into the country, which attracted Soviet youth more than the boring official statements of the party. Young people were developing interests in non-communist pursuits such as heavy metal, rock music and even break-dancing. In the 1970s with the growing accessibility of Western technology, young people liked to gather in a friend's apartment or room to listen to music and, in the case of teenagers with wealthy parents, watch videocassettes. While parents were at work or out of town, teenagers drank alcohol, smoked marijuana and even did hard drugs.[2]

The youth of the 1960s and 1970s was less sexually conservative and more open to sexual experimentation. The word "sex" became more widespread and it was widely associated with Western culture, which many Soviet youths mimicked and imitated.[3] To the dismay of Soviet officials, the younger generation preferred temporary liaisons to permanent commitments, evading their responsibilities to create families and have children.

This is the context in which Lenya (Leonid), a young man born in 1952, was growing up. He was very lucky as he was born into a well-to-do, by Soviet standards, family. Lenya's father worked as a doctor and their family lived in a spacious apartment in a good neighbourhood of the small town of Orenburg, never knowing financial hardships.

From the age of nine however Lenya started to feel that he was different. He felt that he was physically attracted to his male peers to the point of developing a strong emotional attachment to them and even falling in love with them. Believing that this was wrong and hoping that this desire would disappear by itself, he went all out to date girls.[4]

One of them was Masha, a pretty, smart girl with blonde hair. At the age of fourteen Lenya started dating her and, although he was fully cognizant of the absence of any sexual attraction towards her on his part, he still entertained a hope that he would rise to the occasion and would be able to consummate sexual intercourse. Once, at her flat, when her parents were at work, they lay on the sofa and watched television. Wrapping his arms around Masha, Lenya started sliding his hands down her waist, expecting that this would arouse him sufficiently to induce erection, but, to his disappointment, to no avail. Undeterred, he slid his hand under her skirt, but on seeing her pink panties he experienced a sharp feeling of disgust, which killed his desire completely. Although Masha clearly expected him to proceed, Lenya pulled his hand away and, without explaining anything, said he did not feel like doing anything.[5]

After this incident, Lenya made no more attempts to have sex with girls, but at the age of sixteen he was again compelled to think about it as most of his classmates had already been dating girls, bragging about their sexual feats during the class breaks. Their stories made Lenya feel inferior, and urged him to prove to others, and most importantly to himself, that he was a normal man who could have sex. But deep inside he knew that, instead of girls, boys prevailed in his sexual fantasies.

One evening, Lenya's father invited his colleagues, other doctors from the hospital where he worked, for dinner. They were sitting in the kitchen, discussing work and recent medical developments in Soviet medicine. Lenya, meanwhile, was lying in the adjacent room, lazily watching television. Suddenly, a curious snippet of their conversation reached Lenya's ears. His father mentioned the word homosexuality and some of his colleagues said that it was a terrible and incurable disease.

Lenya strained the ears to catch the rest of the conversation, but nothing more was said on the topic between his father's guests. What was the name of the disease that they mentioned? Homosexuality? Was he also suffering from it? Was there any treatment available? The word "homosexuality" stuck in his head and Lenya set out to learn more about it.[6]

One day when nobody was at home Lenya slipped into his father's library, in hopes of finding some answers to his questions. The walls of the library had shelves from floor to ceiling, crammed with books and journals. Lenya scanned the shelves and his eyes settled on a row of thick volumes, whose covers bore the title *Great Medical Encyclopaedia*. He pulled several volumes off the shelf, flipped through them and soon found the required entry. His heart sank when he read the definition of the word "homosexuality" – an unnatural desire towards the members of the same sex.

His eyes frantically slid down the page and another line from the entry leapt out at him.

"Treatment of homosexuality is very difficult. It takes a long time and requires a correct combination of drugs, including hormonal ones. The treatment is far from being always successful."

He reread the lines, again and again, trying to process the new information.

Here we are, then – I am ill, with homosexuality! Lenya thought.[7]

This startling discovery shattered him and weighed on his mind continually. Even though he realized that this disease was no laughing matter and apparently required urgent treatment, he didn't know where he could find help. He also felt a deep sense of shame and even guilt.

Then it dawned upon him – his father was a respected doctor and he obviously knew something about this disease and he could probably help. One evening, when his father was working in the library, Leonid carefully broached the subject. He later recalled this incident:

> I decided to carefully ask my father what treatment methods existed …
> [for homosexuality]. I pretended that someone had asked me to approach
> him with this matter. "Son, these people are freaks, they are ridiculed, it is
> a horrible and untreatable illness" – this is what his answer to me was.[8]

His father's response scared Lenya even more. Over the following days, Lenya could not stop thinking about his father's answer, which deeply troubled him. But soon he managed to console himself with the thought that his situation was not as bad as he believed. Yes, doctors said homosexuality was a disease, but he personally did not feel any terrible effects from it. Yes, his sexual desire was shameful, but it felt so natural and innate in him that after several weeks he abandoned his initial attempts to seek medical treatment. Instead, he started exploring his sexual desire for men and soon he even found some male peers, with whom he engaged in mutual masturbation.

At the age of sixteen, Lenya went to a summer camp, where once again he was reminded of the "incorrect" nature of his desire. One day, when he and other boys were camping on the shore, everybody jumped into the water for a swim, while Lenya stayed on the beach. On hearing a whisper from one of the tents behind him, he turned around to see a girl, Nastya, who stuck her head out of her tent and beckoned Lenya with her finger. Lenya obediently crawled inside. Lenya described this incident in his diary:

> When everyone went swimming, a girl from my class invited me to her
> tent. I stepped inside. "Come closer," she moaned, so I did. "I am not feeling

well," she said. "I have a headache" she added. Then she suddenly said: "Kiss me very hard!" I kissed her. And then again. I embraced her. But neither kissing nor embracing her made me sexually aroused. I was hoping for an erection to occur, but it never did … I slipped my hand under her panties and touched her pubis. But I was not aroused at all. I was doing that because she wanted me to … On that occasion I failed to do anything with her.

Sensing that Lenya was struggling to achieve an erection, Nastya sighed and gently let him know that they could try another time.[9]

There was no other time, as after this embarrassing incident Lenya made sure to avoid Nastya and any other young women at all costs. Instead, he spent all his time in the company of his male friends and soon he fell in love with one of them, Petya, who, as he later found out, was also "sick" with the same disease. As Petya struggled in English classes, Lenya suggested that they might study English together in his father's library during the summer.[10]

On one particularly hot summer day, they studied together at Lenya's flat with naked torsos and wearing only their shorts, so strong and unbearable was the heat. After less than an hour of studying, they decided to have a break. Lenya invited Petya to the living room, where they lit a cigarette. Lenya kicked back in his chair and stretched his legs in front of him, taking a drag on the cigarette and watching the blue wisp of smoke curling up in the air. He then passed the cigarette to Petya, who did the same and then, to Lenya's surprise, extended his hand and stroked Lenya on the hip. Lenya instantly felt a strong sexual desire jolting through his body. Without hesitation, Lenya leaned over to Petya and they ardently kissed and caressed each other. After that day, Petya had a standing invitation to Lenya's "English classes" and never skipped any of them. Later Lenya described this incident in his diary:

> One boy from my class sometimes came to my house to study English with me. He was struggling with English and I did very well in this subject. One day when he came over I was walking around my house only in underwear. I decided not to put any clothes on so I sat down like this with him to study. After studying for about forty-five minutes, we decided to take a

break. We started smoking and I kicked back in the chair and stretched out my legs. All of a sudden, he stroked me on my hip. Instantly, I got an erection, which he noticed because I was wearing only my underwear. Then he slightly tickled my penis and my erection became stronger. I couldn't resist the desire that swept over me and we masturbated each other. Subsequently, he often came to my place "to study English".[11]

After the end of school, Lenya and Petya went their separate ways – Petya went to Kyibyshev to study, while Lenya entered a medical university in Orenburg.[12] During the first year at the university, Lenya was entirely consumed with his studies and lacked the time to meet anyone. But during the second year, Lenya fancied a young man in his group named Artem, a handsome man with long hair, blue brooding eyes and slender physique, who now occupied all his thoughts. Although Lenya's feelings were quite strong, Lenya was not showing any signs of affection towards his new friend. They were just friends and Artem did not suspect that Lenya had romantic designs on him.[13]

As a handsome and gregarious man, Artem was invited to many parties. He also enjoyed huge popularity among women, which, of course, aroused intense jealousy in Lenya. Despite being in high demand, Artem never neglected his friendship with Lenya, taking him along everywhere he was invited. Once they came to a house party of one of Artem's friends. They entered a dimly lit flat, where rock music was blasting from a cassette recorder. Through the thick smoke which hung in the air, Lenya discerned couples of young men and women lazily sitting on the floor, with their backs against the wall, taking a puff on their cigarettes. One couple, while feverishly making out, retreated into what appeared to be the parents' bedroom for further love-making. There were empty beer and vodka bottles scattered around.[14]

Artem disappeared from sight, leaving Lenya standing in the corridor, looking at the couples on the floor, consumed with envy. Recalling this moment Lenya wrote in his diary:

A whole new world opened up to me – the world of normal heterosexual relationships, of the normal sexual attraction of a guy to a girl. A man to a woman. I also wanted to be like them … I wanted to be a normal guy with normal feelings and emotions. But, unfortunately, I was not like this at all.[15]

The next day he began his search for a doctor. Lenya knew that there was one good psychiatrist in Orenburg, Vladimir Chernykh, an acquaintance of his father, who could possibly help him with his problem, but the thought of revealing his secret to a stranger made him shiver with fear. Clearly, going to this doctor would be a last resort. After all, he was studying to be a doctor and maybe he could help himself somehow.[16]

Having decided to seek more medical information on the nature of his ailment and the available options for treatment, he went to the university library, where he pored over numerous textbooks on psychiatry. One textbook stated that homosexuality was an illness which could be corrected with hypnosis. Lenya felt a glimmer of hope. Professors at Lenya's university often commended hypnosis in their lectures as one of the best treatment options for psychiatric disorders, and Lenya hoped that this method would be the right one for him.

Maybe those pederasts, who don women's dresses, swing their hips, speak with mannerisms and absolutely despise women are hopeless, but I feel that I am a normal lad, I want to be a real man, my body is young and healthy, my endocrine glands are all in order, so I can be cured, Lenya said to console himself.[17]

Unaware of Lenya's internal emotional turmoil, but clearly aware of his friend's dejected spirits, Artem invited Lenya to pay a visit to his girlfriend Marina one evening. There Lenya met Lisa. They had dinner, drank some wine and then started dancing to slow romantic music coming from the cassette recorder. Swaying to the music with Lisa and gently wrapping his hand around her waist, Lenya was frantically thinking about what he should do next. Should he lean in for a kiss? Or should Lisa take the initiative herself? Or should they just keep dancing and do nothing else? After all it was just the first time they'd met and perhaps rushing things would only ruin everything?

But in a few seconds Lisa suddenly lowered her hand, brushing it lightly against Lenya's crotch and giggling suggestively. Lenya's stomach dropped – he was completely taken aback. Lisa touched Lenya's crotch again, this time harder, apparently hoping to induce erection, but her touch only killed his desire and made him even more distraught. They kept on dancing, while Lenya anxiously anticipated what was coming next.[18]

By midnight, all of them had become tipsy and ready for love-making. Artem and Marina took the parents' bedroom, and Lenya and Lisa were to sleep in the adjacent room on the foldaway sofa. At first, Lenya thought that maybe he could get drunk and then just pretend to be unable to function sexually, but then he decided to bite the bullet and attempt intercourse with Lisa.

They lay in bed and Lenya's ordeal began again. No matter how hard he tried to achieve erection, he failed miserably. Sweat poured down his face and back, while his penis was becoming more flaccid. When Lisa tried to take it in her hands, it shrank completely. Lenya was in despair – he even tried to conjure an image of Artem in his mind, but to no avail. After a few more attempts, they gave up – Lisa turned on her side and fell asleep, while Lenya, embarrassed and upset, lay awake all night.[19]

The next day Lenya was full of determination to make an appointment with the psychiatrist Chernykh and confess everything. A conversation with a medical professional could not be any more embarrassing than his night with Lisa so what did he have to lose? Lenya asked his father to arrange an appointment with Chernykh, without explaining why, and his father willingly arranged it.

Soon Lenya was sitting in front of Chernykh in his room at Orenburg's psychiatric hospital. Seeing how worried Lenya was, Chernykh assured him that whatever he said would remain confidential. At first, Lenya thought that he might take the doctor into his confidence, but on second thoughts, he decided to describe the problem only in general terms, avoiding any explicit terms and especially the word "homosexuality". Chernykh was listening carefully, occasionally nodding his head sympatheti-cally. Lenya began to relate his sexual failures with women and even attempted to tell the doctor about his sexual attraction to Artem. Lenya described this incident in his diary:

[Chernykh] received me very well and assured me that nobody would ever know what was said in his room and that I should not feel shy about telling him anything. I told him some things and answered some questions. But all the same, I was so embarrassed that I ended up not telling him much … I just used general phrases. The doctor assured me that he could guarantee a 100 per cent recovery very soon.[20]

Lenya was completely surprised. Did Chernykh really have many other patients with the same diagnosis – homosexuality? Did he really manage to cure them from their disease? Lenya wanted desperately to believe this, so he refrained from asking any further questions and decided just to trust to Chernykh's experience and expertise. Chernykh scribbled something on a medical form and recommended rubbing the genitals with cold water after waking up in the morning, and doing sports.

I have no problems with arousal – the problem is that I get aroused at the sight of men, same with my erection – it is rather strong, but at the wrong time, Lenya thought, worrying that the doctor could have misunderstood his problem, but then he calmed down. At least Chernykh guaranteed him a complete recovery, and it was unlikely that an expert like this would raise false hopes in his patients.[21]

During the following days, Lenya conscientiously heeded Chernykh's advice and took the prescribed medicine. He then decided to test the results of his treatment with Lisa, desperate to make it up to her and prove that his last sexual failure was just an accident. But to his disappointment, he again failed dismally.

My disease must have progressed to such an extent that no amount of cold rubbing and sedative drugs is going to help me, Lenya thought.[22]

In even greater despair, Lenya showed up at Chernykh's office, demanding that he administer him a session of hypnosis. Lenya recalled in his diary:

I went to the doctor and asked him to hypnotize me. I placed great faith in hypnosis and now believed it to be the only effective method … The doctor told me to set up an appointment with him on the day of my date with a girl, which I did. At the appointment, he instructed me to lie down comfortably on the sofa, brought a lamp … He started by saying that all my muscles were becoming relaxed and that I was gradually falling asleep.

Then he said, "Now you will go to your girlfriend, meet her, a desire will wake up in you, and as she undresses, you desire will grow stronger and stronger. And then you will satisfy it." This is basically what the sessions of hypnosis were like, in a nutshell. They were not what I imagined them to be.[23]

Although Lenya still thought that the session of hypnosis had failed to achieve the result he had expected, he was infused with a degree of optimism nevertheless. He thanked the doctor and went home. Lisa arrived soon.

Again, they listened to some music and went to Lenya's room. They started kissing, pulled the clothes off one another and lay down. Lenya did not have an erection and Lisa had already been somewhat accustomed to that, which gave Lenya some peace of mind. It took Lenya almost forty-five minutes to achieve an erection – he was just lying in bed, next to Lisa, masturbating himself while Lisa was gently stroking his body and occasionally giving him a kiss. She was very patient.

Whenever he felt ready, his penis would just shrink. Lisa would lean back, giving him time to concentrate and then they would try again. And again. Only on his fifth attempt did they manage to have intercourse, which lasted a few seconds and resulted in Lenya's orgasm. Although it occurred purely as a result of Lenya's self-stimulation, he still considered it a victory. More sessions of hypnosis and encounters with Lisa followed, during which Lenya managed to have an orgasm after an extended period of painful and embarrassing self-stimulation next to Lisa. He was cognizant that he had no sexual attraction to her and was forcing himself to have sex with her. Such a state of affairs continued for a least two months.[24]

Meanwhile, Lenya continued his friendship with Artem, feeling more and more enamoured. His failed attempts to achieve intercourse with Lisa did not upset him as long as Artem was by his side. Artem was not doing well at the university, so Lenya always helped him with studies, inviting him home so they could study together. Sometimes, when Artem hugged Lenya to express his appreciation of their friendship and his help, a wave of excitement and enormous pleasure jolted through Lenya's body. But then sadness swept over him as he realized that their friendship would never turn into something more. Soon though, even their friendship ended: Artem was discovered having an affair with a sixteen-year-old girl, and there was a huge scandal which resulted in his expulsion from university. He was then forced to join the army, which meant that Lenya would not be able to see him for at least two years. Lenya was devastated – he felt a tremendous sense of overwhelming loss, and he even stopped seeing Lisa because of his frustration.[25]

But he needed to move on with his life, in spite of what happened. He continued to suffer quietly from the unrequited love he felt towards his male friends, while trying to have sex with other women. His new girlfriend Irina quickly realized that Lenya had trouble maintaining an erection, but, just like Lisa, she was patient: she really liked Lenya – he was a handsome man and a great person to talk to. When Lenya started seeing Irina, it also took him almost forty minutes to "adjust", that is masturbate himself to the point of erection to consummate intercourse, but, as time went on, he managed to reduce this to fifteen and then ten minutes. Once, he even managed to achieve orgasm with Irina four times, albeit the length of his sexual acts was still under one minute. But Lenya still considered it a success, the details of which he related to Chernykh.[26]

However, the situation with sex never improved. During sex with girls, Lenya always had to masturbate himself, which took a long time and then when he finally achieved erection, he immediately had to start intercourse. If he did not, the erection disappeared. He knew that this was not the way other people acted – that sexual arousal was supposed to come from his mind, not from manual stimulation of his penis. Lenya believed that the more he slept with women, the more he would be able to enjoy it, but natural desire never came, leaving him even more frustrated. He was also growing tired of fighting with himself and his own desires. He was suffering, looking surreptitiously at other men, fantasizing about them and realizing that they would never be together.

At the university, Lenya's friends and classmates chattered during the lectures and gossiped about other classmates. On one occasion they started chatting about one of their classmates being a homosexual. Lenya recalled:

Sometimes in the company of friends we talked about sexual perversions and about the homosexuality of one of our mutual friends. One day, at a university lecture, someone made a stupid verse about him: "Our Roma is very strong in economics, he is very familiar with its laws, he is the best economist, homo – he is – sexualist." I had no choice but to take part in these jokes.[27]

Thinking over everything happening around him, Lenya's heart sank. What if one day his classmates discovered that Lenya was a homosexual too? Were they going to bully him the same way? Were they going to make the same mocking verse and pass it around the auditorium?

After the incident at the university Lenya became obsessed with the idea of treating his homosexuality – not only did he dread having a terrible disease, he was trembling with fear that someone would find out about it and he would become the object of everyone's mockery. Maybe Chernykh is not that great a psychiatrist and I should consult someone else, he thought.

Desperate to get an appointment with another specialist, Lenya threw a tantrum in Chernykh's office, sobbing and begging Chernykh to refer him to someone else. Realizing that he was running out of advice on the young man's problem and with nothing else to recommend, Chernykh said: "I will refer you to a real sexopathologist. But this sexopathologist lives in Moscow."[28]

On the same day, Chernykh gave Lenya's father a call, explaining to him that his son was suffering from impotence, and that he could not help him any more as Lenya needed the assistance of a doctor qualified to treat such issues and that these doctors were based in Moscow. Lenya's father took his colleague's advice seriously, booked tickets for himself and his son and a week later they were in Moscow.

The sexologist whom Chernykh recommended was no other than Pavel Posvianskii, the head of the Department of Sexopathology, who, was one of the country's founding fathers of the new science. The Department was located in one of the buildings on the grounds of the Moscow Research Institute of Psychiatry, surrounded by a brick wall. Lenya and his father went there straight from the airport.[29]

On their way, Lenya was overwhelmed with a multitude of thoughts swarming through his mind. What was he going to say to the sexopathologist? Could he confide in him? Could he tell him everything or just describe the problem in general terms? But then again, what was the point of lying if he really wanted the doctor to help him? Would the doctor tell his father everything that Lenya confessed to him?

Soon Lenya was sitting in Posvianskii's office, looking at the big-bellied man with plump cheeks in a white coat. Like Chernykh, Posvianskii started their appointment by assuring Lenya that he should be honest and frank with him for the sake of the treatment's efficacy and all his disclosures would remain private. This time, Lenya decided not to hide anything from the doctor. In fact, he resolved to use the very word that he had found in the encyclopaedia to make the possibility of a correct diagnosis more likely and to avoid describing details that made him blush.

Posvianskii respected his patients' privacy and understood the predicament most of them found themselves in, so he was deeply sympathetic about the young man's problem. Posvianskii was a knowledgeable professor who knew a great deal about sexual perversions. After Lenya regained his composure, Posvianskii asked him a few questions to make sure that his understanding of Lenya's problem was accurate, and then said with a smile, "Well, I am very optimistic about the prospects of your treatment."[30]

Lenya brightened up and Posvianskii's words stirred a glimmer of hope in him.

"There is a doctor, who has a whole system of treating such patients. He lives in Gorkii. His name is Yan Genrikhovich Goland."

I will go anywhere! Lenya thought. If need be, I will drop out of the university, I will do all I can to cure myself of homosexuality.

Posvianskii kept his word – he didn't tell Lenya's father about his son's actual diagnosis.

Lenya and his father spent a couple more days in Moscow and then his father took a flight to Orenburg and Lenya took the train to Gorkii. Lenya was exhausted from the constant referrals and he was very impatient to meet Goland, whom Posvianskii had spoken of so highly. Sitting on the train, watching the fields and forests clad in white snow rush by, he remained hopeful that a solution to his problem would soon be found. If Goland specialized specifically in homosexuality, then he surely knew how to treat it.

Soon Lenya met Goland, who indeed inspired hope and, unlike Chernykh and Posvianskii, oozed some rough charisma. He was also very tall. He seemed to be more alive. But there was also some undue coarseness which Goland displayed in his communication with Lenya, which sometimes bordered on vulgarity.

Lenya was slightly shocked by such crude directness, but, figuring that these details were necessary for effective treatment, he patiently answered Goland's questions.

Goland asked him about his favourites, as in his objects of sexual desire. So Lenya told him about Artem and other men whom he fancied and with whom he had sexual relations.

Goland told him to imagine that there were no criminal prosecution for sodomy in the USSR. He then asked him if he would still be interested in treating his disease, or would he abandon this idea. Lenya said that he had been dreaming of getting rid of this disease from the moment he realized he was ill. Of course he wanted to become cured – he wanted, he said, to be a normal man, to have a normal girlfriend and live a normal life.

Goland congratulated him, saying he met his main selection criterion. He didn't like to waste his time on patients who started treatment only in order to gain immunity from police prosecution. Goland believed that some patients thought that, if they got caught, they could just tell the police they were having treatment for homosexuality, so that they would escape punishment. Goland had little time for such dishonest patients.[31]

If I meet his criteria then I am not a hopeless case, I can be cured, Lenya thought, immediately imagining himself walking around with new girlfriends and getting genuine pleasure from sex with them.

Goland told him that he'd have to stay in Gorkii for treatment so he needed to obtain a leave of absence from his studies of at least six months. He reassured Lenya that his true diagnosis would not be disclosed; they would just write that Lenya was suffering from a neurosis.

Lenya felt himself that his deeply entrenched sexual desire for men could not be cured overnight and it indeed required treatment for an extended period of time, so what Goland was saying was indeed viable. Lenya was impatient to start.

Lenya embarked upon his journey towards heterosexuality with the greatest zeal. His belongings were delivered in the same week and a few days later Lenya found a room, rented by an old woman in the city of Gorkii. His father said he would help him with money as well.

"These are the diaries written by my former patients whom I successfully treated for homosexuality," said Goland, extending a folder with papers with typed text to Lenya. "Your first task will be to read all of them carefully. I want you to see that your problem is not something unique to you, other people also have suffered from the same disease and managed to get rid of it. Once you have read them, start writing your own diary. I want you to describe your childhood with the sexual fantasies that you experienced, everything in great detail. You will be recording the progress of your treatment as well."[32]

On the first night Lenya started reading the diaries of Goland's former patients voraciously and he of course recognized himself in the stories of these men. All of them felt they were different in their early childhood, none of them could figure out what was wrong with them. All of them learnt the word "homosexuality" either accidentally by overhearing the conversations of other people or after studying books on psychiatry. All of them had been referred to Goland by their doctors. And all of them by the end of their journey reported that they finally got rid of their homosexual desire and managed to achieve a strong heterosexual desire. Lenya was hopeful.

Soon Lenya learnt the basics of autogenic training and relaxation, which, Goland explained to him, were needed to relieve stress and tension whenever he slipped into homosexual fantasies or could not take his eyes off a handsome man in the street. He diligently practised this in bed in the evening and in the morning, despite the annoying sound of the television which came from the landlady. Lying in bed, he closed his eyes, he forced his thoughts off his male acquaintances, conjuring up instead images of pretty girls. He noticed that after a few sessions the images of his "favourites", the male objects of his desire, which had hitherto been stuck firmly in his mind, started to slowly fade away and disappear. His emotions about the men whom he previously fancied were not as intense as they were – being in a different city obviously helped him to forget them.

Whenever Lenya saw a man who struck him as handsome he immediately diverted all his thoughts to his hand in the pocket, imagining how it was slowly becoming cold. This helped him distract himself from any unwanted sexual emotions towards men. Instead of fixing his eyes on a man's face, he tried to turn them to young ladies. Goland also gave Lenya magazines with photographs of women and ordered him to observe and examine them intently before going to bed and try to undress them with his eyes.

In an attempt to take his mind off men, Lenya also occupied his mind with his university studies. Although he obtained a medical leave, he was still required to pass mid-semester exams, which meant that he had to study in his free time.

A month went by and Lenya believed that he had managed to achieve some progress. Forcing himself to think repetitively about women, he finally managed to get rid of homosexual fantasies before going to bed as well as homosexual dreams at night. He carefully documented his progress in his diary, which he then read out to Goland, who was also happy that the treatment was working.

But still sometimes Lenya felt that he was experiencing setbacks, which he also documented in his diary:

Today, the night was awful. I went to bed very early, because I was too exhausted from my unsuccessful auto-training sessions. I woke from a very intense homosexual dream and then I could not fall back asleep for a long time. Memories about Orenburg were creeping into my head and I remembered at least five men, with whom I had sexual relations there. I tried to push these thoughts away ... My mind is in a complete disarray now. There is a mortal combat between my heterosexual and homosexual side within me and the victory still remains with the latter ... Lying awake in the morning I am waiting impatiently for my appointment with Yan Genrikhovich [Goland].[33]

After a month of treatment, he was still aware that his homosexual desire remained and berated himself for that in the diary.

> Some evil inner voice told me – can't you see that you will never be cured? If not today then tomorrow the doctor will tell you that nothing can be done and will send you back. Yes, he will, because a month has already passed and there are no results. In Orenburg Chernykh did not even get that you were sick of homosexuality, you struggled the whole year, forced yourself to be with women, then you arrived here in Gorkii, full of hopes and again nothing came of it ... "Yan Genrikhovich, I will do whatever you say, I will practise auto-training day and night, I will drop out of the university if need be, I will spare no effort, resources, I will do anything" – I swore to myself. But no sooner had I closed my eyes than unwanted images started to invade my head.[34]

But then again he thought that he had managed to regain control of his homosexual urges. Although Lenya avoided public toilets and other places of homosexual congregation, one day he still managed accidentally to strike up an acquaintance with another homosexual man named Arthur, whom he met at the university:

> Well, now nothing, absolutely nothing, can surprise me in this life. Today I have learnt such unbelievable news that overwhelmed me. In a casual conversation with one guy in my group, I found out that he was a homosexual too. He described all his feelings to me and told me about his encounters with men and all of that made my memories come flooding back. I also felt a pretty strong sexual arousal. It also turns out that he is acquainted with a whole group of homosexuals ... He doesn't repent being one and does not reproach himself for that. He believes that everyone should be free to satisfy themselves as they please, that there are quite a few homosexuals. He also says that he does not want to receive any medical treatment for that. And then an unpleasant thought entered my mind: "Maybe he is right? No! I have no other choice, except treatment!"[37]

Subsequently, Lenya and Arthur became friends and often spent time together. In his diary, Lenya described the following episode, which happened between himself and Arthur in one of the city's parks:

I point at a pretty girl [in the street] and he says – how disgusting! But I can see that she is pretty. He also says: what a shame, such a nice guy is walking with such a dopey little cow. And I tell him: "It is a shame for you, not for him". So I am trying to "educate" him. One day he suggested: "Hey, let's have some fun, mess around a little, am I a bad candidate for that?" But I didn't give in to his invitations. I just told him: "I just don't feel like it, if I wanted, I would go. I have no desire whatsoever. If we had met a year ago – I would have messed around with you, because you are a really good candidate. But I have absolutely no desire to disrupt my treatment, which, despite all the difficulties, is moving forward."[36]

Lenya was proud of himself as he'd managed to resist temptation and this was very encouraging and reassuring. He was clearly making progress, although he still felt that he lacked sexual desire towards women. But it would come. Although the acquaintance with Arthur shook Lenya's conviction about the need for treatment for his homosexuality, he persevered. On 14 June 1971, almost four months since the start of the treatment, Lenya wrote:

I want to emphasize that my former indecision and shyness with women have disappeared. If before I was forcing myself to date them, I did so with a feeling of dislike and constantly thinking about my favourites, now dates and conversations with women have become natural for me. I don't have a feeling of dislike towards them any more, I have carefree conversations with them, while trying to undress them in my mind ... Whenever I see a young lady, I immediately tell myself "What an amazing girl" and I attempt to find something pretty in her. On the contrary, when I see a handsome man, I tell myself "What a disgusting face!", I try to discern ugly features in him or just turn away from him. This is, of course, rude of me but it helps a lot ... I think that by the end of July I will be able to proceed to a genuine sex life with women.[38]

However, Lenya's ambitious plans of becoming a heterosexual were disrupted by one curious incident. On 18 July, he decided to go to Moscow for a short leisure trip as he needed a change of scene to refresh his mind and gain more mental strength for a final battle with his homosexual desire. He felt that he was behaving like a real heterosexual, but some remnants of homosexual desire still lingered in his mind.

On 18 July, Lenya arrived at the railway station, yet it appeared that it was too early – the train was to depart in two hours. Lenya wandered about the station aimlessly and soon he felt an urge to have a smoke. He bought cigarettes in the nearest kiosk and went to a park sprawling behind the station, where he settled on a bench and lit up his cigarette. He liked moments like this and, although he considered smoking as harmful as homosexuality, he did not feel as guilty about it.[39] He described what happened next in his diary:

Suddenly I noticed a guy, walking along the path in the park, incredibly handsome and tall, slender, muscular, with a clean-shaven intelligent face, neat short hair and elegantly dressed. I followed his gaze and apparently he noticed it. After walking back and forth a couple of times, he came up to me and asked for a light. "I hope I'm not disturbing you," he said politely, sitting down on the bench. Unable to take my eyes off him, I answered: "Certainly, please sit down". He asked me where I was going and when I told him that I was going to Moscow to visit a friend, he seemed pleased. Of course, I understood that he was a homosexual, that it was better to leave before it was too late, but I could not even get up.

To be on the safe side, however, I moved away to the other end of the bench. We talked more about various small things and suddenly he drew closer to me and hugged me by the shoulders. Then I finally understood what was happening so I said that I was leaving. But with his muscular strong hand he pulled me even closer to him. Then my head started spinning, I experienced an instant strong erection ... he was telling me something about great people of "our world" and so on, but I was no longer listening. Meanwhile, his hand slid to my thigh. I was shaking, as if in a fever, and I just kept repeating: "Why are you doing this, I am not a homosexual". But this time he ignored me and began to unbutton my trousers. The only thing I could say amid this terrible arousal was "After all, it is dangerous. Don't you think so?" "I do," he answered, and taking me by the hand, he dragged me into the dense thickets of bushes and trees ...

He squeezed me so tightly in his arms that all my bones cracked. He breathed heavily, kissing my face and my neck. At that time, I forgot about the treatment, the trip to Moscow, and everything else. I felt such bliss and delight that in the end I began to respond to his kisses and caresses. He pulled down my trousers with such force that I thought all the buttons had come off. His cool hand finally reached out to my flaming penis, and a few moments later I experienced a powerful orgasm. Then I helped him to satisfy himself in the same way and we shook hands goodbye. "Have a good trip to Moscow," he said, waved cheerfully and disappeared, leaving the park and mingling with people.[40]

Lenya was deeply frustrated that he had relapsed – he was not supposed to do these things. On the contrary, it was almost five months into his treatment so he was supposed to be getting better, not worse.

But this stranger had been adamant, it was because of his persistence that I gave in, he was holding me tightly and wouldn't let me go, Lenya told himself. Although he first thought that he would hide this incident from Goland, he decided not to, and reported it in his diary. Maybe Goland would scold him, which would also bring its positive results.

Lenya's trip to Moscow went well – he managed to have a good time, without losing sight of his ultimate goal – becoming heterosexual. Moscow offered far more temptations than Gorkii and Lenya was fully cognizant that he was twice as likely to relapse there. But he never did. The incident at Gorkii station planted a feeling of bitter shame in him – he chastised himself for being weak-willed and vowed to himself that this had been the last time he would have sex with a man. He diligently practised auto-training methods, forcing himself not to dwell on handsome strangers' faces, and looking at pretty female faces.

He came back to Gorkii a week later and told Goland about the incident at the station at once. Goland berated him a little and warned him against going to parks and public baths. He also reminded him that their psychotherapeutic sessions would soon be over and he would have to go back to Orenburg to resume his studies and face his homosexual urges solely with auto training. History does not tell us what became of Lenya in later life. But he was now ready for a battle on his own.

While Lenya was desperately trying to rid himself of his "disease" and Goland continued to promulgate his beliefs that homosexuality was a medical condition treatable with psychotherapy, the growing gay movement in the US and elsewhere was ready to challenge the view that homosexuality was a mental illness. In the early 1970s, gay activists attended the conferences of the American Psychiatric Association, the main professional organization of psychiatrists in the US, responsible for issuing the *Diagnostic and Statistical Manual of Mental Disorders*, which classified homosexuality as a mental illness.

Gay activists disrupted the proceedings of the Association, gave speeches and endeavoured to convince its members to remove homosexuality from the *Manual*. In 1973 their efforts finally bore fruit: the majority of the Association members voted for declassifying homosexuality as a mental illness.

16

A jurist proposes to criminalize lesbianism

Moscow, 1970

Although in the 1960s some Soviet scholars were promoting the view that male homosexuality between two consenting adults was their own private affair and should not be regarded as a criminal act, there were certainly those who vehemently rejected such an opinion. Boris Daniel'bek, a criminology scholar from Azerbaijan State University, was one of them – he despised homosexuals and believed that they should be jailed. He expressed this view in his doctoral dissertation, on which he worked from the mid-1960s to the 1970s, and which he titled *Criminal and Legal Struggle with Sex Crimes*.[1]

That Daniel'bek had very strong negative feelings towards homosexuality is understandable – he was born and spent a significant part of his life in the republic of Azerbaijan. In this part of the country, local people associated same-sex relations among men with past traditions of this region – the abduction of male youths and boys for sexual exploitation. Nobody viewed homosexuality as a medical issue as medical experts from other, more "modern" parts of the Soviet Union did.[2] Such views of homosexuality rubbed off on Daniel'bek's perceptions – he never thought that homosexuality could be consensual, instead always picturing it in his mind as a coercive practice, in which one necessarily inflicted harm on someone more vulnerable.

As a specialist in sex crimes, Boris Daniel'bek was aware of the existing debates on the issue of homosexuality within the community of Soviet legal scholars. He was also cognizant that some Soviet jurists went as far as to suggest that the USSR should follow the example of some capitalist and socialist countries and overturn Article 121.1, which prohibited adult men from consensual homosexual relations. Such a proposal seemed entirely unacceptable to Daniel'bek, who believed that the socialist morality governing Soviet society was incompatible with this form of human behaviour.

But what struck Boris Daniel'bek even more was the fact that homosexual relations between women in the USSR were not regulated by law. Nowhere in the Criminal Code could he find any reference to lesbianism and it appeared that the existence of homosexual relations between women did not bother Soviet authorities at all. And there was a reason for this: Soviet women who desired other women did not actively cruise streets in pursuit of partners and sex like homosexual men, remaining therefore off the police's radar. They were more discreet and secretive. Some women who had relations with other women managed to disguise their relationships as friendships.

The court's archives which Daniel'bek consulted for his dissertation were crammed with folders containing Soviet citizens' criminal cases, and they sometimes mentioned female homosexuality as part of the criminal case but not as the actual cause for criminal conviction.

One such case that Daniel'bek came across dealt with a nineteen-year-old woman, G, from Tbilisi, whose stepfather became aware of her clandestine romantic relations with one of her female friends – a woman in her mid-twenties. In an attempt to escape public shame and make his daughter come to her senses, G's stepfather promptly married her off to a man. But on her wedding night, G desperately flung herself off the balcony and tragically died. Eventually investigators ruled that the reason for her suicide was her love for another woman and the marriage which was forced on her.[3]

Poor woman, Daniel'bek thought, poring over the case. If she had not been seduced by an older experienced lesbian, she would not have acquired this vice and would have been alive now. And if this older lesbian had been convicted, she would not have spread her harmful influence on young unstable minds. There needs to be a criminal law, banning lesbian relations in the USSR too.

Convinced that both male and female homosexual behaviour had to be regulated by Soviet law, Daniel'bek proposed two main arguments in his dissertation: that Article 121.1, criminalizing consensual homosexuality in the Soviet Union, contrary to the emerging views of some scholars and despite liberal developments in the West, should stay in place; more importantly, lesbianism should specifically be criminalized.

First, Daniel'bek criticized the opinions expressed by Pavel Osipov in his dissertation *Sex Crimes* (1966), which we discussed in Chapter 13, where Osipov asserted that, even though consensual homosexual acts between adult men were at odds with socialist morality, this alone could not be considered a sufficient reason for making such acts a crime. To this argument, Daniel'bek simply responded: "Negative personality traits, if they infringe on the principles of socialist morality, may be viewed as criminal."[4] Osipov also argued that the private nature of consensual sodomy made it very difficult to investigate and therefore it was better to decriminalize such relations rather than prosecute them. Daniel'bek, of course, disagreed, arguing: "The intimate nature of homosexual acts, conducted on a consensual basis, indeed hampers the prosecution of people involved in it; however, it does not mean that the law against consensual sodomy should be eliminated."[5] Finally, Osipov contended that the existing law had failed to force heterosexuality on to homosexual citizens, so it had to be eliminated. Daniel'bek responded that "criminal prosecution of homosexuality is not the most effective means of its prevention. Indeed, in order to curb this immoral inclination a combination of societal and medical intervention is needed in the first place; however, one cannot dismiss the educational importance of criminal prosecution."[6]

Daniel'bek also attacked another legal scholar, Yakov Yakovlev (whom we also met in Chapter 13), who was calling for the decriminalization of sodomy, stressing that sex education was the most appropriate means of keeping the rate of homosexuality down in society. Daniel'bek's response to Yakovlev's argument was that "Criminal punishment plays an important role in preventing homosexuality and constitutes a restraining factor on those inclined to such vice ... criminalization of consensual sodomy in our legislation is justified and there are no reasons to alter the existing legislation."[7]

Daniel'bek worked on his dissertation for almost a decade and in 1970 he was ready to defend it. For conferring of his degree, Daniel'bek was required to present a detailed summary of his dissertation and defend its main contentions in front of a panel of experts. A few months before the defence, he was also required to send out his dissertation to the members of the panel so they could read it and then write their reviews, which were to be read out at the defence as well.

Daniel'bek was sure that his novel argument on the criminalization of lesbianism would be well received by the expert members of the panel. He was also hoping that, after securing expert backing, he would be able to petition higher authorities with a proposal to introduce a law criminalizing lesbianism as soon as possible. He even thought that he might get an award for such a proposal – after all, he was defending socialist morality and fighting for the cause of healthy sexual relations in the USSR. He was very much looking forward to receiving laudatory reviews for discovering this legal oversight and finally obtaining his scientific degree, which he had worked so hard for.

But when Daniel'bek received the review reports he was astonished, as not only were the experts unimpressed with his proposal to criminalize lesbianism but some of them even questioned his arguments for keeping Soviet sodomy laws in place:

> So despite the very limited prevalence of tribadism [lesbian sexual relations], the dissertation proposes to introduce punishments for actions in which this type of sexual anomaly is present. The analogy between tribadism and pederasty is not convincing given the limited prevalence of the former.
>
> Distinguished jurist of the RSFSR, Doctor of Juridical Sciences
> Professor V. I. Kurlyandskii[8]

> The author of the dissertation considers it necessary to introduce criminal liability for tribadism, whose harm he considers to be equivalent to that of sodomy. The argument that tribadism is equal to sodomy is controversial as the former is less common than the latter.
>
> Distinguished jurist of the RSFSR, Doctor of Juridical Sciences
> Professor Mark Yakubovich[9]

In our opinion there are not sufficient grounds for criminalizing tribadism between adult women, especially since there is no evidence of the prevalence of this phenomenon, while the author of the dissertation advocates its criminalization.

Doctor of Juridical Sciences Professor Grigorii Anashkin[10]

The author's many conclusions should be accepted, with the exception of his proposal to criminalize voluntary tribadism. In our republic we do not have data on the prevalence of this type of perversion and it cannot be considered so dangerous as to be classified as a criminal act.

A.G. Ibragimov, Chairman of the Supreme Court of the Azerbaijan SSR[11]

The author's argument in support of the criminalization of voluntary sodomy is not convincing enough.

V. Kirichenko, Professor and Head of the Department of Criminal Law of the Higher School of the MVD[12]

[T]he dissertation has not refuted with sufficient persuasiveness the statements of a number of authors who argue against criminalization of voluntary sodomy. Decriminalization of voluntary sodomy will undoubtedly allow homosexuals to fearlessly seek medical help for their perversions ... Why do we need to prosecute individuals because of the unfortunate circumstances in their lives, instead of taking appropriate measures to prevent perversions from arising?

Distinguished jurist of the RSFSR, Doctor of Juridical Sciences, Professor Mark Yakubovich[13]

Elaborating on controversial issues of criminal responsibility for sodomy, Daniel'bek is trying to prove the need to maintain criminal responsibility for consensual pederasty between adult men without aggravating circumstances. He notes that supporters of the abolition of such responsibility, among whom is the author of this review, consider homosexuality to be a specific type of sex drive characteristic of some individuals and embedded in them by nature itself. Meanwhile, none of the modern Soviet medical scientists and lawyers adhere to such an opinion. They believe that the biological forms in which sexual intercourse occurs between adults should be subject to legal regulation only if it affects the social side of sexual relations, that is, impinges on sexual freedom, sexual integrity or normal sexual development and upbringing of minors. At the same time, they emphasize that homosexual relations certainly contradict socialist morality and it is necessary to fight them. However, the struggle should be carried out not in the form of criminal repression, but through proper sex education in the family and at school.

Doctor of Juridical Sciences Y.M. Yakovlev[14]

Daniel'bek never suspected there would be so many reviewers who were against criminalizing any type of consensual homosexuality. He just assumed that most experts would support his views and even credit him for identifying an important legal oversight – the lack of legislation on lesbianism. But he was wrong. Many legal scholars had long been entertaining the idea that sexual relations, if they did not harm anybody else, should not be regulated by law.

Presenting the summary of his dissertation in front of the panel of experts and listening to the reviews being read out to him, Daniel'bek was compelled to admit that his views on the necessity to criminalize lesbianism were indeed ill-thought and that this was more a medical problem than a legal one. Yet he still stood by his conviction that legal punishment for male homosexual acts should stay in the Soviet Criminal Code. Although most experts on the panel disagreed with Daniel'bek on this, none of them dared to initiate a discussion on the issue. Experts recommended that Daniel'bek should modify his arguments on lesbianism in accordance with the panel's recommendations, and after a unanimous vote conferred the degree of a Doctor of Juridical Sciences on him.

A former soldier is crippled with internalized homophobia

City of Vladimir, late 1970s

Pavel, like most other Soviet boys born in 1938, had a deprived childhood.[1] His family was poor and his father had perished in the Second World War in 1943 when he was just five years old. Pavel often suffered beatings at the hands of his rarely sober stepfather. In 1949, unable to support her eleven-year-old son financially, Pavel's mother sent him to the Suvorov boarding school.[2] Named after Alexander Suvorov, a prominent eighteenth-century Russian general and established in 1943, these schools provided boys with military training and secondary education. Most cadets in these schools, like Pavel, were orphans or had only a surviving mother.

Pavel grew up in the austere and busy military environment of the boarding school. He wore a military uniform, got up early in the morning and marched in formations. His life was that of a soldier and consisted almost entirely of training and classes; only rarely did he have time for himself.

Almost immediately after being admitted into the boarding school, Pavel started experiencing strange feelings towards other cadets. Looking at them and thinking about them gave him strange pleasant emotions. Despite their growing intensity, Pavel did his best to bury these feelings, distracting himself with a devotion to military training.[3]

In 1957, when Pavel was nineteen, he discovered that he was the only one among his cadet friends without a girlfriend. Although he'd never had any real desire for one, he knew that, in order to conform to the expectations of his friends, he had to be going out with a girl. Almost all of his friends, fellow cadets, had a story to tell about their sexual adventures. Pavel alone had nothing to contribute to such conversations, which frustrated him immensely and made him feel out of place.

And then one night a petite pretty girl called Masha turned up in the grounds of the military school. She was a daughter of one of the school's educators and Pavel ran into her after an evening class. They struck up a conversation and chatted until very late. Pavel suspected that Masha fancied him, but he was unsure about how to proceed. On the one hand it was high time for him to start dating someone and Masha seemed to be a decent girl, but on the other hand he had no genuine desire to do so and he was not even sure if Masha attracted him sufficiently. Sitting next to Masha on the couch in the corner of the classroom, under Lenin's portrait, Pavel couldn't muster the courage to lean in and give her a kiss. In the end, Masha just fell asleep on his shoulder.

Pavel shut his eyes as well in a fruitless effort to sleep, and remained there in an uncomfortable position for the rest of the night, trying not to make any move that might wake her up. After this, rumours about Pavel's "night adventures" with Masha began to circulate in the boarding school and among his friends. Although Pavel neither confirmed nor denied them, he eventually acquired a reputation as an expert in love affairs.[4]

Despite his enviable and completely unearned reputation, Pavel still struggled with women. He tried to approach them at parties, kiss and even touch them up, emulating the behaviour of his friends, who seemed to do these things more naturally, but all the women rejected him.

Perhaps they sense my defect, Pavel thought with a sense of relief that he didn't have to go on trying. Maybe it's just my mind telling me what to do, but my body wants something else. That is probably why all my attempts to court women never come to fruition.[5]

In 1957, Pavel acted on his desire for men for the first time. In winter, when most of his friends had gone home to visit their families, Pavel stayed in the school's dorm. His roommate Dmitrii did not go home either. One evening both of them lay in their beds, which stood around one metre apart, and talked about their plans for life. Pavel recalled later:

Once, he and I ended up alone in the dorm in the evening. Everyone else had left. It was winter and we went to bed early and naturally we started a conversation about sex. I was considered an expert, and he, although older than me, but since he was more honest, said that he had never slept with a girl. I went into his bed and, caressing and touching his genitals, began to lie about my adventures. A few minutes later we had an orgasm. This went on for several days. It was he who put an end to this relationship.[6]

In the same year, Pavel returned to civilian life, landing a job as an electrician in the small city of Vladimir, commencing engineering courses at an adult-learning night school. Here he also found new friends. After leaving the Suvorov school Pavel expected that his desire for men would subside, because he would not be surrounded by them any more, but he was wrong. On the contrary, it seemed that his desire for men was only becoming stronger. In an attempt to suppress it, he dated women, but whenever he tried to have sex with them he just could not get an erection.

At the school he made a friend called Yegor, an amicable young man who often invited Pavel to join his group of his friends on their weekend trips to the countryside, where they usually spent the night and slept in tents by the river. Pavel always happened to share a tent with Yegor and sometimes, when they were lying close together, Yegor would unexpectedly throw out his arm in his sleep and embrace Pavel. Pavel was not sure whether this was an accidental touch during Yegor's sleep or if he was trying to hug him under the pretence of being asleep. This ambiguity only fuelled Pavel's feelings towards Yegor. During their trips they often took pictures of themselves in swimming trunks and Pavel cherished these photos and often kept them to hand – looking at them lifted his spirits and pulled him out of sad thoughts that often overwhelmed him. However, to Pavel's frustration, Yegor got married and, as family life began to consume him, their friendship dissolved and they slowly grew apart.[7]

After finishing his courses at evening school, Pavel joined the army. This was a familiar environment – after all he'd graduated from the Suvorov Military School and everything around him now felt like home. Although, once again, he was surrounded by men, he never had any sexual liaisons with other soldiers as he managed to distract himself from his desires by again focusing mainly on military training.[8]

After two years in the army, Pavel returned to civilian life and entered university, where he formed new social circles. Still haunted by a strong sexual desire for his male classmates, Pavel resumed his attempts to date women, but all of them ended in failure. He was almost losing heart when he met Valeria. When Valeria witnessed Pavel's inability to sustain an erection during intercourse, she didn't appear offended, nor did she scold him for a "lack of manhood" as Pavel's former girlfriends had done. Instead she displayed great sensitivity and understanding, making it clear to him that sex did not matter to her very much and a failed attempt at intercourse was no big deal. Valeria's patience soon paid off – after a series of unsuccessful attempts, Pavel finally managed to have sexual intercourse with her, albeit with a very weak erection. But for Pavel this was a victory – for the first time in his life he had managed to achieve heterosexual intercourse.[9]

But in spite of Pavel's renewed confidence that from now on the situation would improve, all his subsequent attempts to maintain an erection for intercourse with Valeria proved a disaster. One evening, finally losing her patience, Valeria snapped at Pavel: "Don't make yourself do it if you don't want to, you either don't desire me or you are just a sick person ..."[10]

And it suddenly struck him – was he indeed ill? Was his inability to achieve heterosexual intercourse some terrible disease that had to be urgently treated? Was his desire for men also a disease? It had never occurred to him before that it could be an illness and not any fault of his own. Valeria's words rang in Pavel's ears for several weeks. This incident was the end of their relationship: Valeria was no longer willing to put up with Pavel's sexual difficulties, while Pavel was too embarrassed to keep trying.

In 1968, at the age of thirty, Pavel was still single, which was very uncommon for Soviet men. All of his peers were married and most of them were now raising children, enjoying the benefits bestowed upon young families by the Soviet government. Desperately trying to fit in,

Pavel threw all his efforts into finding the "love of his life", who would settle for his impotence and accept him the way he was. As women outnumbered men in the USSR, and most Soviet families lived unexciting sexual lives anyway, Pavel stood a good chance of finding a spouse. And eventually he found Angela, a woman his age who also faced societal pressure for being a single woman and fretted at the idea of being one for ever. After a brief dating period, they tied the knot.

Angela took Pavel's impotence for granted and resigned herself to a sexless family life. She strove to appreciate Pavel's other qualities – he was a hardworking man with a promising career as an engineer and, despite widespread consumption of alcohol among Soviet men, he almost never drank. Although Angela indeed had some misgivings about the underlying causes of Pavel's sexual struggles, she never put any uncomfortable questions to him. After all, it was difficult to find a decent husband in the USSR and Angela was grateful for what she had.

Pavel also learnt to derive happiness from his "faulty" marriage and even managed to convince himself that he loved his wife and that life without her was meaningless. On several occasions, he summoned all his strength to have sex with Angela in an attempt to conceive a baby and eventually Angela became pregnant. Having a child further solidified Pavel's confidence and gave him a feeling that he was a healthy man capable of having sex with a woman. Sex with Angela was still an onerous duty, which he knew he had to fulfil. Sometimes it was extremely difficult, excruciating and suffocating, but Pavel had no other choice. Otherwise he felt swamped by guilt for not satisfying his wife.[11]

Despite the marriage, Pavel's desire for sexual intimacy with men never left him and only grew stronger, threatening to get out of control. In July 1970, while Angela went to visit her mother in the countryside with the baby, Pavel ventured into the city's park, where he knew he would find men like himself. He had often felt their piercing gazes when he'd strolled there with his wife, but he had always avoided them. In the park he soon met a man, and, after a short exchange, Pavel took him home. Pavel knew that he was acting recklessly, but his desire was so overwhelming and strong that it eclipsed all his apprehensions. At home, Pavel and the man, whose name Pavel did not remember, downed two glasses of vodka each and got down to business.

Although alcohol dampened Pavel's fears and instantly gave him a sense of liberation, he did not dare to engage in anal sex as the mere thought of it frightened and disgusted him. After a couple of minutes, they both achieved orgasm and, for the first time in his life, Pavel learnt what genuine satisfaction from sex felt like. They lay in bed for about ten minutes in silence, their chests rising and falling as they got their breath back. Then the man pulled his pants up and left, leaving Pavel lying in bed naked. Pavel stayed like this for at least half an hour, relishing every second of this hitherto unknown but highly pleasurable feeling that lingered in his body, and that he had never known existed.

Soon the effects of alcohol began to wear off and Pavel's state of bliss began to give way to bitter remorse for what he'd done. He jumped off the bed, grabbed the sheets, filled the bathtub with water and soap and threw them in. He hoped that Angela wouldn't notice anything when she returned. He vowed to himself that this was only a one-off encounter and that he would never again let his desire get the better of him.

A few days later Angela returned. The minute she appeared at the door, Pavel rushed to her, gave her a tight hug, kissed her hard on her mouth and then, holding her against him, clumsily started unbuttoning her blouse. Such a fervent reception caught Angela off guard – she'd never viewed her husband as an ardent lover; if anything she was always the one who asked for sex. But now here he was, kissing her deeply and hungrily all over her body and dragging her into the bed.

Little did Angela know that Pavel's unusual passion was not due to joy on her arrival, but his desperate attempt to prove to himself that he was still capable of having sex with a woman. He also wanted to make it up to her for cheating on her. Their sex on this occasion was not perfect, as Pavel's penis was almost flaccid, but he still managed to achieve orgasm and remove the feeling of guilt.[12]

Despite promises to himself that he would never sleep with men again, Pavel failed to hold himself to them. In the same year, 1970, he was appointed a supervisor of a construction site in Kovrov, a nearby small town, where he had to spend five days a week. Work in a different city, away from Angela and their son, provided him with an opportunity for a respite. In Kovrov Pavel was assigned a small room in the dormitory, where he could now bring men. Even so he was still hesitant to take advantage of this newly found privacy as he did not want his desire to lead to an entrenched habit. He worried that the more he indulged in same-sex liaisons, the more addicted to them he was becoming, which was why, during 1970, he brought only three men to his room.[13]

When the construction work in Kovrov was finished, a commission of officials arrived from Moscow to inspect and inaugurate the place. One of the officials, named Eduard Petrovich, a man in his forties, stood out from other members of the commission, most of whom had grim faces which matched their grim grey suits. Eduard Petrovich seemed livelier; he smiled and wore a colourful shirt and a scarf around his neck. There was something different about his gestures and voice too, although Pavel was unable to pinpoint what exactly. Eduard Petrovich was in turn greedily eyeing Pavel at the inauguration ceremony and, when all the members of the commission proceeded to the local canteen for celebratory drinks of vodka, he approached Pavel, introduced himself and asked if he knew of any bathhouses in town. Pavel hesitated, trying to fathom what sort of interest this man from Moscow had. Then he said that there was indeed a bathhouse in town and offered to take Eduard Petrovich there.

Their further conversation in the bathhouse confirmed his suspicions – Eduard Petrovich was also interested in men and he had designs on him. While washing Pavel's back, he started gently moving and sliding his hands across his back, lingering on his buttocks and down to his hips. Pavel wanted to sink through the floor from embarrassment as he did not expect his superior to be so bold as to start touching him up in the public washroom amongst other men. Pavel did not find the Moscow boss attractive and he made that clear to him by washing his back without any sensual gestures. Eduard Petrovich took the hint and abandoned his intentions. This bathhouse experience planted a feeling of guilt and disgust in Pavel that lingered for several months and put him off meeting other men.[14]

Although Pavel tried to erase this unpleasant experience from his mind, it made him wonder what life was like in Moscow for men like him. In his imagination, based on his experience with Eduard Petrovich, Moscow men were bold and audacious; they could have well-paid jobs and respect in society despite their overtly effeminate behaviour. For a small city like Vladimir, where Pavel lived, meeting a man as effeminate as Eduard Petrovich was unimaginable.

Soon Pavel got a chance to explore life in Moscow himself as he had to travel there for work. On the first day of his trip, when his work was done for the day, Pavel went to the city's Kazansky railway station, where he hoped to meet men like him. The massive structure of the Kazansky station, crowned with a clock tower, stunned Pavel with its beauty and glory – never in his life had he seen a railway station like this. Never-ending streams of people hurrying in different directions made Pavel feel dizzy at first, until he got used to the hectic pace of the station. He ventured into the station's mazes and its numerous ornate waiting halls, gawking at their architectural grandeur. He even forgot what he had come here for – so magnificent was the place.

Then in the corner of one waiting room he glimpsed a sign: "TOILETS". Pavel started towards the sign, pulled the door open and stepped inside. A foul odour stung his nostrils and made him wince with disgust. Despite its location in one of the most beautiful railway stations that Pavel had even seen, this toilet reeked of tobacco and urine and in this regard was no different from other toilets. Pavel covered his nose with his hand and started towards the urinals.

Standing at the urinal, he heard the sound of a creaking door and heavy steps behind his back. A moment later a man appeared beside him, fumbling with his belt. Pavel turned his head towards him and shuddered: the man was staring at him, winking suggestively and smiling with his crooked teeth. Repulsed, Pavel quickly finished his business and dashed out of the toilets without washing his hands. He just wanted to leave the place as quickly as possible and erase that ugly face from his mind.[15]

Moscow's homosexual world did not seem to be as alluring as Pavel had pictured it in his mind. His business trip lasted only three days and as soon as he was done with his business he boarded the train back to Vladimir.

Several months later Pavel travelled to Moscow on business again. Although he initially pushed the idea of visiting the toilets out of his mind, he eventually went back to the Kazansky station. This time he did not set foot in the toilets, but loitered in one of the waiting rooms. Soon a handsome man in his thirties approached him, introducing himself as Anton, and, as usually happens between two homosexual men who have just met, they struck up a conversation.

Anton invited Pavel to his flat. Pavel nodded and they left the station. Anton took Pavel to a Stalin-era skyscraper – a tall, imposing building, which looked like a palace, a far cry from the cramped Khrushchev-era apartment blocks Pavel and most Soviet citizens inhabited. In the porch a concierge greeted them. They ascended in the lift and soon found themselves in a spacious dimly lit flat with wood-panelled floor and high ceilings. The apartment apparently belonged to someone from the Soviet elite and the apartment's furnishings attested to that: embossed wallpaper covered the walls, huge carpets covered the floor, cupboards with inlaid fronts stood here and there. There were even antique columns in the apartment's hallway.

Anton gave Pavel some slippers and led him to the kitchen, which was almost as big as Pavel's entire flat. Soft opera music played faintly. A large table stood in the middle of the kitchen set for dinner. Bottles of alcohol on the table bore foreign names that most Soviet citizens had never heard of: Hennessy VS, Red Label, Jameson.

There was someone else in the kitchen. At the stove stood a stylishly dressed person, whose gender Pavel struggled to discern. Wearing an exotic lounging robe, the person, who seemed to be in their sixties, was holding a frying pan in one hand and turning something over with his spatula. Pavel soon realized that this was a man who looked like a woman. Later Pavel recalled in his diary: "I could not stay long at his [Anton's] house … His friend was wearing a woman's robe, had a very, very unpleasant face and in general, all this seemed awful to me and I persuaded him [Anton] to leave. We left – I said goodbye to him at the subway station."[16]

Again, after a short respite, Pavel had business in Moscow to attend to. His third visit to Moscow ended in making the acquaintance of Kirill, a handsome young man, whom he also met at the Kazansky railway station. This time Pavel invited Kirill to the hotel Leningrad, where he stayed. No longer squeamish about anal sex, Pavel allowed himself to cut loose. From their subsequent conversation, Pavel learnt that Kirill worked as a cameraman at Moscow's Ostankino television tower, where Soviet television programmes were mounted and filmed. Kirill invited Pavel to sit in the audience of a programme that he was going to film the next day, to which Pavel agreed.

The next day they were in Ostankino, a tall concrete skyscraper, on the set of the USSR's news and current affairs show. Pavel took his seat in the audience while Kirill and the other cameramen froze behind their cameras, which were pointed at a grim-looking television presenter in a grey suit, who reeled off the day's so-called highlights.

After the shoot, Kirill showed Pavel around. Among the faces of hurrying assistants, decorators, make-up assistants and many other Ostankino staff members Pavel recognized some famous people he'd often seen on television. After their excursion around Ostankino, Kirill saw Pavel off to the railway station. There he suddenly started begging Pavel to stay. It even looked as if tears were welling up in his eyes, but, far from touching Pavel's heart, they made the whole situation even more uncomfortable. Incapable of offering any kind of affectionate response, Pavel waved Kirill goodbye and got on his train.[17]

Pavel decided to refrain from further forays in Moscow for some time in order to detach himself from his Moscow experiences emotionally and let himself "regain his normality". His hopes that spending more time with his family would diminish the intensity of his desire to have sex with men, however, were disappointed. In the mid-1970s, his family life began to suffer significant setbacks. After a series of blazing rows, Angela left Pavel and moved to her mother's house in the countryside with their son.[18] Although his family had fallen apart, Pavel made adroit use of his newly acquired freedom. He went travelling around various cities across the USSR as part of his work and for leisure, during which he ventured into local public toilets and bathhouses in search of men for sex.[19]

After a series of such trips and a number of anonymous encounters with men, Pavel realized that he did not want to live that way any more. His desire had got the better of him, as he'd feared, and he seemed incapable of stopping himself from falling deeper into its trap. He had no desire whatsoever to return to his wife and son or to find another woman, but the whirlwind of anonymous encounters with men only made him feel more depressed. He needed help.

From one of his homosexual friends, he learnt of the existence of a doctor in Gorkii, Yan Goland, who provided homosexuals with medical treatment. Without hesitation Pavel went to Gorkii, where he found Goland's clinic and secured an appointment with him. After listening to Pavel's story and making some notes, Goland asked his key question: "If tomorrow, our government announces that criminal penalties for sodomy in our country are removed from our Legal Code, will you still be interested in my therapy?"

"Of course, doctor. Sometimes I think that maybe it would be better if police caught me and threw me in jail – at least this would help me stop."

"Then I think we can start our therapy. I am sure that we can help you," said Goland, with a smile.

We do not know how or whether Pavel responded to Goland's treatment.

18

In which we learn about emerging gay activism in the USSR

Moscow, 1975

Under Brezhnev, the state apparatus was growing ever bigger, while the Communist Party was expanding and becoming more bureaucratic. Far from projecting the image of ascetic revolutionaries, Soviet officials now showered themselves with never-ending privileges, which the majority of Soviet people could only dream of. They lived in luxurious houses, travelled overseas, went to special stores with no food shortages, received high-quality medical treatment in elite hospitals filled with the latest Western technology and sent their children to prestigious universities, whose doors were typically closed to those not from elite circles. This annoyed Soviet people and left them disgruntled as many of them saw few material prospects for themselves. The economic decline, which began to affect the Soviet economy in the mid-1970s, also fuelled their hatred and resentment towards the Soviet regime.

Realizing that the government had failed to adequately reward their labour, many Soviet citizens began to withdraw their energy from state-sanctioned work, channelling it instead into illegal economic activity, which seemed far more rewarding. This degraded and diminished Soviet society: work ethics were being destroyed, corruption abounded, while many skilled people with stifled motivation were demoralized and disappointed. Alcoholism was also becoming more common, especially among factory workers.

For these reasons, Soviet homosexuals could never have mobilized in the way that gay people did in the US and other Western countries in the mid-1970s. The economic decline, widespread Soviet pessimism and cynicism and withdrawal from public life in the pursuit of individual benefits were all to the detriment of the public good. There was also continued repression of overt political activism. In a society afflicted by so many problems, and where political freedom in any case was suppressed, any gay activism was out of the question.

Unlike in the USSR, where homosexual people made no attempts to self-organize in any meaningful way, gay people in the US were, by the mid-1970s, actively standing up for their rights, engaging in activism and protests against the government's homophobia. Their concerted efforts led to a number of breakthroughs, one of which was pressuring the American Psychiatric Association into removing homosexuality from the official list of mental illnesses in 1973. In European countries, with the backing of sympathetic medical professionals and jurists, gay people also had managed to overhaul anti-sodomy legislation: male homosexual acts became legal in England and Wales (1967), East Germany (1968), Bulgaria (1968), West Germany (1969), Austria (1971), Norway (1972) and other countries. Meanwhile in the USSR male homosexuality continued to be prosecuted, and the number of criminal convictions for this type of crime actually rose from the late 1960s.[1]

Despite this, Soviet homosexuals actively tapped into the growing unofficial life in the USSR, using gathering places in big cities, which they called *pleshkas* where they could socialize, meet one another and establish their networks for contacts. Certainly those homosexuals who lived in large Soviet cities like Moscow or Leningrad possessed a greater self-awareness than those in smaller cities, fully embracing their homosexual lifestyle. Some of them were deeply aware of being victims of the state's homophobic oppression and even occasionally stood up for themselves.

In the early 1970s, a lexicographer from New York interested in Soviet homosexual subculture, Vladimir Kozlovskii, ventured into Moscow's gay street life and there he encountered "Mama Vlada", a big-bellied, flamboyant openly homosexual man with a deep, booming voice, who did not shy away from using female grammatical inflections when talking about herself and her fellow homosexual friends. Mama Vlada took Kozlovskii on a tour around the Bolshoi Theatre, one of Moscow's main gay cruising spaces, telling him about the trial of a group of homosexual men in Leningrad, against whom local police had fabricated a criminal case. Many other homosexual men showed up in court to support their wrongly accused friends and heckle the judge:

> Have you heard about a show trial of our people in Leningrad? The audience began to whistle. It was all fake through and through with false witnesses … the state security organs issued a directive to conduct a show trial and carried it out in the best traditions of 1937. Blackmail, falsified facts and presumption of guilt for homosexuals.[2]

> We are expanding no matter how hard the devil is trying to oppress us. In the last month alone, there have been five round-ups here! There, on the *pleshka*, where our gals usually promenade … street vigilantes apprehended every single one of them in tight jeans and with a made-up face. And how many of our guys are in prisons and labour camps? How many of our guys are mortally afraid of approaching our places?[3]

Mama Vlada also told Kozlovskii about the constant harassment on the part of the KGB, which, despite its lack of interest in homosexuals in the 1960s, seemed to change its attitude to them in the 1970s:

> In Leningrad the situation is even worse. There the KGB started sending their plainclothes agents into our territory to fight our people, although not as fiercely as before. They suffer losses too. They say that one such agent had the misfortune of running up against one of our guys, a karate aficionado. Once the agent flashed his red KGB card, the guy smacked him so hard that the agent's thigh bone jumped out of his arse! The guy also took a 20-ruble note out of the cop's wallet – as a compensation for the discomfort caused … Next time, the cop will think twice, if he is ever discharged from hospital.[4]

> We have grown bolder, but the pressure on us is growing. Instead of adult agents, they are now sending little boys eighteen years old into our territory. With their affectionate stares and put-on shyness, they are trying to cling to our guys … There are at least five of them on each bench here. But we know them all here – can you see the one, there, in jeans and a blue T-shirt? Innocence personified! But all our guys around here avoid him like a leper. And the agents are also here, staking out the place, wearing hats and spying from behind their newspapers.[5]

Mama Vlada demonstrated a deep awareness about the growing Soviet homophobia:

> So what did we ever do to deserve such harsh treatment? Well, because we are nonconformists compared to all this fucking proletariat, whose boozing saw their legs fall through their arses! We are not politically reliable and we are difficult to manage. A barbaric country! And we are suffering from this in particular! They say that either in Sweden or Holland marriages between two men are legally allowed ... and here our guys are scared to walk arm in arm in the street.[6]

> Our fucking leaders don't understand that they can lock me up and work me over as much as they like, but they will never get me to change. It's just not my fault. I was born this way. For me, anything you call normal sex is unnatural and disgusting. Oh, if only the authorities up there knew how many celebrated names there are in our ranks ... Their own KGB people, police, some people in the government, singers, celebrities.[7]

Although similar sentiments prevailed among many Moscow homosexual men, they did not develop into any homophile movement.

But sometimes help came from overseas. As more foreign tourists were now able to visit the USSR, with them came foreign gay activists, sympathetic to the plight of Soviet homosexuals. Under the pretence of being devout communists, they obtained permits to enter the USSR and there they met homosexuals in large cities and expressed support for them, interviewed them and on some occasions openly defied the Soviet authorities' homophobia.

One such activist, an Italian named Angelo Pezzana who visited the USSR in 1977, even dared to take to the streets and stage a one-man protest against the Soviet state's oppression of homosexuals. A few days before the event, he went to visit Andrei Sakharov, a prominent Soviet dissident and activist for human rights, at his apartment in Moscow in the hope of securing his support for the forthcoming homosexual protest.

Although Sakharov commended Pezzana on his idea, he showed considerable reluctance to stand up for the rights of homosexuals and associate his name with their cause: "I cannot support you publicly, they would say I am a homosexual, I have to fight for everyone's civil rights.

But you are doing it very well." Disappointed but undeterred, Angelo decided to proceed with his plan without Sakharov's support.[8]

As he wanted to attract as much attention as possible, he chose Red Square, the very heart of Moscow, as a venue for his protest. But on the day of the planned event, the KGB officers foiled Angelo's plans. They apprehended him as he was walking out of the Metropol Hotel, tore his placard "FREEDOM FOR HOMOSEXUALS IN THE USSR" from him and bundled him into their car. Pezzana was then taken to the KGB's headquarters on Lubyanka Square for interrogation.

"Give us a list of homosexuals that you personally know in Moscow," the KGB officers demanded through the translator.

Pezzana shrugged nonchalantly and said he did not know any.

"Do you realize that you will never be able to get back into this country?"

"I don't want to come back until there is a true libertarian socialism here," he announced and refused to speak with them further. On the same day Pezzana was put on a plane and flown out of Moscow back to Milan.[9]

Soviet legal scholars sympathetic to homosexuals, as in the 1960s, continued to push for the removal of Article 121.1. Aleksei Ignatov, a scholar who in the 1960s, as we saw in Chapter 13, had called on the judges not to prosecute men for homosexual behaviour such as oral sex and sexual touching, now argued that any consensual sexual activity, including anal sex, had to be decriminalized. He expressed this view in his doctoral dissertation *Problems of Criminal Liability for the Study of Causes of Crime and Developing Measures of Crime Prevention* at the All-Union Institute for the Study and Prevention of Crime. Devoting a whole chapter to the issue of homosexuality in the USSR, Ignatov wrote:

> At present, we may consider it to be an established fact that a certain number of people suffer from a congenital perversion of sexual desire … As it stands, people with psychological deviations are most predisposed to homosexuality. Therefore, criminalisation of homosexuality is not just a matter of law. It goes without saying that such perversion is of a pathological nature and legal sanctions are not only useless, but unjust. The fear of criminal punishment prevents homosexuals from resorting to medical help.

In the medical and legal literature, it has been stated multiple times that consensual homosexual liaisons between adults neither pose societal danger nor damage the state.[10]

In recent years, the People's Republic of Bulgaria and the German Democratic Republic along with a number of other foreign countries have abolished criminal liability for voluntary homosexual relationships. Currently, of the European socialist states, only Romania and Yugoslavia retain criminal liability for voluntary homosexuality.[11]

In 1974, several weeks before the scheduled day of Ignatov's dissertation defence, one of his colleagues at the All-Union Institute for the Study and Prevention of Crime received a phone call from a high-ranking Party official, who accused Ignatov of "propagating immorality" and "undermining the foundations of socialist law in the country".[12] Ignatov understood very well that his arguments were not to the Party's liking. Now he faced a difficult choice – either to give in to the pressure of the officials, backtracking on his bold proposals, or else defy the party officials, putting his career in danger.

On 6 May 1974, Ignatov's defence took place. As the conventions of such an event dictated, Ignatov first delivered a speech for the panel of distinguished experts, outlining the key proposals of his dissertation and then experts began to ask him questions.

"In criminal law, does homosexuality violate the basic norms of socialist morality?" one of the experts enquired.

Ignatov flashed back to the call that his department had received a few weeks ago and hesitated for a moment. He had to say something. Part of him longed to speak his mind and express his disagreement about the relevance of socialist morality to the issue of sodomy, but the other part warned him to comply and pay lip service to the ignorant party officials. He decided to avoid making any clear statements regarding the issue, and said evasively:

The issue of homosexuality is very complex and very difficult to solve. My thesis proposes to eliminate criminal responsibility for consensual sodomy between adult men. On the other hand, criminal liability should be imposed for all types of homosexual behaviour associated with the use of violence against a person. I am receiving both support and criticism in response to my abstract and this dissertation and it has made me think through and consider this issue once again.[13]

Ignatov swallowed his pride and continued:

It seems to me that the problem of responsibility for homosexuality and in general the issue of sodomy should be addressed comprehensively. It goes beyond the scope of a purely legal perspective and requires a further, deep and comprehensive study. It seems premature to put forward a proposal to eliminate the criminal responsibility for sodomy. Public consciousness and public opinion are not yet ready for such a solution to the problem. And in this regard, you correctly said that indeed this act is condemned by socialist morality and that our criminal code considers it as a violation of the basic principles of socialist morality.[14]

Ignatov quickly scanned the experts in the room – it was unlikely that any of these conservative scholars, most of whom had received their education during Stalin's time, would welcome his call for tolerance towards homosexuals. Yes, Ignatov had supporters, but he doubted that any of them was in the room among this panel of experts who would get to decide his academic career. Silently scolding himself for betraying his ideas, Ignatov conceded:

Studying the reviews and their arguments made me once again carefully think over this problem and led me to the conclusion that the proposal to completely abolish criminal liability for voluntary sodomy was put forward somewhat prematurely. It seems to me that public consciousness is not ready for such a decision.[15]

On the same day, the panel of experts conferred his doctoral degree on Ignatov. Despite the positive outcome, Ignatov felt humiliated – he had succumbed to censorship and was pressed and bullied into capitulation. It took Ignatov several weeks to overcome his frustration and accept the fact that conformity was the only way for him to retain his privileged position within Soviet academia and continue to fight for the removal of Article 121.1.

Over the following years Ignatov continued to advocate for the decriminalization of sodomy. In 1974, Ignatov published a pamphlet based on his dissertation titled *Classifying Sex Crimes* (1974), where he again openly argued that consensual sodomy had to be abolished.[16] Several years later, in 1979, Ignatov sent a letter to the Interior Ministry, in which he again drew the authorities' attention to the importance of repealing Article 121.1. His letter, of course, was never responded to.

Part IV

Under Gorbachev

19

A strange patient from Africa baffles Soviet doctors

Moscow, 1982

On 14 August 1982, doctors and interns working at the Moscow Hospital of Infectious Diseases Number 2 received a patient who had just landed at the Sheremetyevo airport and was rushed to their hospital by ambulance. The patient was a man named Vladimir, thirty-two years old, who had just returned from Tanzania, where he'd been working in the Soviet embassy as a translator and interpreter. The initial examination showed that Vladimir was extremely unwell and was suffering from some unknown disease.[1]

Following Vladimir's hospitalization, doctors submitted him to a battery of tests and performed examinations of his body to learn more about his mysterious affliction. Vladimir was losing weight due to unrelenting diarrhoea and was suffering from unexplained fatigue, the origins of which the doctors struggled to identify. According to Vladimir, the first symptoms of the disease had presented themselves in July 1982, a month before his return to the USSR, and included fatigue, headache, insomnia and persistent diarrhoea. Local Tanzanian doctors suspected malaria, and, after several unsuccessful attempts to treat Vladimir, advised him to urgently seek treatment in Moscow.[2]

After many tests and endless investigations of Vladimir's body, Soviet doctors pronounced bacterial dysentery as a tentative diagnosis, which initially assuaged Vladimir's fears for his life as bacterial dysentery did not sound like a horrible disease that people died of.[3] But after his initial relief, Vladimir began to worry that this diagnosis was incorrect and that he was suffering from something far more serious. He was worried because he knew that he had wilfully concealed from the doctors an episode during his life in Africa – an event which might have triggered his ailment and the knowledge of which could have possibly helped doctors to establish the correct diagnosis. But Vladimir was far too embarrassed to mention it to anyone. He knew that if he had told his secret to the doctors he would have been in serious trouble and possibly ended up in jail.

He tried not even to call this episode to mind in the presence of doctors, fearing that somehow they would be able to read his mind and find out the truth. Doctors treated Vladimir with antibacterial drugs and his diarrhoea did indeed begin to subside over the coming days. Noting the improvement, Vladimir felt more optimistic and entreated doctors to discharge him. The doctors, however, were not as eager to discharge their patient and convinced him to remain under their observation for at least another week. And they had grounds for their caution.

To Vladimir's horror and the doctors' astonishment, a week later Vladimir developed a fever and his body broke out in a rash, especially on his arms and legs. Doctors also discovered that Vladimir had enlarged lymph nodes, and blood tests showed an increase of lymphocytes. Again, doctors managed to treat his rash and bring down his temperature so that once again it seemed that the patient was ready to start convalescing. Yet soon another serious symptom presented itself – blood in Vladimir's stool. This discovery prompted a colonoscopy, which doctors did not conduct until four weeks after Vladimir's admission to the hospital due to his refusals to undergo the procedure. The colonoscopy revealed lumps in Vladimir's colon and led doctors to revisit their previous diagnosis.[4]

After further tests and assessments, doctors suspected a new diagnosis – a tumour in the rectum – so they transferred him to the department of proctology in Moscow's Hospital Number 2, where he again developed fever and sharp unrelenting pain in the stomach. After more tests, doctors again changed their diagnosis, this time to Crohn's disease.[5] Vladimir was in for a long and unpleasant treatment. He was growing tired of the uncertainty, endless examinations and the doctors' inquisitive and judgemental stares, which he found humiliating. He was also suffering from insomnia and nightmares. He knew that he should not have done what he did in Tanzania. He deeply regretted it. Lying in his drab hospital room, he was reminiscing about the start of his career and how not that long ago he had lived in Moscow, dreaming of leaving the USSR for some exotic country.

From his early childhood, Vladimir had been fascinated by foreign languages, especially English, and he had always dreamt of travelling around the world. In the 1970s and early 1980s, the average Soviet citizen was not allowed to travel overseas, and foreign trips were available only to a privileged minority. In order to be able to leave the USSR, one had to apply for a special permit providing ironclad reasons why a journey outside the country was necessary. Applying for travel to capitalist countries was especially difficult and the person seeking to travel to the capitalist world needed to demonstrate exemplary credentials, a clean past, political connections and evidence of previous travel to Eastern Europe. Those applying for travel to these parts of the world had to fill in five pages of forms with questions about their family and work history, whether they had ever violated the Soviet law or had any family members living abroad. Finally, aspirants for foreign travel needed to demonstrate evidence of being in good health. The whole process was difficult and stressful and it was very common for travel permissions to be refused or delayed.[6]

With such a stringent system in place, Soviet authorities weeded out untrustworthy applicants who were likely to betray the Motherland by permanently leaving the country and settling in capitalist countries. Indeed, it was much easier for foreign tourists to visit the USSR than vice versa.

But there were some exceptions – representatives of certain professions directly linked to foreign countries had little trouble obtaining travel permissions. These were elite professionals and included international pilots, sailors and, of course, diplomats. Getting into any of these professions usually happened through one's connections or exceptional talent and achievements.

Vladimir, though, was born to an average family and had no influential relatives who could help him with his career, so he had to rely on himself alone. Despite the cronyism and nepotism flourishing in the diplomatic ministry, after university Vladimir managed to get a job as a translator in the Ministry of Foreign Affairs and was offered a job in Tanzania in 1980.[7] When Vladimir received his job offer, he couldn't have been happier.

Working as part of diplomatic and military services in African countries was quite prestigious and promised considerable material benefits. Those who were offered such work had the opportunity to see a country whose culture was totally different from that of the USSR as well as to improve their financial situation significantly. For instance, after one and a half years' work in Angola, some diplomats could afford to buy a car. The salary of Soviet representatives in African countries depended on the position they held, whether there were military conflicts there or whether climatic conditions were severe. Some Foreign Ministry officials, when calculating salaries for Soviet diplomatic and military workers in African countries, believed that those working in countries closer to the equator deserved higher pay due to the harsh climate compared to those working further away.[8]

African countries constituted a special strategic interest for the USSR, which supported them in their struggles against colonialism and actively participated in their post-colonialist reconstruction. Many African students received their education in the USSR as well. Compared to other countries in the region, Tanzania was relatively safe for working and living in as there were no ongoing hostilities there and it even had access to the ocean, which meant that Vladimir could relax on the beach in his holidays.

To be cleared for work in Tanzania, Vladimir had to jump through many hoops as well. After numerous medical examinations, filling in endless papers and forms and sitting through interviews with the KGB, Vladimir was finally ready for his trip. His boss had issued him a foreign passport and had withheld his internal passport and Communist card from him until his return. He had also handed him plane tickets. Holding them tightly, Vladimir could not contain his excitement as he had never even travelled by plane before.

The Soviet embassy was located in the picturesque port city of Dar es Salaam, a former capital of Tanzania, on the shores of the Indian Ocean. Vladimir obtained a separate room in the embassy and soon got to know all the other officials who worked and lived there. Most of them were married, had children and had been serving in Tanzania as diplomatic workers for a long time. They preferred to stay on the territory of the embassy in the company of their colleagues, complaining about being bored, missing the USSR and drinking vodka. As a young single man, Vladimir struggled to find common topics of conversation with them and preferred to explore the city and surroundings during his free time.

Contrary to Vladimir's expectations, Tanzania turned out to be a country with a rich culture, impressive colonial architecture and pristine sandy beaches, which impressed him the most. Tired of urban landscapes and the hectic pace of life in Moscow, Vladimir appreciated and enjoyed Tanzanian beaches.

Before leaving Moscow, KGB officers had instructed Vladimir not to mingle with the locals and to keep in mind that he was there for work not for leisure. Vladimir pledged to heed their advice, but once he found himself in Tanzania he immediately forgot about his promises. The friendly manners of the locals enchanted him and tempted him to communicate with them. Needless to say, Vladimir also attracted a great deal of attention from the locals, who gave him all kinds of furtive looks and inquisitive stares. Vladimir felt them everywhere: at the markets, at the museums and especially on the beaches, where his naked fair-skinned body stood out conspicuously. It was on the beach that Vladimir met a tall broad-shouldered dark-skinned man in his forties with a charming smile, whose name he struggled to remember ... Vladmir suspected that his terrible disease was somehow related to this encounter.

On 28 April 1983, almost nine months after his admission to hospital, Vladimir was discharged.[9] The symptoms of his disease seemed to have finally subsided. He was immensely relieved, and above all glad that he had managed to keep his secret to himself. He still felt fatigued, but he longed to be discharged and erase the memories of his long hospital ordeal. He planned to return to his native town in the Moscow region and start working there as a teacher in a secondary school. We shall return to Vladimir's story in Chapter 22.

Little did Vladimir's doctors know that the disease they had encountered in their unusual patient had already been baffling American doctors for almost two years. In May 1982, the *New York Times* had published an article titled "New Homosexual Disorder Worries Health Officials", which broke the news to the public about an unknown immune disorder that had affected 335 people and killed 136 of them. People stricken with this disease suffered from a rare type of cancer called Kaposi's sarcoma as well as a number of serious infections and disorders.

Since the new disease seemed to affect mostly homosexual men, doctors initially called it GRID, which stood or Gay Related Immune Deficiency.[10] In September the year, the Center for Disease Control and Prevention used the term AIDS (Acquired Immune Deficiency Syndrome) for the first time to describe this puzzling disease. By the end of 1982, AIDS cases were being reported in a number of European countries. But the overwhelming majority of Soviet doctors remained unaware of these developments – for the present.

Soviet officials try to protect the USSR from AIDS

1982–1985

On 10 November 1982, Leonid Brezhnev, who had been ruling the USSR for almost two decades, passed away. A few hours after his death the members of the Politburo gathered in the Kremlin to decide who was going to be the new leader of the country. All members of the Politburo took the floor, delivering eulogies to Brezhnev and proposing candidates who in their opinion were best suited to fill the role. It was decided that sixty-eight-year-old Yuri Vladimirovich Andropov, the chairman of the KGB, would be Brezhnev's successor.

Andropov had a reputation for being an honest and highly intelligent man with solid experience in internal and international affairs. As a KGB chief, he was well informed about the many problems besetting the country. Soviet society had been in a deep economic crisis; the country was descending into an embarrassing decrepitude; shortages were becoming part and parcel of Soviet life; and people had to spend hours in long queues at stores for food and other consumer goods. The country's economic growth had ground to a complete halt.

Soviet ideology was in deep crisis too. Soviet people, stripped both of initiative and spirituality, had lost faith in the bright future of communism, regarding their leaders' slogans about socialist construction with cynicism and mockery. As society headed towards its inevitable moral and economic decline, Soviet people invented their own survival strategies, including absenteeism, pilfering and illegal commercial activity; others found solace in guzzling rotgut vodka on a daily basis. Meanwhile, corruption among

Soviet officials was growing to unprecedented levels. Bringing order and discipline to society as well as boosting the Soviet economy were key goals Andropov hoped to accomplish.

The USSR's international affairs were also in dire straits. Despite the easing of hostility between the US and the USSR during the 1970s, in the early 1980s they again started to deteriorate following the Soviet invasion of Afghanistan in 1979. The newly elected president of the US, Ronald Reagan, at his first press conference in January 1981, dubbed the USSR "an evil empire" and "the focus of evil in the modern world", which only further fuelled Andropov's belligerence towards his American counterpart.

In mid-1981, a group of Soviet virologists headed by Rem Petrov at Moscow's Institute of Immunology began to receive reports from abroad about a strange virus, which had first been noted and described by American doctors and, according to their observations, seemed to specifically afflict homosexuals. Taking the reports seriously, Petrov decided to discuss them with his colleagues at one of the sessions of the Soviet Academy of Medical Sciences, but he immediately drew harsh criticism from fellow academics, especially the president of the Academy, Nikolai Blokhin, who interrupted him by saying: "Somewhere in America … a handful of queers got sick and you are making such a big deal out of it …."[1] The vast majority of doctors in the Soviet Union remained unaware of the new disease.

But as the number of cases in the US was growing and the disease, which now had a name – AIDS – was found to afflict heterosexual people and children, it became increasingly clear to Petrov that soon the disease would appear in the USSR. But whenever Petrov approached officials of the Health Ministry with requests for permission for the publication of a series on articles on AIDS, he was met with assurances that AIDS could strike only homosexuals, prostitutes and drug addicts, and there were no concomitant social conditions in the USSR for such a disease to proliferate.

After numerous attempts on the part of Petrov and his colleagues from Moscow's Institute of Immunology to lobby the publication of materials on AIDS, the Health Ministry allowed Petrov to publish only one article.

He was warned not to spread panic and, despite the emerging scientific evidence about everybody's vulnerability to AIDS, he was urged to underscore the fact that this disease was still largely prevalent among American homosexuals.

On 22 June 1983, a major Soviet newspaper, *Literaturnaya gazeta*, published Petrov's article under the rather dull title "Immunodeficiency: What Is It?", in which he broke the news about AIDS to the Soviet public for the first time:

> A peculiar type of immunodeficiency found in adults, which was described three years ago in the US, is attracting the attention of scientific journals and the wider press of the United States. The unique manifestations and dissemination of this illness gave it a special name, which distinguishes it from primary and secondary disorders of the immune system. This immunodeficiency is called acquired [immunodeficiency syndrome] AIDS ... It is common among drug-addicts, homosexuals and immigrants from Haiti, who settled in the US.
>
> The spread of this type of immune system disease among a limited number of individuals ... makes some American researchers suspect the existence of an unknown virus. It is assumed that the virus selectively affects the immune system, causes the development of immunodeficiency and dooms the infected person to the disease, depriving him of protection against any otherwise harmless microbes. If this assumption is confirmed, the social danger of homosexuality will be greater than previously thought, since it is possible for the virus to spread beyond the named circle of people. Of course, this type of immunodeficiency may simply be the result of the detrimental effect on the body of these vices.[2]

Soviet Health Ministry officials believed that this information was already enough to raise people's awareness about AIDS and any further mentions of the disease would only spread unnecessary panic.

While the Soviet Health Ministry preferred to disregard the problem of AIDS, gloating over the misfortunes of capitalist countries, the Soviet KGB watched the news about AIDS in the US with great interest, wondering how to use it to their own advantage. Soon, as a response to Reagan's belligerent rhetoric towards the USSR, the KGB launched an international disinformation campaign accusing the US of creating AIDS in Pentagon labs. The Soviet KGB had already orchestrated various disinformation campaigns against the US and for this purpose had set up and funded newspapers in other countries, then citing them as foreign "independent" sources for their allegations. One such newspaper was called *Patriot*, which KGB agents had set up in India as early as 1967.[3] In 1983, this newspaper was used for an AIDS disinformation campaign.

Soviet KGB officials composed an article with the alarming title "AIDS May Invade India: Mystery Disease Caused by US Experiments" which claimed that AIDS was created in the Pentagon and that Americans were about to transfer their AIDS laboratories to Pakistan, close to the Indian border. The article was then covertly planted in *Patriot* and published in 1983, but, despite its sensational allegations, neither the Indian nor the international press picked it up at that time. After all, *Patriot*'s print-run was only thirty thousand copies and in 1983 AIDS was not yet a problem on the subcontinent.[4]

Meanwhile, the USSR was about to face another succession crisis. Yuri Andropov's health was swiftly deteriorating as a result of diabetes and chronic kidney dysfunction, which confined him to a hospital bed and kept him away from public functions for six months. On 9 February 1984, after a short fifteen-month reign, he passed away.

Andropov was succeeded by Brezhnev's protégé, seventy-two-year-old Konstantin Chernenko, who, like his predecessor, remained ill for the duration of his thirteen-month tenure. Predictably, Chernenko left little imprint on Soviet affairs – things remained almost the same and the problem of AIDS continued to be an unmentionable taboo in public sources. Chernenko died of heart problems, hepatitis and cirrhosis in March 1985.

After yet another death of an ageing Soviet leader in such a brief period, Politburo members realized the urgency of breathing new life into the ranks of these old, tired and sick Soviet leaders. Very shortly after Chernenko's death, the Politburo nominated fifty-four-year-old Mikhail Gorbachev as Communist Party General Secretary. Energetic, lively and ambitious, Gorbachev was the youngest Soviet leader since Stalin. He was impatient to extricate the USSR from its crises and reset the stalled US–Soviet relations.

While Soviet leaders were sorting themselves out during the interregnum, the problem of AIDS was becoming more urgent worldwide. By 1985, cases of AIDS had been registered across various continents and in different countries. The disease was spreading and had already taken the lives of some high-profile men, including Klaus Nomi, the famous German counter-tenor, and the French philosopher Michel Foucault, who died in 1984. Then in July 1985, the American actor Rock Hudson, adored globally as the stereotypically straight, square-jawed leading man, publicly announced that he was infected with AIDS. Hudson's admission, and his subsequent death, brought AIDS to the forefront as nothing else had done. It was killing people – people everyone admired – and it had to be acknowledged.

The international community of medical researchers had also now discovered the cause of AIDS – a human immunodeficiency virus – and this discovery led to the mass production of commercial human immunodeficiency virus (HIV) blood tests in the US in early 1985. Even the US President Ronald Reagan, who had never publicly spoken on the problem since the first reports about the disease, was pressured to break his silence during a press conference on 17 September 1985, calling the AIDS issue, ironically, his "top priority".

In the USSR, officials did not appear overly alarmed about the news from the West. Instead, they busied themselves with clearing the decks for a major international event – the 12th World Festival of Youth and Students, which was to take place in Moscow from 27 July to 3 August 1985. Soviet authorities anticipated around eighteen thousand participants from some 150 countries along with thousands of tourists. Predictably, Soviet authorities used this festival as an instrument of ideological propaganda against the West and most festival attenders came from pro-communist countries. They were to attend concerts, political lectures and exhibitions devoted to the issues of anti-imperialism.

In an attempt to prevent foreigners from bringing AIDS on to Soviet soil, a couple of weeks before the festival officials from the Health Ministry ordered staff at Soviet international airports to monitor and examine arriving foreign nationals for traces of AIDS.[5] They also placed two small articles on AIDS in newspapers, which, apart from claiming that AIDS was caused by promiscuous sexual behaviour, warned readers not to shake hands with foreigners.[6] Despite these and many other precautions and preventive measures, the week-long festival did bring people carrying AIDS to the Soviet Union. Some of them were identified by Soviet doctors and immediately deported, but some, as doctors had suspected, could have fallen through the cracks of the precautionary measures and passed it on to Soviet citizens. All the same, Soviet health officials continued their silence on AIDS and Health Ministry officials continued banning articles and items on AIDS in Soviet newspapers to avoid stoking panic, hoping to tackle the epidemic without attracting public attention.

In November 1985, the Soviet Health Ministry dispatched two officials, Professors Fedotenkov and Agranenko, to the US in order to gain first-hand knowledge on how Americans were combating the virus through observation and participating in medical conferences. In December, they returned from the US and reported their observations to the officials of the Soviet Health Ministry:

> We have taken part in a series of conferences and we have seen things on their television. Many people are dying, but at the same time extensive research on the problem is being conducted. The President is constantly informed on the problem – some congressmen are accusing him of not disclosing the true state of affairs in the country and glossing over the mortality statistics in particular. American doctors are also conducting the screening and medical examinations of high-risk groups – prostitutes, homosexuals and drug addicts, which also seems to curb the rate of the infection.[7]

Inspired by their observations in the US, Health Ministry officials decided to implement similar measures and even enlisted the help of Soviet police. The Soviet Health Ministry sent numerous memos to the Interior Ministry of the USSR, urging police to "take necessary measures for detection of groups considered to be 'high risk' – homosexuals, prostitutes, drug-addicts – with a view to examining them and curbing their activities that may lead to the spread of the viral infection".[8]

That the Soviet Health Ministry chose to rely on the police in order to screen and examine the so-called "risk groups" was not unexpected as in previous decades the police and doctors had conducted joint operations aimed at identifying sources of venereal diseases among urban populations. At the instigation of doctors, police organized surveillance of cities' bus and railway stations, parks and squares, known as places of congregation of homosexuals and prostitutes. As a result of extensive round-ups, police captured suspicious individuals and confined them to STI hospitals, where doctors examined them for venereal disease. If further investigation confirmed their engagement in homosexual acts, such individuals stood trial and were sent to jail.[9]

The threat of AIDS dissemination, and the Soviet medical authorities' conviction that homosexuals were to blame, unleashed a new wave of harassment and entrapment of homosexual people in big Soviet cities. In 1987 in many large cities, local police departments set up commissions on "AIDS dissemination prevention", which included the entrapment of homosexuals and prostitutes.[10] The Interior Ministry even published specialized pamphlets for the police, one of which was called *Tasks of the Police for AIDS Prevention* (1988), which openly blamed homosexuals for the transmission of AIDS in the community and called on the police to prevent their pernicious activities.[11] So, punished already by lack of appropriate help and the silence around this spreading disease, and discriminated against for their lifestyle, homosexual men were now even more threatened by harassment, arrest and imprisonment. They were to carry the blame and the burden of shame that accompanied the emergence of AIDS for many years.

The response of gay men and women in other countries, however, was different. After the Stonewall riots in 1969 and during the 1970s, a new lesbian and gay consciousness had been emerging in the US and other Western countries, which facilitated the development of a well-organized press, social and political groups and a highly visible gay commercial world.[12]

Almost immediately, in 1982, when the first reports about AIDS began to emerge, concerned gay men in New York formed the Gay Men's Health Crisis Group, which, apart from being focused on research and education, also established a variety of services for people affected by the virus.[13] Soon similar organizations were formed in other American cities as well as in Canada, Australia and northern Europe, where gay men and women had been organizing during the previous decades. With a tangible enemy to fight, there was now a strong impetus to organize as a community.

The Soviet KGB becomes inspired by the American gay press

1985–1987

On 30 October 1985, a major Soviet newspaper, *Literaturnaya gazeta*, featured a long article with the screaming headline "Panic in the West, or What Is Hidden behind the Sensation around AIDS?" Citing an obscure Indian newspaper, *Patriot*, the author of the article, a certain Valentin Zapevalov, speculated that AIDS was a biological weapon created in the laboratories of the Pentagon.[1] Zapevalov's article was the first major article on AIDS published in Soviet newspapers since Petrov's first article in 1983. The publication of Zapevalov's article was initiated by the Soviet KGB, which decided to resume its plans of launching the disinformation campaign conceived back in 1983. Although the new Soviet leader, Mikhail Gorbachev, was about to initiate liberal reforms in society and improve the relations between USSR and the US, during his first year in office he didn't intervene in the workings of the KGB, which acted pretty much independently and still had great power.

Although Zapevalov's story originated from an obscure source, it spread like wildfire. Millions of Soviet people who read *Literaturnaya gazeta* every day were terrified by the news, which, against the backdrop of the deteriorating relations between the US and USSR, seemed quite credible. Many were scared that the US had created and would use this weapon against the USSR.

The article also confused Soviet doctors, who obviously knew nothing about the intentions of the KGB to use the issue of AIDS in its disinformation campaign. To counteract the misleading claims about AIDS being a biological weapon and to assuage people's fears, the Soviet Health Ministry began publishing newspaper articles with scientific information on AIDS, but without questioning Zapevalov's disinformation article. Soviet doctors, at the instigation of the Health Ministry, also began to deliver public lectures on AIDS, which attracted many people who wanted to know how they could protect themselves from the disease.

In December 1985, a large crowd of people attended one such lecture in a large auditorium at Moscow's Vishnevsky Institute of Surgery, delivered by a doctor who was taken aback by such a diverse and large audience. Some people sat but most stood, trying to get closer to the stage to hear the doctor. An American correspondent, Gary Lee, who was present at the lecture, described it thus:

> A rare public lecture here two weeks ago on the AIDS epidemic packed a large auditorium so tightly that the crowd of nearly 1,000 – professionals, students, men in military uniform, housewives and others – spilled into the aisles and kept yelling for the Soviet doctor on the podium to speak up.
>
> After the 1½-hour talk, including an extensive question-and-answer period, the audience's curiosity seemed hardly satisfied.
>
> "This disease has been known for a long time," said a middle-aged man, who had pushed through the crowd and grabbed the microphone, "but not here, unfortunately. We have only known about it for the last hour. That's why … all of us are scared."
>
> The lecturer, who was introduced as "Arkady" but not fully identified, said there were cases of Kaposi's sarcoma, a skin cancer that can be especially deadly in AIDS patients, in Moscow, but he knew of no registered cases of AIDS.
>
> Near the end of his lecture last month, the doctor topped his list of preventive measures with a recommendation to avoid contact with foreigners and undesirable elements. He added that blood for transfusions should be drawn from women, who he said are less likely to be carriers of AIDS.[2]

Despite people's confusion, fear and a lack of reliable information on AIDS in the Soviet Union, the KGB went ahead with its disinformation campaign, planting more articles in the Soviet press with falsehoods about it being artificially cultivated in American labs. Soon the international press also picked these stories up and by late 1987 they had appeared in the media of 80 countries and in 25 languages, sowing panic not only among Soviet people but also in citizens of other countries.

The KGB's propaganda, which had now acquired international dimensions, significantly hampered international efforts to fight the epidemic and wrought extensive damage to America's reputation. Since the USSR had long been engaged in disseminating various falsehoods about the US, Americans maintained a pool of qualified experts in Soviet disinformation campaigning, who worked tirelessly to punch holes in Soviet propaganda stories.

After conducting extensive research on the possible origins of the Soviet allegations regarding AIDS, an American expert in Soviet propaganda, Todd Leventhal, came to the astonishing conclusion that, for their initial 1983 *Patriot* article, Soviet KGB officials had lifted quotations from an American gay magazine called the *New York Native*! Because during the early days of the pandemic AIDS had been a great mystery, seeming to afflict only homosexual men, some American gay journalists speculated a lot about the origins of the disease. One gay author, who subsequently published an article in the *New York Native*, indeed suggested that AIDS could have been a result of Pentagon experiments.[3] And this article somehow appeared on the radar of Soviet security services, who decided to use it as the main source of their allegations.

Leventhal quickly realized that his discovery could be used against strait-laced Soviets to embarrass them into ceasing their disinformation campaign. He pitched the idea to his colleague, another Soviet propaganda expert, the writer and ex-communist Herb Romerstein, who was just about to leave for Moscow for negotiations about Soviet's recent publications which accused the US of manufacturing AIDS in its laboratories. With a grin, Leventhal tossed the issue of the *New York Native* to Romerstein, motioning him to have a look at its cover, which featured three men in drag – one wearing a long gown and cowboy hat, while the other two wore cowboy boots and jockstraps.

"Why don't you take them with you to Moscow?" Leventhal suggested. "I can't use *these* in the meeting," Romerstein replied. "Take them with you," Leventhal insisted "You never know."[4]

So Romerstein flew to Moscow with the journal in his briefcase straight to the meeting at the headquarters of the *Novosti Military Bulletin*, which had been circulating articles with falsehoods about US biological warfare. Several men in overcoats were present in the meeting room, who, Romerstein immediately realized, were KGB agents. Upon the arrival of journalists and the main editor of the *Novosti Military Bulletin*, Romerstein cut to the chase.

"You've been publishing stories that the AIDS virus was created as a biological weapon by the United States and that it was caused by U.S. nuclear testing," he began. "We've seen this crazy story – stay away from it because it's not true."

"We didn't create the AIDS disinformation story," a Soviet man in an overcoat chuckled. "It was in your press."

With that, Romerstein opened his briefcase and pulled out the issue of the *New York Native* and held it up for everybody to see its cover. "This is your source," Romerstein said. "Now, we want to save you embarrassment. We don't want you to be known for quoting *this* as your source. It's not good for your image. Anytime you have a question about a source in America, you can call us and we'll be happy to help!"

"Since you do us a favour," said one of the men in overcoats, "We will give you a year's free subscription to *Novosti Military Bulletin*. It normally costs $200."[5]

Romerstein's knowledge about the provenance of Soviet AIDS disinformation from an American gay magazine had indeed embarrassed Soviet KGB officials, who subsequently felt compelled to explain themselves in an attempt to salvage their reputation. Commenting on the theory that AIDS was created in American laboratories, the author of a Soviet pamphlet on AIDS, published in 1988, wrote: "This version appeared in the pages of our press, and it originated ... among American homosexuals ... who began to argue that this virus was created in the laboratories of the US Special Services in order to physically destroy them. Our newspapers only reprinted messages from American newspapers and other Western press."[6]

As Mikhail Gorbachev was working hard to improve Soviet–US relations and initiate democratic reforms at home, the Soviet AIDS disinformation campaign gradually became pointless and the story had gently faded from Soviet outlets by 1988.

22

Soviet doctors find Soviet "Patient Zero"

Moscow, 1987

"We need to find our first AIDS patient; I am convinced that he is already on Soviet soil," said Vadim Pokrovskii to his audience – dozens of doctors in white coats who had come to hear a lecture on AIDS in 1987. All the doctors were listening to him carefully and taking notes.[1]

Vadim Pokrovskii, aged thirty-two, was a crucial figure in the Soviet fight against AIDS. A son of a prominent Soviet epidemiologist and president of the Soviet Academy of Medical Sciences, Valentin Pokrovskii, Vadim decided to follow in his father's footsteps and devote his life to studying viruses. The news about the mysterious disease AIDS, which was later found to result from a virus, mystified and intrigued Pokrovskii, compelling him to stake his whole medical career on the study of this novel virus. By 1987, Pokrovskii had successfully defended a dissertation on AIDS and even inaugurated an AIDS testing laboratory in Moscow, where Soviet citizens could have their blood screened for viral antibodies anonymously.

Although most Soviet senior doctors were still reluctant to admit in public that AIDS could be of concern in the USSR, confidently proclaiming that, out of a handful of AIDS cases registered on Soviet soil, most were foreigners, behind the scenes they urged their colleagues to take action against the epidemic. By the end of 1987, when the Soviet disinformation campaign had significantly subsided, the Soviet Health Ministry launched an extensive AIDS public education campaign and inaugurated a network of AIDS testing centres, which were concerned primarily with screening donated blood. Most health officials were also convinced that foreigners should be the main target of testing, introducing stringent testing requirements for foreigners coming from abroad.

Despite this, Pokrovskii was convinced that Soviet health officials were barking up the wrong tree. He believed that the virus was most certainly already circulating among Soviet people and it was just a matter of time before this first Soviet AIDS case surfaced. He knew that no Soviet case had yet been officially recorded only because of the lack of testing equipment in Soviet clinics and the ignorance on the part of most doctors about the virus. Pokrovskii was also aware that the appalling state of Soviet hospitals, with their constant shortages, poor sanitary conditions and faulty sanitary procedures, especially in hospitals far from big cities, created propitious conditions for the spread of the virus. On top of that, there was a severe shortage of condoms in the country and those that were produced in the Soviet Union were mostly of substandard quality.

In 1987, Pokrovskii began to deliver a series of lectures on AIDS in an attempt to raise awareness about the virus along with the latest medical information on it for doctors in Moscow and other large cities. Pokrovskii believed that some doctors could already have AIDS patients in their care without knowing it due to their ignorance about the disease. The correct diagnosis of AIDS patients could have also been hampered by the placating statements of Soviet officials in newspapers, who asserted that this disease afflicted only foreigners, and stating there were in any case no conditions for such a disease to proliferate in the USSR.[2]

After one such lecture delivered in Moscow in late February 1987, Pokrovskii was approached by a young doctor named Elena Fabrikova.[3] She reported that one of her patients' symptoms seemed to match everything he had described. She also added that they were running tests on him, trying to contact doctors who had previously treated him in Moscow. Pokrovskii asked Fabrikova to allow him to meet the patient.

So Fabrikova invited Pokrovskii to the proctology clinic where she worked and, on examining the patient in question, he was sure that Fabrikova was correct. The patient, named Vladimir, whose story was told in Chapter 19, presented with all the typical symptoms of AIDS: his face, torso, arms and legs had broken out in a rash, which merged into plaques in some places. Fabrikova also briefed Pokrovskii on the particulars of Vladimir's medical history – he had been treated for Crohn's disease from August 1982 to April 1983 in Moscow. Then he returned to Rybinsk, his native town in the Moscow region, where from 1983 to 1985 he had two episodes of shingles and pneumonia. In early 1985 he started developing symptoms of Kaposi's sarcoma, a usually benign reddish skin cancer that generally affected older Mediterranean and Jewish men. In 1986, he sought medical treatment in Rybinsk, but local doctors failed to help.[4] Then he came back to Moscow and ended up in Fabrikova's care.

Pokrovskii noticed the patient's somewhat effeminate behaviour, and, although he'd wondered for a split second whether it might be connected to his state of health, he had initially dismissed the idea. Pokrovskii now advised Fabrikova that Vladimir should be tested for AIDS but, when she attempted to explain this to the clinic's chief doctor, he flew into a rage.

With Pokrosvkii's backing, Fabrikova managed to convince her boss to sanction Vladimir's testing. The test, on 7 March 1987, showed the presence of HIV antibodies in his blood. Doctors also established that what afflicted Vladimir was indeed Kaposi's sarcoma and that Vladimir was indeed suffering from advanced AIDS.[5] He was transferred to Moscow Hospital of Infectious Diseases Number 2, where doctors who had treated him in 1982 immediately recognized their former patient. After short deliberations, Fabrikova and Pokrovskii broke the news to Vladimir, who already suspected that he had AIDS – he read newspapers too.

Although Vladimir was devastated, he tried to keep himself together and not lose heart.

So Pokrovskii took Vladimir under his care and answered all his questions about the disease, explaining what he could expect in the following years. Unlike other doctors, who seemed to have little sympathy for Vladimir, Pokrovskii treated him with a certain kindness and compassion.

The democratic reforms, including the liberalization of the press, which Gorbachev initiated in 1987 led to more publications about AIDS in Soviet newspapers and magazines. The information that the first Soviet AIDS patient had been officially identified attracted a lot of attention to Vladimir. At first, he even felt flattered, but soon he grew tired of the constant questions and annoying intrusions in his private life.[6] He declined all requests for interviews. In search of sensation, journalists, who were now free to write about whatever they wanted, turned for comment to the doctors who had treated Vladimir in 1982. One doctor, whose interview was published in *Ogonek*, a Soviet weekly magazine, found it difficult to conceal her contempt of Vladimir:

> I have seen him – our first patient, the one who brought that terrible disease to us. Sickly, with protruding shoulder blades, with red spots on his face … He looks more like an infantile adolescent than a thirty-six-year-old man … He readily showed himself to the many doctors from the clinic and others who had come to have a look … and in his readiness to expose himself there was also something unnatural … He was complaining in a high-pitched voice.[7]

Vladimir's personal tragedy had become a horror story, which Soviet journalists and doctors promulgated to demonstrate that it was those cunning homosexuals who were to blame for the spread of AIDS in the USSR. An educational pamphlet titled "AIDS" (1988) for example, made a number of damming and highly fictitious claims about their Soviet Patient Zero:

> The fate of the first Soviet AIDS patient is instructive. He grew up a spoiled and pampered child … an American magazine fell into his hands and after reading it he drew the conclusion that he was a homosexual. At this time, he was abroad, where he easily managed to find a male sexual partner. Unaware that he had become infected with AIDS, he returned to his homeland and here skilfully made use of the knowledge gained abroad. With the help of small gifts, pornographic publications brought from abroad, alcohol and eloquence, he inclined young people of eighteen to twenty years to sexual relations. During a period of three years, he managed to find more than twenty partners, five of whom became infected with the AIDS virus.[8]

As for Vladimir himself, who was far from the fictional spoiled child and predatory cunning monster portrayed in this pamphlet, he died in 1991. After being diagnosed with AIDS, he spent his last years in one of Moscow's hospitals, battling with unrelenting infectious diseases, under Pokrovskii's supervision and the curious gaze of scientists, doctors and medical interns.

Soviet homophobia hits its peak

Moscow, 1988

In April 1985, at the Plenum of the Communist Party's Central Committee, Mikhail Gorbachev famously announced: "We strive for greater transparency ... People should know both the good and the bad."[1] In May of the same year Gorbachev delivered another speech in Leningrad, in which he openly criticized the slowing down of the Soviet economy and the inadequate living standards of Soviet people. Finally, Gorbachev signalled his intention to improve relations with the Western world. Despite the scepticism of Western politicians about Gorbachev's statements, which most of them considered more shallow words from yet another deceitful Soviet leader, Gorbachev meant what he said and indeed delivered on his promises.

In early 1986 Gorbachev adopted *perestroika* ("restructuring") of Soviet society as his key political slogan, hoping to revitalize the country's stalled social and economic development. He also announced the importance of *glasnost'* ("openness") – the policy of promoting open and honest discussions about the country's problems. Gorbachev believed that by liberalizing the press and television, which had hitherto been under strict Party control, the country would be able to find effective ways of resolving problems which prevented Soviet economic and social development. Honesty in the press was also supposed to restore public confidence in political leaders and their statements, which most Soviet people believed to be lies. To demonstrate his commitment to openness and liberalization, Gorbachev did something that previous Soviet leaders had never done – he travelled around the USSR, meeting with people from all strata of society to hear their opinions about the reforms.

In 1987, the Soviet media landscape began undergoing swift and dramatic transformations. For the first time in Soviet history, newspapers started to openly criticize the government's failures in economy, healthcare and culture, while shedding light on taboo issues of troubled Soviet history such as Stalin-era atrocities and repressions. AIDS, which had hitherto been an unmentionable subject, also came under the spotlight of the Soviet press.

A barrage of articles now began to appear in the press with detailed medical information on the virus, its methods of transmission, the first AIDS-related death and statistics on HIV infections on Soviet soil. Newspapers also discussed the case of the Soviet "Patient Zero", Vladimir, dwelling on the details of his personal life and his homosexuality and hinting that his sexual orientation predisposed him to catching the disease. Other journalists openly blamed the representatives of so-called "risk groups" – homosexuals, prostitutes and drug-addicts – for the spread of the virus, so that now these already despised individuals were seen as even more of a threat to Soviet society. Enraged Soviet readers wrote impassioned pleas to newspapers, wanting to execute homosexuals or send them to an island, isolating them from the rest of society. The degree of hatred towards homosexuals in the USSR during this time was so high that even some medical professionals did not shy away from public statements such as the following:

> Dear colleagues! We, graduates, of a medical institute (sixteen men) are categorically against the fight against a new "disease" – AIDS! We intend in every way to hinder the search for means of combating this noble epidemic. We are confident that AIDS will destroy all drug addicts, homosexuals and prostitutes in a short time. We are convinced that Hippocrates would have approved of our decision. Long live AIDS![2]

Many readers supported the doctors and commended them on the proposal. One reader, aged twenty-six, wrote:

I fully support the opinion of sixteen medics that AIDS is a natural doctor of humanity, which will save it from drug addicts, homosexuals and prostitutes ... The virus will help us kill two birds with one stone: get rid of the scum of humanity and resolve a number of vital problems.[3]

Other readers proposed equally inhumane measures. Writing about the risk groups, one reader proposed:

If we believe their [representatives of risk groups'] shallow promises to start leading a normal life, then soon we will have millions of infected, just like in the United States. These people will never become decent ... All homosexuals, prostitutes and drug addicts got stuck in their sexual liaisons and do not even attempt to limit themselves ... They don't need any anonymity and they should be screened forcibly! These bastards will never go to the doctor to have their blood screened! What for? If you are sick, there is no cure anyway, so it is better not to know and live without fear. It is also terrible that they seduce innocent teenagers! Urgent measures must be taken immediately to isolate them ... My suggestion: somewhere in remote Siberia, from where it is difficult to escape, set up camps like a leper colony and let them live, work and communicate with each other ... and slowly die out until an effective method of treatment is found![4]

Unlike in the US, where the AIDS epidemic and the predictable public backlash only made the gay community stronger and more fierce, the arrival of AIDS in the USSR only angered the public while making the position of homosexual people more precarious. While most Soviet homosexuals preferred to continue living closeted lives, very few tried to defend themselves in the pages of Soviet newspapers.

In December 1988, a Soviet magazine, *Molodoi Kommunist*, published a letter from a Russian man called Volodya who openly confessed his homosexuality and gave vent to his anger at the barrage of homophobic articles in Soviet newspapers:

Let me introduce myself: my name is Volodya D. I am twenty-seven years old, and most importantly, I am a homosexual, which means that in your opinion I am a creature from a "high risk group". I would never have written to you, but your article drove me around the bend. It just infuriated me. For a very long time I was discouraged from writing this letter, I was told that it would not change anything and that I could pay dearly for such audacity. And I'm not going to change anything, I just want people to understand everything impartially ... How else can one interpret V.I. Pokrovskii's words ... that the internal affairs organs, the justice organs and the councils of people's deputies should deal with the AIDS problem? Don't you think that this is way too much?

We are being chased away, and harassed, everywhere. Our lives are hard even without AIDS. Even without AIDS, the police are not letting us live, there is already an Article 121 in the Criminal Code, which says that, if two men who have never harmed and do not harm anyone (that is, they don't kill, rape or rob anyone), but simply live and love each other, then they need to be punished! And this means – imprisonment for at least three years, although now, I think, the prison term will be longer. But all the same, it is very unreasonable of you, gentlemen from police and Ministry of Internal Affairs.

I have been a homosexual for fifteen years – no nobody corrupted me – I knew I was a homosexual as early as twelve years old. Because of my homosexuality I was kicked out of the Young Communist League (I cried like a fool) and because of my homosexuality I was sent to prison (where I spent a year and six months and where I was given treatment). There, I learned to hate our law enforcement agencies, which, in my opinion, have been created specifically to humiliate, insult and ruin people's lives...

... I am sure that the number of suicides will increase, and if I get AIDS, then forgive me, but I will not go for treatment ... I will try to infect as many of you as possible – [the] honest and morally stable [people]... I have nothing more to say... I will add only one thing: homosexuals are people too and they have the same right to life as everyone else, just try to understand this.[5]

Another homosexual man, who wrote to the same newspaper, and whose letter was published in the same issue, didn't have the same anger, but was crippled with fear for his life. Convinced that his homosexual desire was a disease, he implored the editors of the newspaper to interview doctors and publish their opinions on the problem:

I am very concerned about the emerging publications on AIDS. It is certainly good that you warn about this threat, but not a single word about where people from the risk group can turn to – I mean prostitutes, drug addicts and homosexuals. I am also from this group and would really like to get rid of my habit. I am young and handsome and this makes my situation even worse. At the university, girls offer me their friendship, but I try to stay away from them as far as possible. I've tried to commit suicide several times but someone always prevented me from doing it. Indeed, you can't overlook this problem: public toilets are filled with homosexuals – the same is the case on the buses – they always try to rub against you ... I myself, however, have not done this yet and I will not do this – most likely I will commit suicide. But many homosexuals would be happy to seek medical help – but only if they knew that this would be anonymous and would yield results. I don't even know whether homosexuality is curable or not. Dear editors, if you are not afraid to publish an honest interview with a specialist on this topic, you will bring many people like me back to life.[6]

Aleksei Novikov, a journalist working for *Molodoi Kommunist* who received these young men's letters, decided to respond to their requests and interview Soviet jurists and doctors knowledgeable about the issue of homosexuality. The first person Novikov interviewed was jurist Aleksei Ignatov, who, as we saw in Chapters 13 and 18, had been trying to achieve the abolition of Article 121.1 from the Soviet Legal Code for almost two decades. Before Gorbachev's policy of *glasnost'*, he could only discuss the problem of homosexuality either in close specialist circles or in specialist literature unavailable to the wider public. Now, for the first time, he could express his views on the pages of a popular Soviet magazine with a print-run of more than a million copies.

"Most authors who write on this topic conclude that criminal liability for homosexuality is inappropriate," Ignatov began. "But, why? Firstly, if it is a medical pathology, then why should we punish for the disease? Secondly, this phenomenon is not socially dangerous. You know, those who argue for criminalization of homosexuality give several reasons. They say that homosexuality results in a decline in the nation's masculinity. But the example of Sparta testifies to the contrary. Another argument they present is that it leads to a decrease in birth-rates, but this claim is not supported by the existing statistics. They also say that homosexuality leads to a person's degradation, but we know there are many examples of great people who were homosexuals – Tchaikovsky, Leonardo da Vinci ..."[7]

"So do you think that this law is completely unnecessary?" Novikov asked.

"Well, the corruption of minors – whether a boy or a girl – and their involvement in homosexual and heterosexual relationships, attempts to involve them in debauchery – all this, of course, must be punished by the law. But as for the consensual homosexual relations between two adults – who are they doing harm to? They do these things in private – we are trying to peep through the keyhole here and when we see that they are not like everybody else, we want to punish them."[8]

Novikov nodded in agreement.

"Now, let's say that we label a person as a homosexual and send him to prison, which, by the way, has not yet corrected a single homosexual," Ignatov continued. "This means that we leave this person at the mercy of the men, who for many years have been deprived of the normal outlet to satisfy their sexual needs. In prison even normal people are routinely raped, and homosexuals are even more so."[9]

"So what is homosexuality in your opinion?"

"Here we are talking about a significant disorder in the sexual sphere and it is not clear if a legal punishment is justifiable here. After all, it is all about the psyche, the nervous system and you can't correct it with any type of punishment. Many such people have a natural aversion to relationships with the people of the opposite sex. We break their nature and make them submit themselves to a torture. Some people just think that if Article 121 of the Criminal Code is removed, then almost everybody will immediately begin to engage in homosexuality! Nonsense! Criminal punishment makes little difference here – it does not reduce or eliminate homosexuality …"[10]

"And what about AIDS?"

"Criminal prosecution can only do harm because it leads to a kind of vicious circle. For example, some homosexuals are quite amenable to medical treatment, but now they will never ever go to the doctor, because, if they do, there is a possibility that from the doctor's office they will go straight to the prison cell. The same with the threat of AIDS. It is one thing to do anonymous screening, but it is completely different if you go and ask for treatment and have to admit that you are a homosexual ..."[11]

"So do you think that consensual sodomy will ever be legalized?"

Ignatov shrugged.

"It is difficult to say if the article on consensual sodomy will be removed from the Criminal Code ... at least the new version of the Criminal Code contains this article, but in a different form. It is still a draft and the relevant commission has agreed on it, but it will still have to go through other relevant authorities ... In former times, a person who was not a jurist, but who held a senior position, could say something like this at the last moment: 'And what is this? Let's cross this out!' Or, conversely, 'Let's add something!' As a result, a well-thought-out and well-substantiated proposed law was suddenly changed."[12]

The next person Novikov interviewed was Dr Lev Gertsik from the Moscow Psycho-Endocrinological Centre, who espoused sympathetic views towards homosexuals and was very well aware of their predicament:

"To be honest, I think that homosexuals per se are not a problem, but their hyper-sexuality is," Gertsik said, concluding, "As research shows, most of them are far more sexual than the rest of the people. Anonymous relationships are very common among homosexuals, when partners don't even know each other. But their hyper-sexuality ... stems from society's hostility towards them and their desire to get away from loneliness and feeling of inferiority. And in this way, Article 121.1 for homosexuality does only harm, because such a law terrorizes them, embitters them and drives them underground along with their many unresolved issues. I personally don't have any problem if homosexuals create a family, as this will not hurt our society in any way, although I understand that my stance will be received with hostility. There are a lot of social prejudices against these people in the public consciousness, which will only get worse with the spread of AIDS. Mass media have a lot of work to do here – they have to foster the correct attitude towards this issue. I believe that anybody has the right to do what they please, and the more tolerant our society is, the fewer problems it will face."[13]

Novikov even managed to interview Aron Belkin, who during the Stalin years had treated homosexuals in Siberia under the supervision of his mentor Igor Sumbaev, as we saw in Chapter 6. Belkin also deplored the fact that for many decades the problem of homosexuality in the USSR had been ignored:

"We have been turning a blind eye to the issue of homosexuality, sweeping it under the carpet ...," said Belkin. "Only a small circle of scientists attempted to study it. And mentioning the word 'homosexuality' in the press was simply out of the question!"

"However, now the situation is beginning to change and my interview with you attests to that," Novikov said. "Maybe now is the time to think about how we can arrange medical treatment for homosexuals, at least for those who want this and have a chance to be cured? Don't Soviet doctors have any experience in this area at all?"

"We do," Belkin said. "In the 1920s, doctors treated homosexuals quite successfully. In the late 1940s Professor Sumbaev also treated them successfully in Irkutsk, and Professor N.V. Ivanov from Gorkii also achieved good results. If a person wants to receive treatment, we should not question their desire to do so and we must help. But we need qualified medical specialists. Professor Ivanov designed a special therapy for treating homosexuality, which, after his death, was taken up by his trainee Yan Goland. I am a pupil of Ivanov too, by the way. In addition to this, doctors have to be familiar with psychoanalysis ... Psychotherapy is a very democratic science and any ideological obstacles raised only reduce its efficacy. Soviet psychotherapy is limited to a very small set of methods focused mainly on treatment in a group (because it is cost-effective) and we don't have in-depth psychotherapy, the type that is required for correction of sexual orientation. This field of knowledge, like no other, requires a serious educational basis, which we are lacking in our country."[14]

"So you are saying that these two men who wrote letters to our newspaper cannot be helped?"

"I am a doctor and I am familiar with psychoanalysis. But I can't afford to see a patient for an hour and a half three times a week for a year, because I have an hourly workload and if I don't fulfil it, then it means I am not fulfilling my duties ... If our country is freer, richer and we are freed from bureaucracy one day, then maybe I will be able to help the guy who wrote you the letter. I will not make any appointments with anyone for the entire week and will devote myself entirely to treating him."[15]

"It follows from your words that the emergence of professional psychotherapy in our country will take at least a decade, or decades ... As you can see, right now a young man is writing to us entreating us to help him get rid of homosexuality. What can we offer him?"[16]

"Nothing ... we can't do anything to help him. I am not taking on such patients, even though I could. Even those doctors who can render such treatment, will not do that. This issue will always boil down to funding ..."[17]

In December 1988, Novikov published a long and weighty article, "Three Monkey Syndrome", in *Molodoi Kommunist*, in which he presented letters by two homosexual men along with his interviews with Ignatov, Gertsik and Belkin. His article began:

> For many decades, our government has been forming a very negative public sentiment about homosexuality – as something disgusting, absolutely unacceptable, criminal – while public conscience regarded homosexuals as cattle and the scum of the human race. I had a chance to see these sentiments in the readers' letters ... The overwhelming majority of the readers demanded that the representatives of the "risk groups" should be punished by various means – ranging from sending them off to the North Pole to shooting them. Being the most accessible victim for this terrible disease, homosexuals suddenly turned into scapegoats and the main culprits of the spread of AIDS in the USSR. Without going into a long discussion, I just want to say that this is not the case: although the first person to bring AIDS into the USSR was homosexual, now, according to the statistics, its main transmitters are women who have sexual relations with foreigners.[18]

The ending of the article was equally thought-provoking:

> According to scientists, around two to six per cent of people are homosexual or have homosexual tendencies. And what if we project these figures on the Soviet population? In this huge group of people ... there are many individuals who need help, but at the moment, left to the mercy of fate. Will society help them?[19]

Although Novikov was guided by benevolent intentions to help Soviet homosexuals by instigating an expert discussion about the topic and invoking sympathy for them, he also unwittingly spread misconceptions about it. Certainly he called for compassion, but only based on the premise that homosexuals were sick and needed help. He would have done better to argue that homosexuality was just a normal variant of human sexuality, so people who possessed this variant were being unjustly oppressed by society. Soviet citizens, despite the recent swift democratization and honest public discussions on hitherto forbidden topics, still had a lot to learn about the homosexual citizens among them.

24

Soviet homosexuals finally speak about themselves in public

Moscow, 1989

In January 1989, shocking news spread across Soviet newspapers – twenty-seven babies in a children's hospital in the city of Elista, in the Russian republic of Kalmykia, were found to have been infected with AIDS. A commission of Moscow doctors was dispatched to Elista, and discovered that the babies' infection with AIDS was entirely the fault of the hospital staff, who had used unsterile needles for the children's injections and continually reused the same syringes.[1] Similar incidents later occurred in children's hospitals in other Soviet cities, as no doubt they did in other parts of the world, where equipment shortages and a general ignorance about AIDS transmission combined to create a perfect storm. The chain of these horrible incidents shocked Soviet society to the core.

Journalists unleashed a new barrage of criticism of the Soviet government and the appalling state of Soviet healthcare in the pages of increasingly liberalized Soviet newspapers. Soviet journalists and correspondents were finally admitting that the spread of AIDS was occurring due to the crumbling system of Soviet healthcare with its endemic shortages and corruption, rather than due to the existence of homosexuals, drug addicts and prostitutes:

> We are used to the idea that AIDS threatens mainly risk groups: prostitutes, drug addicts and homosexuals, forgetting that there are more "innocent" ways of infection. How did the virus find its way into a children's hospital?[2]

A correspondent of the newspaper *Trud* also sharply criticized the indifference and cynicism of Petr Burgasov, a high-ranking Health Ministry official, who had publicly commented several times that AIDS was the product of homosexuality and "the Western and American way of life". The correspondent then exclaimed:

> How can I believe in our "bright future" when there is no guarantee that a nurse will not use a syringe many times instead of once and sell the rest of the syringes to drug addicts? The recent cases of AIDS infections – in Leningrad, Odessa and Elista – prove that this disease is not just something overseas, but here, at home.[3]

The growing hatred towards the inefficiency of the Soviet system and its failures managed to decrease homophobic rhetoric in Soviet press and helped people realize that homosexuals were not responsible for the spread of AIDS in the country. Still, homosexuality remained a frequent topic of discussion in the context of AIDS, and one which, after many decades of stifled freedom and censorship, the ambitious and hungry Gorbachev-era journalists were keen to pursue.

Oleg Moroz, a journalist from *Literaturnaya gazeta*, had been interested in the topic of AIDS and its impact on social relations ever since he began to receive letters from the newspaper's readers in early 1987, complaining about a lack of public information about the virus and especially its social aspects. Although initially Moroz, like most of his readers, had very little sympathy towards the representatives of "the risk groups", he soon changed his mind. This happened after he started receiving anonymous letters from homosexual men telling the unfortunate stories of their lives and how AIDS had rendered their already miserable lives even worse. One letter touched Moroz in particular – it was a letter from the mother of a man who'd been jailed for homosexuality:

> I am a mother of three children and it is very difficult for me to write about this, but I cannot be silent about this issue either. When it comes to these issues, you will not find any advisers, you will not find anybody to share this problem with, you have nobody to ask how to continue living with it and what to do.

I want to tell you about my son Igor. He graduated from high school with excellent grades and then served in the army. Then he graduated from a university with excellent grades too. He was always active, cheerful, intelligent and sociable. He easily got on with people, but he did not have close friends. And he often felt lonely. I began to tell him that it was time to start a family, to introduce his wife to me. But he always answered somewhat evasively that it was too early, that he was not ready for family life. And I stopped broaching the subject.

And then out of the blue I am summoned to the police station for a conversation with the inspector about my son. It turns out that one of Igor's friends was undergoing treatment in a venereological hospital and he told the police that he had a homosexual contact with my son. Interrogations and cross-examinations began. Igor could not bear all that – he broke down and wanted to commit suicide. I cried, I begged of him not to take his life, at least for me, and he promised to me that he would not do that. He was expelled from the Party and fired from his job.

The investigator concocted a criminal case of twenty pages. Igor was sentenced to a year of imprisonment. When I went to the prosecutor and said that we would file a complaint and appeal against the verdict, he replied: "Well, go ahead if you are not ashamed. I would shoot such scum myself."

I cannot say that I sympathize with such people. But I am his mother and I feel sorry for my child. He told me that he cannot do otherwise, and not because he has been spoilt or perverted, but because it is his need.

I wanted to know if it is a disease or really a crime. I haven't found any literature on this issue. I just realized that there are many such people. But why has not science yet said anything on this issue! I hope that some scientists will have their say regarding the issue in the pages of your newspaper.[4]

The letter shook Moroz to the core and compelled him to start working on a pamphlet titled *Risk Group*, examining the lives of Soviet homosexuals, drug-addicts and prostitutes and featuring the author's conversations and informal interviews with them.[5] Nowhere before in the Soviet press had such individuals been allowed to speak for themselves, which made Moroz's pamphlet even more sensational.

In order to find homosexual men for an interview, Moroz contacted Dr Vadim Pokrovskii, one of the leading Soviet specialists on AIDS, who invited him to his hospital and introduced him to his patients – Aleksei, Mikhail and Pavel. All were openly homosexual men in their early thirties, and all HIV-positive. When Moroz saw them for the first time, it struck him how different they looked from his stereotypical perception of a "typical homosexual" with soft feminine voice and behaviour. All men looked quite conventional and Moroz caught himself thinking that he would have never thought that they were homosexuals if they hadn't told him so themselves. They also seemed intelligent and smart young men. Mikhail worked as an engineer and even had a family with two children. When talking about their diagnosis they used sophisticated medical jargon, and from their speech it was clear that they were university-educated. "So much for Soviet propaganda which always casts homosexuals as depraved degraded individuals," Moroz thought. Mikhail, Pavel and Aleksei consented to an interview, which Moroz conducted in the hospital corridor.

"Have you had many sexual contacts?" Moroz asked Mikhail, hoping he didn't sound too blunt.

"Well, if you want to know … so from the age of sixteen, I think approximately three persons a month," said Mikhail pensively.

"New ones?"

"Sometimes new, sometimes the same … Maybe actually two a month," Mikhail said, still thinking.

"Do you think it is normal for a homosexual to have two or three partners a month?" Moroz asked, trying to disguise his astonishment.

"I think it's normal not only for a homosexual," Aleksei cut in. "It is normal for anybody, for a normal young man, regardless of who he is."

"Ordinary men and women change their partners no less frequently than homosexuals," Mikhail added.

I disagree, Moroz thought. Homosexuals tend to change their partners more frequently.

"Social conditions play an important role here …" Aleksei tried to explain. "If I had my own flat, I would not run from one guy to another and would live with only one guy."

"Yes, if only we lived the way people in the West do," Pavel continued. "Homosexuals there live officially … Without hiding. And their living arrangements make it possible for them."

"We also have couples like this …" Moroz tried to argue.

"Yes, but there are very few of them," Aleksei interrupted. "Most homosexuals in our country live with their parents. In order to meet they need to look for an apartment, somewhere on the side or visit someone … Or wait until their parents go out. So this is why it happens thus: today you are with one, tomorrow with another …"

"How many pairs do you know who are in a committed relationship?" Moroz asked.

"I know at least four couples," Mikhail said. "Two of them have been living together for a long time – probably about ten years. Now they are about thirty-six years old. I do not know what kind of relations they have with their neighbours and how they sort out the legal side of the issue. But all these problems are not important in a big city. But in small towns, I simply can't imagine such a thing. Everyone there knows each other, everyone pokes their noses everywhere."[6]

"How well do you know the people whom you have sex with? Do you often have casual sex?"

"Of course it happens," Pavel said. "Most often it takes place on holidays, in the southern part of our country. But if a guy seems to be a good person, then we maintain our friendships. I have friends with whom I had sexual contacts five or six years ago … you know, sex is not the most important thing in the world. Apart from sex, people share common interests too …"

"Have you ever had sex with a woman?" Moroz continued.

All three men replied in the affirmative, confessing that during their teenage years they had sex with women, but now considered themselves to be "genuine homosexuals".[7]

"And where are you all living now?"

"I am still living with my mum," said Aleksei.

"I am living with my wife in her flat, but I am going to file for divorce," Mikhail said.

"My mum passed away not that long ago," said Pavel. "So I am living alone now. You know what they say, 'Homosexuals are mostly those who grow up without a father.' I told my mother about this when she was alive. Women, of course, don't want to admit that they are to blame."

"Does your mother know that you are a homosexual? What is her opinion about that?" Moroz asked Aleksei.

"She certainly does, but her opinion on this issue is not very positive. But she can't do anything about it and is forced to accept everything as it is. Now she tells me all the time: 'I warned you that you would contract some nasty thing!'"

"Mikhail, aren't you afraid that somebody at work may find out that you are homosexual?"

"Well, if they do, then I won't be able to do anything. I am not advertising this though."

"In our country there's still a law criminalizing such relations between men," Moroz reminded his interlocutors.

"That is outrageous! I think it's a violation of human rights!" exclaimed Mikhail.

"You know that some say homosexuals don't leave progeny?" Moroz continued.

"Most homosexuals are married. They have completely healthy children, in contrast to those whom you consider to be normal – who eat, drink and give birth to scum ..." Aleksei sounded angry now and Moroz felt he'd gone too far.[8]

"Do you drink?" Moroz continued.

For a second Mikhail, Aleksei and Pavel exchanged looks and even giggled. This question seemed so off topic and unexpected that it left them wondering what relevance it had to their conversation.

"I have heard that homosexuals drink very little," Moroz explained.

"I would say this: they drink less than other people," Mikhail said. "If a homosexual drinks all the time – he won't be able to have sex. There are drinkers of course, but there are fewer of them."

"You may wonder why I am not getting married now?" Aleksei said unexpectedly. "Well, how am I going to sustain myself financially? With the stipend I am receiving? On my mother's pension? And then we will have children ... I manage to get by, but neither my wife nor my child can live on this money. Even if my wife starts working." Apparently remembering that he'd contracted the AIDS virus, he added, somewhat saddened: "To be honest, I've stopped thinking about these plans for now … Temporarily I hope."[9]

Thinking that it would somehow help distract Aleksei from his sad thoughts Moroz decided to steer the conversation in a different direction.

"I don't understand how you can marry and live with a woman if you are all indifferent to the opposite sex," Moroz said.

"Well, why indifferent? Sex is not the most important thing!" Pavel objected. "Most people get married not only because they need to satisfy their needs, but because they don't want to be lonely. Loneliness is a terrible thing. So when love, or what they considered to be love, evaporates, the husband and wife sometimes cheat on each other, but then come back to each other. Because nobody cares for them the way they do for one another."[10]

"You know there are many reports about the prevalence of prostitution among homosexuals," Moroz said. "What do you know about it?"

"You know the development of homosexual prostitution is a recent phenomenon and usually foreigners are the main clients," Aleksei said. "Guys from outside Moscow, from small cities, usually work as prostitutes. They start chasing foreigners, offering themselves and their services to them in return for presents …"

"And have you ever dealt with a homosexual prostitute yourselves?"

"What for? They're too expensive," said Pavel. Then their conversations shifted to AIDS.

"Of course, if we're talking about AIDS, homosexuals are more susceptible to it," Pavel said. "But our authorities have gone too far here – indiscriminately declaring that only homosexuals are to blame for this. As a result, homosexuals are crippled with fear, while normal people continue living with their wives thinking that this problem will never concern them."

"When did the fear of AIDS emerge among our Soviet homosexuals?" Moroz asked.

"I think this year, 1988," Aleksei responded.

"Do homosexuals use condoms?" Moroz continued.

"Now they do," Pavel said. "Now they have started to."

"And you know what," Aleksei cut in, somewhat annoyed. "You know I can tell you that when homosexuals are brought here from other cities, they are escorted here by the police. That is, they are not treated as victims, so nobody sympathizes with them. Instead, they are viewed as criminals. They think that we deserve it."

"I think all such people should be treated with tolerance," Pavel continued. "Not only homosexuals, but people already infected. Because these people are in a very unfortunate position. For example, here in our hospital there was a woman with a baby, I can't recall which city she was from. She also carried the infection. So you think someone will treat her with compassion? Absolutely not. She will be treated the same way I am. That means that her life has been completely ruined. She has to flee her city to avoid disgrace – this is the kind of atmosphere created around this issue."[11]

"How did your comrades react to the news that you became infected?" Aleksei shrugged.

"Everybody reacts differently," Aleksei sighed. "Although I try not to divulge this information among my friends, but rumours are rumours, you know. Many already know about me, trying to cut off all contact and running away from me in different directions. I have one friend who knows everything about me and who, despite everything, has not turned his back on me. At least now I know who is a real friend and who is not."

"Do you think that homosexuals are now trying to cut down on the number of contacts they have because of AIDS?"

"They're doing everything the way they used to …," Aleksei sighed. "And I think they will continue behaving the way they have always done. Not only homosexuals, but all other people too. Everyone will have the same number of contacts they've always had."[12]

A few days after his interview with the three men at Pokrovskii's hospital, Moroz decided to meet Aleksei's friend, another homosexual man named Maksim, who had just returned from the army. Maksim also displayed no effeminate traits, and, like Aleksei, Mikhail and Pavel, looked like any other Soviet man.

"How many partners do you have every month?" Moroz opened with his usual question.

"Approximately two," said Maksim.

"And is it so because you are living with your parents?"

"No, it's my physical necessity," Maksim said, somewhat embarrassed.

"Do you think that such frequent change of partners is normal?"

"I think it is normal yes. For homosexuals. And even for straight people too. Do you think it's a lot – two persons a month? Some people have more partners than that."

Although Moroz tried hard not to judge his interviewees, he still struggled to accept their way of life and agree that a constant change of partners was normal. Even though at the beginning of the chapter on homosexuality in his pamphlet *Risk Group*, he assured his readers that his intention was not to scapegoat them, in the final section Moroz couldn't help but judge:

> These guys are weird. Human civilization has existed for thousands of years and at no point of its existence has it ever been the norm for a man to meet a woman, go to bed with her and then just move on and find another one … If you say that it is deviation from the norm and an anomaly – I will agree. But the norm is a completely different thing.[13]

Still, Moroz's pamphlet *Risk Group*, published in 1990, despite its (for the USSR) small print run of six hundred thousand copies and the author's self-righteous tone, was an important attempt to break the stereotypical image of homosexuals as pariahs, showing instead that they were no different from any other Soviet citizens.

Epilogue
In which Boris Yeltsin decriminalizes consensual homosexuality – but homophobia remains
Moscow, 1989–1993

Glasnost' and liberalization produced a political and cultural awakening the likes of which the Soviet state had never seen during the seven decades of its existence. In 1989, for the first time in its history, the USSR held relatively democratic elections. But while political and social life was becoming livelier, Gorbachev's disastrous economic reforms plunged the country into a deeper crisis. Basic consumer goods and food disappeared off the stores' shelves, prices skyrocketed and unemployment was spreading like wildfire. The sharp decrease in people's standards of living and swift impoverishment of the nation caused strong frustration with Gorbachev's reforms and made him increasingly unpopular.

Although Gorbachev managed to put an end to the arms race between the USSR and the US, the prestige of the USSR and the appeal of communism started to diminish in socialist countries. In 1989, revolutions swept across pro-communist East European countries, which led to the toppling of their communist dictatorships and democratic elections in these countries. Unlike his predecessors who crushed dissent in satellite countries with tanks and military force, Gorbachev did not intervene.

Apart from the economic turmoil, the USSR was descending into political chaos. The swift fall of communism in the countries of the Eastern bloc sparked local movements for independence in fifteen Soviet republics.

Fearing that Gorbachev was going to give in to their pressure, and infuriated by the USSR's loss of control in hitherto communist East European nations, a group of Soviet hard-liners organized a coup in 1991, trying to take control of the country from Gorbachev. Although the coup failed and Gorbachev managed to regain control, the political unrest further empowered republican leaders, who now saw that the USSR was weak and so they pushed for independence. In December 1991, the leaders of the Russian, Ukrainian and Belarusian republics signed a treaty, declaring that the USSR had now ceased to exist, disintegrating into fifteen independent countries. Seeing that he was no longer able to change or control the situation, Gorbachev resigned as Soviet leader.

During the last tumultuous years of *perestroika*, Soviet homosexual men and women attempted to organize themselves, forming various alliances and organizations and even publishing their own newspapers. On 23 July 1991, the International Gay and Lesbian Symposium and Film Festival took place in Moscow and Leningrad. Although sodomy laws were still officially on the books, they were rarely enforced.

On 29 April 1993, Russia's new president, Boris Yeltsin, facing pressure from the Council of Europe, repealed Article 121.1 which had criminalized consensual sex between men, as part of an omnibus package rushed before parliament. Just as Stalin had decided without consultation to adopt the sodomy law in 1933, Yeltsin and his team didn't consult any Russian gay organizations or provide any explanation as to why the law was repealed. Although gay men and lesbians all over Russia celebrated this move, they were also caught by surprise. The abolition of the law took place quietly without their participation or any debate even though this law directly affected their lives. Gay people in the new Russia realized that they were still excluded from power, and their fates were still being decided by non-gay, and invariably homophobic politicians.

Many officials were not ready for the abolition of the law, just like 1933, when many officials were not ready for its adoption. Indeed, consensual sodomy was suddenly decriminalized but there was no concomitant order for prison officials to release people convicted under the Article 121.1 and no guidelines on how to make this process smooth and complete.[1] Neither officials nor the media followed up on the enforcement of the repealed legislation.

In the absence of any directives from authorities on how to conduct the release of the prisoners, the Ministry of Internal Affairs was expected to inform the officials of Russia's 744 prisons about the legal reforms, who would then have to identify inmates convicted under Article 121.1 and send their cases to local courts for review. But nothing like that happened. Unsurprised by the government's indifference towards imprisoned homosexual men, the activists of the Moscow Prison Working Group began contacting colonies for clarifications on what was being done to release the prisoners. One of the members of the Group, Masha Gessen, recalled:

> When we contacted facility 389/40 in the city of Kungur of the Perm region, a surprised woman ..., when asked whether anyone was serving time in the facility under Article 121.1, said, "We have a thousand inmates here. Do you want me to look through everybody's file?". When I answered in the affirmative, she made me repeat that this search of the card catalogue was indeed necessary and then instructed me to call her back two hours later. At that point, she told me she had found two men mentioned above – and that their cases would now be forwarded to the sentencing court for review.[2]

When activists contacted another colony in the city of Severo-Onezhsk in the Arkhangelsk region, a certain Anatoly Tretyak picked up the phone. Masha Gessen recalled:

> Contacted under similar circumstances ..., Anatoly I. Tretyak of facility OU-250/4 of the city of Severo-Onezhsk in the Arkhangelsk region told us, in July 1993, that a search for Article 121.1 inmates was undertaken following our request and would be completed by the following week. He gave me a phone number at which no one picked up the phone for the next six weeks, and the colony did not respond to repeated follow-up telegrams and written requests for information.[3]

Other gay activists working in Russia also tried to facilitate the release of prisoners convicted under Article 121.1. When Yuri Yereyev, president of the Tchaikovsky Foundation for Cultural Initiative and the Defence of Sexual Minorities, visited Yablonevka prison with a Western journalist, the prison director stepped outside and screamed: "I don't care what has been repealed. They are still in there, and they will stay in there." He never allowed activists to enter the prison.[4]

Reflecting on the removal of Article 121.1 from the Russian Criminal Code and its impact on the lives of Russian gay people, Masha Gessen wrote in 1994:

> Until now, the existence of Article 121.1 has been the single most significant threat, impediment and motivator to action in the gay and lesbian community in Russia. With the repeal of this law begins the process of questioning the de jure and de facto status of gays and lesbians in Russia – and comes the uneasy realization that much remains to be done before gays and lesbians in Russia enjoy fundamental rights and freedoms ... The repeal of Article 121.1 fell far short of guaranteeing gays and lesbians equality before the law in the area of private conduct.[5]

Although Soviet law criminalizing consensual homosexual behaviour was repealed almost three decades ago, this statement holds true even today. Life remains extremely difficult for Russian LGBTQ citizens, who are constantly harassed and scapegoated by the government and in some republics of the country are even killed. The rise of modern Russian state homophobia began in the early 2010s, when Vladimir Putin, Russia's then Prime Minister, who had already served as President for two years, decided, in a highly controversial move, to re-elect himself in 2012 for a third term. Despite widespread anti-Putin demonstrations and diminished popularity, Putin won the elections in March 2012, which, according to independent observers, were rigged. Aware of his flimsy electorate base, Putin decided to increase his popularity and distract public attention from Russia's declining living standards by unleashing a campaign of hatred towards LGBTQ people, casting them as a great threat to Russian society on Russian state-controlled television and newspapers.

In June 2013, the Russian Federal Parliament, controlled by Putin, unanimously adopted a law prohibiting "propaganda of non-traditional sexual relations" among minors. Although the makers of the law argued that it was aimed only at the protection of children from information that could damage their health and hamper their development, the adoption of the law made it illegal to equate straight and gay relationships and effectively prohibited LGBTQ rights and culture in the country. Most importantly, the law led to a sharp spike in homophobic violence across the country.

In 2017, Russian homophobia developed and gained even more gruesome dimensions. In that year, the authorities of the Russian republic of Chechnya initiated a brutal prosecution of its LGBTQ people, arresting and torturing hundreds of Chechen men suspected of being gay. Some of these men went missing and were even killed.[6] Gay prosecution in Chechnya still continues and the all-powerful Russian president, in whose hands lie the decision-making power regarding all matters in Russia, prefers to turn a blind eye to the reports about killings, torture and mysterious disappearances of LGBTQ people in the republic of Chechnya.

In 2021, Putin overhauled the Russian Constitution, creating a new one which would allow him to extend his more than twenty-year rule. It also contained two hundred new amendments, among which was a ban on same-sex marriage. The new Russian Constitution now explicitly states that marriage is possible only between a man and a woman and underscores the importance of God as well as educating children about patriotism.

Despite the ever-increasing state-sponsored homophobia and its aggressive policies of instilling "traditional" and "conservative" values in younger generations, young Russians, especially in large cities, seem to be growing increasingly intolerant of Putin's regime and more accepting of LGBTQ people. Western social media platforms such as YouTube, Facebook and Instagram do their share of fostering a positive image of LGBTQ life, openly showing gay-friendly materials, shows and podcasts which Russia's law on gay propaganda is unable to take down. Still, much work remains to be done, in order to make the lives of Russian LGBTQ people safer, allowing them to pursue lives as fulfilling as those of their heterosexual counterparts. This requires an end to the dangerous new state-sanctioned homophobia.

Dan Healey, a pioneering scholar of Russian LGBTQ history, argues that in order to combat present-day Russian homophobia and begin an intelligent and well-informed dialogue about the place of LGBTQ citizens in Russia today, we need "a rich and sophisticated account of the history of popular homophobia in Russia, Ukraine and the other societies of the USSR".[7] Healey then writes:

> In order to combat present-day hostility to LGBT citizenships, activists must be equipped to explain how Russian/Soviet prejudices were constructed and evolved, as part of a modern heteronormativity. Human rights activists also need more stories of individual prosecution and endurance, to enrich a threadbare narrative and to inspire the next generation of young LGBT citizens and democrats of all sexualities.[8]

We must also remember that writing LGBTQ history in Russia is not just an ordinary exercise in historical writing and a way of enhancing one's academic career, but an urgent enterprise which will have serious implications for the present and the future of Russia's LGBTQ communities. Therefore, activists and scholars should strive to write engaging accounts of homosexual prosecution in the USSR, using accessible and clear language, which can be read and understood outside as well as within academia and appeal to LGBTQ people without an academic background but with a deep interest in gay politics in Russia today.

I submitted the manuscript of *Red Closet* to Manchester University Press in mid-February 2022, when the prospect of Putin's comprehensive military invasion of Ukraine still seemed quite unlikely if not downright impossible. But unfortunately, the worst prognosis and predictions of Western and Russian observers and politicians came true – on 24 February Putin launched an unprecedented attack on Ukraine, which continues as I write this.

On the day of the invasion, Putin delivered a speech announcing that Russia was commencing "a special military operation" (his euphemism for war) in Ukraine. In this speech, quite unsurprisingly, Putin accused the West of undermining Russia's "traditional values", "eroding Russian people from within" and "aggressively imposing" its own Western values, "leading to degradation and degeneration, because they are contrary to human nature".

Those following Russian politics know that by "traditional values" Putin means Russian patriotism, spirituality, respect for his leadership and compliance with heteronormative and patriarchal ideals of family and gender. Over the last decade Putin has been working hard to promulgate these "traditional values" in Russian society and make them an essential part of Russian people's identity. He has been doing so, in part, by infusing Russians with homophobia and intolerance of various kinds. And now, once again, to justify his military invasion of Ukraine, Putin evokes homophobic discourse and tries to convince Russians that LGBTQ people are threatening the country. Putin's discourse has already inspired the members of the lower chamber of the Russian parliament to consider the adoption of harsher penalties for disseminating "any propaganda of non-traditional sexual relations".

Under such circumstances, the importance of knowing and uncovering Russia's LGBTQ history is more important than ever. Such history will add another dimension to our knowledge about classified Soviet atrocities and injustices upon which the Putin regime rests, and will hopefully encourage more Russians to engage in the fight for real freedom and genuine peace. But most of all, this history will be useful to Russian LGBTQ people who are yet to begin their own fierce battle for acceptance and equality in Russian society.

Notes

Preface

1 Simon Karlinsky, "Russia's Gay Literature and Culture", in *Hidden from History: Reclaiming the Gay and Lesbian Past,* edited by Martin Bauml Duberman, Martha Vicinus and George Chauncey, Jr (Chicago: University of Chicago Press, 2002), p. 349.
2 Karlinsky, "Russia's Gay Literature and Culture", p. 357.
3 Dan Healey, *Homosexual Desire in Revolutionary Russia* (Chicago: University of Chicago Press, 2002), p. 3.

Chapter 1

1 John Simkin, *The Individual in History: Stalin* (Skipton: Spartacus Educational, 1987), p. 50.
2 Robert Service, *Stalin: A Biography* (Cambridge, MA: Belknap Press, 2004), p. 264.
3 Benno Ennker, "The Stalin Cult, Bolshevik Rule and Kremlin Interaction", in *The Leader Cult in Communist Dictatorships: Stalin and the Eastern Bloc,* edited by Balázs Apor, Jan C. Behrends, Polly Jones and E.A. Rees (Basingstoke: Palgrave Macmillan, 2004), p. 84.
4 Dan Healey, "Homosexual Existence and Existing Socialism: New Light on the Repression of Male Homosexuality in Stalin's Russia", *GLQ* 8, no. 3 (2002): 358.
5 John D'Emilio, *Sexual Politics, Sexual Communities: The Making of a Homosexual Minority in the United States, 1940–1970* (Chicago and London: University of Chicago Press, 1983), pp. 14–15.
6 D'Emilio, *Sexual Politics.*
7 Healey, "Homosexual Existence and Existing Socialism", 360.

8   Healey, *Homosexual Desire*, p. 184.

9   Healey, *Homosexual Desire*, p. 329.

10 Healey, *Homosexual Desire*, p. 190.

11 G. Morev, *Mikhail Kuz'min i russkaya kul'tura XX veka* (Leningrad: Muzei Anny Akhmatovoi v Fontannom Dome, 1990), p. 144.

12 Sergei Kunyaev, *Nikolai Kliuev* (Moscow: Molodaya gvardiya, 2014), p. 467.

13 Sheila Fitzpatrick, *Everyday Stalinism: Ordinary Life in Extraordinary Times: Soviet Russia in the 1930s* (Oxford: Oxford University Press, 2000), p. 26.

14 Fitzpatrick, *Everyday Stalinism*, p. 27.

15 Laurie Essig, *Queer in Russia: A Story of Sex, Self, and the Other* (Durham, NC: Duke University Press, 1999), p. 6.

16 Leonid Maksimenkov, *Sumbur vmesto muzyki: stalinskaya cul'turnaya revolyutsiya, 1936–1938* (Moscow: Yuridicheskaya kniga, 1997), p. 204.

17 Maksimenkov, *Sumbur vmesto muzyki*, p. 206.

18 Simon Sebag Montefiore, *Stalin: The Court of the Red Tsar* (London: Phoenix, 2003), p. 223.

19 Nikita Petrov and Mark Iansen, *"Stalinskii pitomets" – Nikolai Yezhov* (Moscow: ROSSPEN, 2009), p. 156.

20 Petrov and Iansen, *"Stalinskii pitomets"*, p. 203.

Chapter 2

1   This chapter is based on the events described by Harry Whyte in his letter to Joseph Stalin. See: Garry Uait, "Mozhet li gomoseksualist sostoiat' chlenom kommunisticheskoi partii?", *Istochnik* 5–6 (1993): 185–191.

2   Jeffrey Meek, *Queer Voices in Post-War Scotland: Male Homosexuality, Religion and Society* (London: Palgrave Macmillan, 2015), pp. 13–39.

3   In his letter to Stalin, Harry does mention, in passing, that a friend of his, with whom he "engaged in homosexual liaisons" had been arrested. Harry does not mention the name of his friend and does not elaborate on the nature of their relationship. The story in this chapter is based on my own understanding of Harry's letter. See Uait, "Mozhet li gomoseksualist sostoiat'", 186.

4   Harry's letter does not contain any details on Ivan's sister or the phone call described. But one can imagine that, after having discovered the disappearance of his friend, Harry could have tried to call him and it is likely that someone like Ivan's relative would have informed him about Ivan's disappearance.

5   Uait, "Mozhet li gomoseksualist sostoiat'", 186.

6   Mark Sereiskii, "Gomoseksualizm", *Bol'shaya sovetskaya entsiklopediya* (Moscow: Sovetskaia entsiklopediia, 1930), pp. 596–598.

7   See Uait, "Mozhet li gomoseksualist sostoiat'", 189.

8   Uait, "Mozhet li gomoseksualist sostoiat'", 188.

9   Uait, "Mozhet li gomoseksualist sostoiat'", 186.

Notes

10 Healey, "Homosexual Existence and Existing Socialism", 358.
11 Uait, "Mozhet li gomoseksualist sostoiat'", 186.
12 Oleg Khlevniuk, "Letters to Stalin: Practices of Selection and Reaction", *Cahiers du Monde Russe* (2015): 327–344.
13 This is an abridged version of the letter. The whole letter can be found in Uait, "Mozhet li gomoseksualist sostoiat'", 185–191.
14 Healey, *Homosexual Desire*, p. 231.

Chapter 3

1   This chapter is based on a criminal case, which can be found at the Central Municipal Archive of Moscow. F. 819, op. 2, delo 51.
2   Clayton J. Whisnant, *Queer Identities and Politics in Germany: A History 1880–1945* (New York: Harrington Park Press, 2016), pp. 204–242.
3   See Central Municipal Archive of Moscow. F. 819, op. 2, delo 51, l. 104.
4   Central Municipal Archive of Moscow. F. 819, op. 2, delo 51, l. 102.
5   Central Municipal Archive of Moscow. F. 819, op. 2, delo 51, l. 106.
6   Dan Healey, "Moscow", in *Queer Sites: Gay Urban Histories since 1600*, edited by David Higgs (London: Routledge, 1999), p. 44.
7   Healey, *Homosexual Desire*, pp. 30–36.
8   Central Municipal Archive of Moscow. F. 819, op. 2, delo 51, l. 14.
9   Central Municipal Archive of Moscow. F. 819, op. 2, delo 51, l. 14.
10 Central Municipal Archive of Moscow. F. 819, op. 2, delo 51, l. 17.
11 Peter H. Solomon, *Soviet Criminal Justice under Stalin* (Cambridge: Cambridge University Press, 1996), pp. 458–459.
12 Eugene Huskey, *Russian Lawyers and the Soviet State: The Origins and Development of the Soviet Bar, 1917–1939* (Princeton: Princeton University Press, 1986), p. 189.
13 Central Municipal Archive of Moscow. F. 819, op. 2, delo 51, l. 106.
14 Central Municipal Archive of Moscow. F. 819, op. 2, delo 51, l. 106.
15 Central Municipal Archive of Moscow. F. 819, op. 2, delo 51, l. 103.
16 Central Municipal Archive of Moscow. F. 819, op. 2, delo 51, l. 93.

Chapter 4

1   Boris Savchenko, *Vadim Kozin* (Smolensk: Rusich, 2001), pp. 78–79.
2   Savchenko, *Vadim Kozin*, p. 80.
3   Boris Savchenko, *Proklyatoe iskusstvo* (Moscow: Vagrius, 2005), p. 14.
4   Savchenko, *Proklyatoe iskusstvo*, p. 14.
5   Savchenko, *Proklyatoe iskusstvo*, p. 15.
6   Savchenko, *Proklyatoe iskusstvo*, p. 16.

7   Savchenko, *Proklyatoe iskusstvo*, p. 16.
8   Sebag Montefiore, *Stalin*, pp. 517–518.
9   Savchenko, *Vadim Kozin*, p. 130.
10 Dan Healey, *Russian Homophobia from Stalin to Sochi* (London: Bloomsbury, 2018), pp. 77–78.
11 Savchenko, *Vadim Kozin*, p. 130.
12 Translation from Healey, *Russian Homophobia*, p. 83. Healey's account is based on Savchenko, *Vadim Kozin*.
13 Translation from Healey, *Russian Homophobia*, p. 85.
14 Translation from Healey, *Russian Homophobia*, p. 85.
15 Translation from Healey, *Russian Homophobia*, p. 86.
16 Savchenko, *Proklyatoe iskusstvo*, pp. 364–365.
17 Healey, *Russian Homophobia*, p. 79.

Chapter 5

1   This chapter is based on archival material: GARF, f. P-9474, op. 13, delo 1077.
2   Mie Nakachi, "Population, Politics and Reproduction: Late Stalinism and Its Legacy", in *Late Stalinist Russia: Society Between Reconstruction and Reinvention*, edited by Juliane Fürst (London and New York: Routledge, 2006), p. 23.
3   Donald Filtzer, "Standard of Living versus Quality of Life: Struggling with the Urban Environment in Russia during the Early Years of Post-War Reconstruction", in *Late Stalinist Russia: Society Between Reconstruction and Reinvention*, edited by Juliane Fürst (London and New York: Routledge, 2006), p. 85.
4   GARF, f. P-9474, op. 13, delo 1077.
5   Daniel P. Schluter, *Gay Life in the Former USSR: Fraternity without Community* (London: Routledge, 2001), p. 102.
6   Healey, *Russian Homophobia*, p. 63.
7   See GARF, f. P-9474, op. 13, delo 1077, l. 7.
8   See GARF, f. P-9474, op. 13, delo 1077, l. 7.
9   GARF, f. P-9474, op. 13, delo 1077, l. 15. In a similar appeal, Kravtsov also argued that investigator Gryaznykh, "taking advantage of Oshurkov's juridical illiteracy and threatening him, forced him into providing false testimony against me". See GARF, f. P-9474, op. 13, delo 1077, l. 23.
10 GARF, f. P-9474, op. 13, delo 1077, l. 8.
11 GARF, f. P-9474, op. 13, delo 1077, l. 21.
12 GARF, f. P-9474, op. 13, delo 1077, l. 8.
13 GARF, f. P-9474, op. 13, delo 1077, l. 23.
14 GARF, f. P-9474, op. 13, delo 1077, l. 8.
15 Rustam Alexander, "New Light on the Prosecution of Homosexuals under Brezhnev", *Russian History* 15, 3 (2019): 16.
16 GARF, f. P-9474, op. 13, delo 1077, l. 21.

17 GARF, f. P-9474, op. 13, delo 1077, l. 22.
18 Peter H. Solomon Jr, "The Case of the Vanishing Acquittal: Informal Norms and the Practice of Soviet Criminal Justice", *Soviet Justice*, XXXIX (1987): 531.
19 Solomon, "The Case of the Vanishing Acquittal", 533.
20 Solomon, "The Case of the Vanishing Acquittal", 533.
21 Whisnant, *Queer Identities and Politics in Germany*, p. 217.
22 D'Emilio, *Sexual Politics*, p. 15.

Chapter 6

1 Aron I. Belkin, *Freid Z. "Izbrannoie"* (Moscow: Vneshtorgizdat, 1989), p. 14.
2 Belkin, *Freid Z. "Izbrannoie"*, p. 18.
3 Igor S. Sumbaev, "K psikhoterapii gomoseksualizma", *Sovetskaya Psikhonevrologiya*, 3 (1936): 60.
4 Sumbaev, "K psikhoterapii gomoseksualizma", 60.
5 Sumbaev, "K psikhoterapii gomoseksualizma", 59–60.
6 Sumbaev, "K psikhoterapii gomoseksualizma", 61–62.
7 Aron I. Belkin, *Tretii Pol: Sud'ba pasynkov prirody* (Moscow: Olimp, 2006), p. 260.
8 Belkin, *Tretii Pol*, p. 260.
9 Mikhail O. Gurevich, *Psikhiatria: Uchebnik dlia meditsinskikh institutov* (Moscow: Medgiz, 1949), p. 471.
10 Belkin, *Tretii Pol*, p. 261.
11 Belkin, *Tretii Pol*, p. 265.
12 Belkin, *Tretii Pol*, p. 267.
13 Izmail F. Sluchevskii, *Psikhiatriya* (Leningrad: Medgiz, 1957), p. 343.
14 Belkin, *Tretii Pol*, p. 270.

Chapter 7

1 Richard Cavendish, "Death of Joseph Stalin: The Soviet Leader Died on March 5th, 1953", *History Today* 53, 3 (2003). www.historytoday.com/archive/months-past/death-joseph-stalin.
2 Jeffrey S. Hardy, *The GULAG after Stalin: Redefining Punishment in Khrushchev's Soviet Union, 1953–1964* (Ithaca and London: Cornell University Press, 2016), p. 27.
3 GARF, f. P-9414, op. 1, delo 2882, l. 78.
4 Rustam Alexander, *Regulating Homosexuality in Soviet Russia, 1956–91: A Different History* (Manchester: Manchester University Press, 2021), p. 28.
5 GARF, f. P-9414, op. 1, delo 2888, l. 91.

6 Golfo Alexopoulos, *Illness and Inhumanity in Stalin's GULAG* (New Haven and London: Yale University Press, 2017), p. 163.

7 GARF, f. P-9414, op. 1, delo 2896, ll. 234–235.

8 GARF, f. P-9414, op. 1, delo 2896, ll. 234–235.

9 GARF, f. P-9414, op. 1, delo 2896, l. 214.

10 GARF, f. P-9414, op. 1, delo 2896, l. 215.

11 GARF, f. P-9414, op. 1, delo 2896, l. 164

12 GARF, f. P-9414, op. 1, delo 2896, ll. 207–215.

13 GARF, f. P-9414, op. 1, delo 2896, l. 215.

14 GARF, f. P-9414, op. 1, delo 2896, l. 193.

15 GARF, f. P-9414, op. 1, delo 2896, l. 193.

16 GARF, f. P-9414, op. 1, delo 2896, l. 228.

17 GARF, f. P-9414, op. 1, dop., delo 608, l. 76.

18 Hardy, *The GULAG after Stalin*, p. 194.

19 David K. Johnson, *The Lavender Scare: The Cold War Prosecution of Gays and Lesbians in the Federal Government* (Chicago: University of Chicago Press, 2004), p. 1.

20 D'Emilio, *Sexual Politics*, p. 49.

21 D'Emilio, *Sexual Politics*, p. 53.

Chapter 8

1 This chapter is based on the criminal case of David Morozov located in the State Archive of Leningrad Province in the City of Vyborg (LOGAV, f. 3820, op. 2, d. 4471), and is examined in the chapter "Comrades, Queers, and 'Oddballs': Sodomy, Masculinity, and Gendered Violence in Leningrad Province in the 1950s", in Dan Healey's book *Russian Homophobia from Stalin to Sochi*, pp. 51–73. In 2015, I attempted to obtain these materials in the archive myself, but archive workers denied me access to the file.

2 Healey, *Russian Homophobia*, p. 51.

3 See Healey, *Russian Homophobia*, p. 51.

4 Healey, *Russian Homophobia*, p. 52.

5 Healey, *Russian Homophobia*, p. 68.

6 Healey, *Russian Homophobia*, p. 61.

7 Healey, *Russian Homophobia*, p. 61.

8 Healey, *Russian Homophobia*, p. 61.

9 Healey, *Russian Homophobia*, p. 56.

10 Healey, *Russian Homophobia*, p. 55.

11 Healey, *Russian Homophobia*, p. 56.

12 Healey, *Russian Homophobia*, p. 68.

13 Healey, *Russian Homophobia*, p. 68.

14 Healey, *Russian Homophobia*, p. 68.

Notes

15 Healey, *Russian Homophobia*, p. 69.
16 Healey, *Russian Homophobia*, p. 69.
17 Healey, *Russian Homophobia*, p. 56.
18 John Howard, *Men Like that: A Southern Queer History* (Chicago: University of Chicago Press, 1999).

Chapter 9

1 Peter H. Solomon Jr, *Soviet Criminologists and Criminal Policy: Specialists in Policy-Making* (New York: Columbia University Press, 1978), pp. 52–53.
2 GARF, f. A-385, op. 26, delo 153, ll. 182–183.
3 Georgii B. Karnovich and Mikhail G. Korshik, *Rassledovanie polovykh prestuplenii: posobie dlia sledovatelei* (Moscow: Gosudarstvennoe izdatel'stvo iuridicheskoi literatury, 1958), p. 77.
4 Mikhail I. Avdeev, *Sudebnaia Meditsina* (Moscow: Gosudarstvennoe izdatel'stvo yuridicheskoi literatury, 1951), p. 376.
5 See GARF, A-385, op. 26, delo 152, ll. 292–293.
6 State Archive of Latvia, f. 938, op. 6, delo 66, l. 82.
7 D'Emilio, *Sexual Politics*, p. 81.
8 On West German homophile groups see Whisnant, *Queer Identities and Politics in Germany*, pp. 64–112. On French homophile movements see Julian Jackson, *Living in Arcadia: Homosexuality, Politics, and Morality in France from the Liberation to AIDS* (Chicago: Chicago University Press, 2009).
9 Tommy Dickinson, *Curing Queers: Mental Nurses and Their Patients, 1935–74* (Manchester: Manchester University Press, 2015), pp. 57–61.
10 Kateřina Lišková, "Now You See Them, Now You Don't: Sexual Deviants and Sexological Expertise in Communist Czechoslovakia", *History of the Human Sciences* 29, 1 (February 2016): 54.

Chapter 10

1 D. Gorfin, "Polovaia zhizn", in *Bol'shaia sovetskaia entsiklopediia*, vol. 46 (Moscow: Sovetskaia entsiklopediia, 1940), pp. 163–169.
2 Ronald Bayer, *Homosexuality and American Psychiatry: The Politics of Diagnosis* (New York: Basic Books, Inc., 1981), p. 43.
3 Elizaveta M. Derevinskaia, "Materialy k klinike, patogenezu, terapii zhenskogo gomoseksualizma" (Dissertatsia na soiskanie uchenoi stepeni kandidata meditsinskikh nauk, Karaganda State Medical Institute, 1965), p. 253.
4 Derevinskaia, "Materialy k klinike", p. 39.
5 Derevinskaia, "Materialy k klinike", p. 117.

6 Derevinskaia's dissertation did not feature her patients' names, which I have invented for the sake of the story. Derevinskaia, "Materialy k klinike", p. 117.

7 Derevinskaia, "Materialy k klinike", p. 119.

8 Derevinskaia, "Materialy k klinike", p. 254.

9 Derevinskaia, "Materialy k klinike", p. 73.

10 Derevinskaia, "Materialy k klinike", pp. 129–130.

11 Derevinskaia, "Materialy k klinike", p. 139.

12 Derevinskaia, "Materialy k klinike", p. 121.

13 Derevinskaia, "Materialy k klinike", pp. 211–212.

14 Derevinskaia, "Materialy k klinike", p. 195.

15 Derevinskaia, "Materialy k klinike", p. 197.

16 Katherine B. Eaton, *Daily Life in the Soviet Union* (London: Greenwood Press, 2004), p. 198.

17 Derevinskaia, "Materialy k klinike", p. 199.

18 Derevinskaia, "Materialy k klinike", p, 201.

19 Derevinskaia, "Materialy k klinike", p. 204.

20 Derevinskaia, "Materialy k klinike", p. 204.

21 Derevinskaia, "Materialy k klinike", pp. 215–217.

22 Derevinskaia, "Materialy k klinike", pp. 217–218.

23 Derevinskaia, "Materialy k klinike", p. 219.

24 Derevinskaia, "Materialy k klinike", p. 221.

25 Derevinskaia, "Materialy k klinike", p. 227.

26 Derevinskaia, "Materialy k klinike", p. 232.

27 Derevinskaia, "Materialy k klinike", pp. 235–236.

28 Derevinskaia, "Materialy k klinike", p. 236.

29 Derevinskaia, "Materialy k klinike", p. 237.

30 Abram M. Sviadoshch, *Zhenskaia seksopatologiia* (Moscow: Meditsina, 1974).

31 Bayer, *Homosexuality and American Psychiatry*, pp. 52–53.

Chapter 11

1 Julie Fedor, *Russia and the Cult of State Security: The Chekist Tradition, from Lenin to Putin* (London: Routledge, 2013), p. 33.

2 Fedor, *Russia and the Cult of State Security*, p. 38.

3 State Archive of the Security Service of Ukraine, delo 66876, volume 6, l. 270. Hereafter "Petrenko's case". Names have been changed.

4 Petrenko's case, volume 4, l. 95.

5 Petrenko's case, volume 3, l. 57.

6 Petrenko's case, volume 3, l. 103.

7 Petrenko's case, volume 3, l. 123.

8 Petrenko's case, volume 5, l. 113.

9 Petrenko's case, volume 6, l. 114.

Notes

10 Petrenko's case, volume 6, l. 117.
11 Petrenko's case, volume 6, l. 88.
12 Petrenko's case, volume 6, l. 89.
13 Petrenko's case, volume 6, l. 20.
14 Petrenko's case, volume 6, l. 89.
15 Petrenko's case, volume 3, l. 256.
16 Petrenko's case, volume 4, l. 1.
17 Petrenko's case, volume 4, l. 1.
18 Petrenko's case, volume 4, l. 1.
19 Petrenko's case, volume 4, l. 1.
20 Petrenko's case, volume 4, l. 1.
21 Petrenko's case, volume 4, l. 1.
22 Petrenko's case, volume 6, l. 106.
23 Petrenko's case, volume 6, l. 270.
24 Petrenko's case, volume 6, l. 69.
25 Petrenko's case, volume 6, l. 62.
26 Petrenko's case, volume 6, l. 120.
27 Petrenko's case, volume 6, l. 181.
28 Petrenko's case, volume 6, l. 182.
29 Petrenko's case, volume 2, l. 109.
30 Petrenko's case, volume 2, l. 109.
31 Petrenko's case, volume 3, l, 21.
32 Petrenko's case, volume 6, l. 125.
33 Petrenko's case, volume 3, l. 32.
34 Petrenko's case, volume 6, l. 224.
35 Petrenko's case, volume 6, l. 270.

Chapter 12

1 Mikhail Stern and August Stern, *Sex in the USSR* (New York: Times Books), pp. 88–89.
2 Igor Kon, *The Sexual Revolution in Russia: From the Age of the Czars to Today* (New York and London: The Free Press, 1995), p. 172.
3 Kon, *The Sexual Revolution in Russia*, p. 172.
4 Pavel B. Posvianskii, "Sovremennye problemy seksopatologii", in *Aktual'nye voprosy seksopatologii: Sbornik statei*, edited by Dmitrii D. Fedotov (Moscow: Moskovskii nauchno-issledovatel'skii institut psikhiatrii, 1967), p. 17.
5 Nikolai V. Ivanov, *Voprosy psikhoterapii funktsional'nykh seksual'nykh rasstroistv* (Moscow: Meditsina, 1966), p. 4.
6 Il'ia M. Porudominskii, "Kto zhe lechit polovye rasstroistva?", *Meditsinskaia gazeta* 96, 29 November 1963, 3.
7 Alexander, *Regulating Homosexuality*, p. 87.

Notes

8 Alexander, *Regulating Homosexuality*, p. 87.
9 Ivanov, *Voprosy psikhoterapii*.
10 Ivanov, *Voprosy psikhoterapii*, pp. 133–139.
11 Ivanov, *Voprosy psikhoterapii*, pp. 133–139.
12 Ivanov, *Voprosy psikhoterapii*, pp. 133–139.
13 Ivanov, *Voprosy psikhoterapii*, pp. 133–139.
14 Ivanov, *Voprosy psikhoterapii*, pp. 133–139.
15 Ivanov, *Voprosy psikhoterapii*, p. 137.
16 Ivanov, *Voprosy psikhoterapii*, p. 138.
17 Alexander, *Regulating Homosexuality*, p. 104.
18 See Yan G. Goland, "O stupenchatom postroenii psikhoterapii pri muzhskom gomoseksualizme", in *Problemy Sovremennoi Seksopatologii*, edited by Anatolii A. Portnov (Moscow: Moskovskii nauchno-issledovatel'skii institut psikhiatrii, 1972), p. 477.
19 Goland, "O stupenchatom postroenii", p. 479.
20 Goland, "O stupenchatom postroenii", p. 480.
21 Goland, "O stupenchatom postroenii", p. 483.
22 Goland, "'O stupenchatom postroenii", pp. 473–486.
23 Goland, "O stupenchatom postroenii", p. 485.
24 Alexander, *Regulating Homosexuality*, p. 214.

Chapter 13

1 Natalya Chernyshova, *Soviet Consumer Culture in the Brezhnev Era* (London and New York: Routledge, 2013), pp. 2–3.
2 Joshua Rubenstein, *Soviet Dissidents: Their Struggle for Human Rights* (Boston: Beacon Press, 1980), pp. 31–44.
3 Rubenstein, *Soviet Dissidents*, pp. 63–97.
4 Günter Bischof, Stefan Karner and Peter Ruggenthaler (eds), *The Prague Spring and the Warsaw Pact Invasion of Czechoslovakia in 1968* (New York: Lexington Books, 2009).
5 Healey, *Russian Homophobia*, p. 98.
6 Mikhail N. Khlyntsov, *Rassledovanie polovykh prestuplenii* (Saratov: Privolzhskoe knizhnoe izdatel'stvo, 1965), p. 145.
7 Khlyntsov, *Rassledovanie polovykh prestuplenii*, p. 147.
8 Khlyntsov, *Rassledovanie polovykh prestuplenii*, p. 145.
9 Khlyntsov, *Rassledovanie polovykh prestuplenii*, p. 152.
10 Aleksei N. Ignatov, *Otvetstvennost' za prestuplenia protiv nravstvennosti: Polovye prestupleniya* (Moscow: Yuridicheskaya literatura, 1966), p. 180.
11 Pavel P. Osipov, "Polovye prestupleniia: obshchee poniatie, sotsial'naia sushchnost' i sistema sostavov" (Dissertatsiia na soiskanie uchenoi stepeni kandidata iuridicheskikh nauk, Leningrad, 1966), p. 202.

12 Osipov, "Polovye prestupleniia", p. 202.

13 Osipov, "Polovye prestupleniia", p. 204.

14 Yakov M. Yakovlev, "Otvetstvennost' za muzhelozhstvo po sovetskomu ugolovnomu pravu" in *Voprosy kriminalistiki i kriminologii* (Dushanbe: Izdatev'stvo Tadzhikskovo universiteta, 1968), p. 45.

15 D'Emilio, *Sexual Politics*, p. 144.

16 D'Emilio, *Sexual Politics*, p. 145.

17 D'Emilio, *Sexual Politics*, p. 145.

18 D'Emilio, *Sexual Politics*, p. 146.

Chapter 14

1 This chapter is based on a typewritten medical report of Yan Goland's former patient Andrei Tarasov, who underwent psychotherapy for homosexuality in 1968. Hereafter I refer to it as "Tarasov, *Report*". The chapter is also based on typewritten feedback from his wife Nadezhda (hereinafter "Nadezhda's feedback"), which she provided in September 1968 after Andrei had completed a psychotherapy course for homosexuality. Both files are contained in the private collection of Yan G. Goland and are used with his permission. Names have been changed.

2 Nadezhda's feedback, pp. 1–4.

3 Nadezhda's feedback, pp. 1–4.

4 Nadezhda's feedback, p. 2.

5 Nadezhda's feedback, p. 2.

6 Tarasov, *Report*.

7 Nadezhda's feedback, pp. 3–4.

8 This is my own understanding of how Andrei's and Nadezhda's marital life developed after Andrei finalized his treatment for homosexuality.

9 D'Emilio, *Sexual Politics*, p. 147.

10 D'Emilio, *Sexual Politics*, p. 196.

11 D'Emilio, *Sexual Politics*, p. 239.

Chapter 15

1 This chapter is based on the autobiography of Leonid (Lenya) Bykov, contained in the private collection of Yan G. Goland; used with his permission. Hereafter I refer to it as "Bykov, *Avtobiografiia*". It also deals with Bykov's diary, which he kept while receiving medical treatment for homosexuality. Hereafter I refer to it as "Bykov, *Diary*". Names have been changed.

2 Eaton, *Daily Life in the Soviet Union*, p. 267.

Notes

3   Anna Rotkirch, "What Kind of Sex Can You Talk about? Acquiring Sexual Knowledge in Three Soviet Generations", in *Living through the Soviet System*, edited by Daniel Bertaux, Paul Thompson and Anna Rotkirch (New Brunswick: Transaction Publishers, 2005), p. 106.

4   Bykov, *Avtobiografiia*, p. 2.

5   Bykov, *Avtobiografiia*, p. 4.

6   Bykov, *Avtobiografiia*, p. 7.

7   Bykov, *Avtobiografiia*, p. 7.

8   Bykov, *Avtobiografiia*, p. 7.

9   Bykov, *Avtobiografiia*, p. 8.

10   Bykov, *Avtobiografiia*, p. 9.

11   Bykov, *Avtobiografiia*, p. 9.

12   Bykov, *Avtobiografiia*, p. 9.

13   Bykov, *Avtobiografiia*, p. 10.

14   Bykov, *Avtobiografiia*, p. 10.

15   Bykov, *Avtobiografiia*, p. 10.

16   Bykov, *Avtobiografiia*, p. 10.

17   Bykov, *Avtobiografiia*, pp. 10–11.

18   Bykov, *Avtobiografiia*, p. 11.

19   Bykov, *Avtobiografiia*, p. 11.

20   Bykov, *Avtobiografiia*, p. 12.

21   Bykov, *Avtobiografiia*, p. 12.

22   Bykov, *Avtobiografiia*, p. 12.

23   Bykov, *Avtobiografiia*, p. 12.

24   Bykov, *Avtobiografiia*, p. 12.

25   Bykov, *Avtobiografiia*, pp. 13–14.

26   Bykov, *Avtobiografiia*, p. 14.

27   Bykov, *Avtobiografiia*, p. 17.

28   Bykov, *Avtobiografiia*, p. 17. Describing this episode in his diary Lenya wrote: "[I thought that] …maybe there are better doctors than Chernykh. Once I threw a tantrum in Chernykh's office and said that I couldn't continue like that any more. He apparently realized that there was little else he could do and he advised me to go to Moscow to see a real sexologist."

29   Bykov, *Avtobiografiia*, p. 17.

30   Bykov, *Avtobiografiia*, p. 17. Describing this episode Lenya wrote in his diary: "On 22 January my father and I were already in the office of Professor Posvianskii. He listened to me, asked several questions and said that he was optimistic. He said that I should go to Gorky, where Y.G.G., a very good doctor 'with a whole system of treatment [for homosexuality]' and 'excellent results', lived. I was so happy!"

31   Although Lenya does not tell us what his initial interview with Goland was like, on the basis of my interview with Goland and my analysis of other sources from Goland's archive, it is very likely that Lenya's initial conversation

with Goland resembled this reconstructed scenario. Lenya also mentioned in his diary: "He [Goland] said that I met his criteria. And I was so incredibly relieved." See Bykov, *Avtobiografiia*, pp. 20–21.

32 Bykov, *Avtobiografiia*, p. 21. Lenya does mention in his diary that Goland instructed him to read his former patients' testimonials: "I read 'the memoirs' of his former patients and they also infused me with confidence."

33 Bykov, *Diary*, 3 March 1971.

34 Bykov, *Diary*, 7 March 1971.

35 Bykov, *Diary*, 19 May 1971.

36 Bykov, *Diary*, 19 May 1971.

37 Bykov, *Diary*, 17 May 1971.

38 Bykov, *Diary*, 14 June 1971.

39 Bykov, *Diary*, 18 July 1971.

40 Bykov, *Diary*, 18 July 1971.

Chapter 16

1 Boris V. Daniel'bek, "Ugolovnopravovaia bor'ba s polovymi prestupleniiami" (Avtoreferat dissertatsii na soiskanie uchenoi stepeni doktora iuridicheskikh nauk, Moscow, 1970).

2 Healey, *Homosexual Desire*, p. 96.

3 Boris V. Daniel'bek, *Polovye izvrashchenia i ugolovnaia otvetstvennost'* (Volgograd: Vysshaia sledstvennaia shkola MVD SSSR, 1972), p. 105.

4 Daniel'bek, *Polovye izvrashchenia*, p. 89.

5 Daniel'bek, *Polovye izvrashchenia*, p. 90.

6 Daniel'bek, *Polovye izvrashchenia*, p. 90.

7 Daniel'bek, *Polovye izvrashchenia*, p. 92.

8 GARF, f. P-9506, op. 75, delo 57, ll. 35–36.

9 GARF, f. P-9506, op. 75, delo 57, l. 97.

10 GARF, f. P-9506, op. 75, delo 57, l. 81.

11 GARF, f. P-9506, op. 75, delo 57, ll. 104–105.

12 GARF, f. P-9506, op. 75, delo 57, l. 110.

13 GARF, f. P-9506, op. 75, delo 57, l. 87.

14 GARF, f. P-9506, op. 75, delo 57, ll. 125–126.

Chapter 17

1 This chapter is based on the autobiography of Pavel Krotov, contained in the private collection of Yan G. Goland; used with his permission. Hereafter I refer to it as "Krotov, *Avtobiografiia*". Names have been changed.

2 Krotov, *Avtobiografiia*, p. 2.

Notes

3 Krotov, *Avtobiografiia*, p. 2.
4 Krotov, *Avtobiografiia*, p. 4.
5 Krotov, *Avtobiografiia*, p. 4.
6 Krotov, *Avtobiografiia*, p. 4.
7 Krotov, *Avtobiografiia*, p. 5.
8 Krotov, *Avtobiografiia*, p. 6.
9 Krotov, *Avtobiografiia*, p. 7.
10 Krotov, *Avtobiografiia*, p. 8.
11 Krotov, *Avtobiografiia*, p. 8.
12 Krotov, *Avtobiografiia*, p. 9.
13 Krotov, *Avtobiografiia*, p. 9.
14 Krotov, *Avtobiografiia*, p. 9.
15 Krotov, *Avtobiografiia*, p. 10.
16 Krotov, *Avtobiografiia*, p. 10.
17 Krotov, *Avtobiografiia*, p. 10.
18 Krotov, *Avtobiografiia*, p. 11.
19 Krotov, *Avtobiografiia*, pp. 11–12.

Chapter 18

1 Healey, *Homosexual Desire*, p. 262.
2 Vladimir Kozlovskii, *Argo russkoi gomoseksual'noi subkul'tury: materialy k izucheniu* (Benson, VT: Chalidze Publications, 1986), p. 16.
3 Kozlovskii, *Argo russkoi gomoseksual'noi subkul'tury*, p. 16.
4 Kozlovskii, *Argo russkoi gomoseksual'noi subkul'tury*, p. 16.
5 Kozlovskii, *Argo russkoi gomoseksual'noi subkul'tury*, p. 16.
6 Kozlovskii, *Argo russkoi gomoseksual'noi subkul'tury*, p. 17.
7 Kozlovskii, *Argo russkoi gomoseksual'noi subkul'tury*, p. 17.
8 Vera Schiavazzi, "L'urlo di Pezzana per la difesa dei gay 37 anni fa a Mosca", *La Repubblica*, 11 February 2014. https://torino.repubblica.it/cronaca/2014/02/11/news/l_urlo_di_pezzana_per_la_difesa_dei_gay_37_anni_fa_a_mosca-78282247/.
9 Schiavazzi, "L'urlo di Pezzana per la difesa dei gay 37 anni fa a Mosca".
10 Aleksei N. Ignatov, "Problemy ugolovnoi otvetstvennosti za prestuplenia v oblasti polovykh otnoshenii v sovetskom ugolovnom prave" (Avtoreferat dissertatsii na soiskanie uchenoi stepeni doktora iuridicheskikh nauk, Moscow: Vsesoiuznyi institut po izucheniiu prichin i razrabotke mer preduprezhdeniia prestupnosti, 1974), pp. 28–29.
11 Ignatov, "Problemy ugolovnoi otvetstvennosti za prestuplenia", p. 29.
12 Masha Gessen, *The Rights of Lesbians and Gay Men in the Russian Federation: An International Gay and Lesbian Human Rights Commission Report* (San Francisco: Gay & Lesbian Human Rights Commission, 1994), p. 10.

13 GARF, f. P-9506, op. 75, delo 296, l. 80.
14 GARF, f. P-9506, op. 75, delo 296, l. 80.
15 GARF, f. P-9506, op. 75, delo 296, l. 105.
16 Aleksei Ignatov, *Kvalifikatsiia polovykh prestuplenii* (Moscow: Iuridicheskaia literatura, 1974), pp. 231–237.

Chapter 19

1 Vadim V. Pokrovskii, "Pervyi sluchai sindroma priobretennogo immunodefitsita u grazhdanina SSSR", *Terapevticheskii arkhiv* LX, 7 (1988): 10.
2 Pokrovskii, "Pervyi sluchai", 10.
3 Pokrovskii, "Pervyi sluchai", 10.
4 Pokrovskii, "Pervyi sluchai", 11.
5 Pokrovskii, "Pervyi sluchai", 11.
6 Anne E. Gorsuch, *All This Is Your World: Soviet Tourism at Home and Abroad after Stalin* (Oxford: Oxford University Press), p. 111.
7 Pokrovskii, "Pervyi sluchai", 10.
8 Svetlana Grigor'ieva, "'Sovetskaia povsednevnos' v afrikanskikh predstavitel'stvakh 1960–1980-kh gg.", *Vestnik Nizhegorodskogo universiteta im. N.I. Lobachevskogo*, 6 (2017), p. 18.
9 Pokrovskii, "Pervyi sluchai", 11.
10 Lawrence K. Altman, "New Homosexual Disorder Worries Health Officials", *New York Times*, 11 May 1982.

Chapter 20

1 Nikolai A. Ivanov and Vladislav V. Bogach, *SPID bez sensatsii* (Khabarovsk: Knizhnoe izdatel'stvo, 1988), p. 15.
2 R. Petrov, "Immunodefitsity: chto eto takoe?", *Literaturnaya gazeta*, 22 June 1983, 15.
3 Thomas Boghart, "Operation INFEKTION: Soviet Bloc Intelligence Disinformation Campaign", *Studies in Intelligence* 53 (December 2009): 6.
4 Boghart, "Operation INFEKTION", 6.
5 GARF, f. P-8009, op. 51, delo 1765, l. 11.
6 Seth Mydans, "Moscow Clears Deck for Anti Imperialist Youth", *The New York Times*, 27 July 1985, 2.
7 GARF, f. P-8009, op. 51, delo 1765, l. 224.
8 GARF, f. P-8009, op. 51, delo 1765, l. 224.
9 GARF, f. 8009, op. 33, delo 1084, l. 57.
10 GARF, f. 8009, op. 51, delo 2954, l. 75.

11 Anatolii V. Zagornov and Viktor S. Kuz'michev, *Zadachi organov vnutrennikh del po preduprezhdeniu SPIDa: Metodicheskaia razrabotka* (Moscow: MVD SSSR, 1988), pp. 10–13.

12 Dennis Altman, *Power and Community: Organizational and Cultural Responses to AIDS* (London: UCL Press, 1994), p. 20.

13 Altman, *Power and Community*, p. 19.

Chapter 21

1 V. Zapevalov, "Panika na zapade ili chto skryvaetsia za sensatsiei vokrug SPID", *Literaturnaya gazeta*, 30 October 1985.

2 Gary Lee, "Soviets Try to Quiet AIDS Fears", *The Washington Post*, 12 December 1985. www.washingtonpost.com/archive/politics/1985/12/12/soviets-try-to-quie t-aids-fears/3550d9d0-19b8-4b0f-9004-4a2c5e140fe4/.

3 Alvin A. Snyder, *Warriors of Disinformation: American Propaganda, Soviet Lies, and the Winning of the Cold War: An Insider's Account* (New York: Arcade Publishing, 1997), p. 113.

4 Snyder, *Warriors of Disinformation*, p. 114.

5 Snyder, *Warriors of Disinformation*, p. 114.

6 Ivanov and Bogach, *SPID bez sensatsii*, p. 13.

Chapter 22

1 Oleg Moroz, *Gruppa riska* (Moscow: Prosveshchenie, 1990), p. 61.

2 Moroz, *Gruppa riska*, p. 61.

3 Pokrovskii, "Pervyi sluchai", 11.

4 Pokrovskii, "Pervyi sluchai", 12.

5 Pokrovskii, "Pervyi sluchai", 12.

6 Moroz, *Gruppa riska*, pp. 60–62.

7 Galina Kulikovskaia, "Obratnogo khoda net", *Ogonek*, 23 (1987): 19.

8 V.I. Pokrovskii and V.V. Pokrovskii, *SPID: Sindrom priobretennogo immuno-defitsita* (Moscow: Meditsina, 1988), p. 18.

Chapter 23

1 Dmitry Strovsky and Ron Schleifer, "Soviet Politics and Journalism under Mikhail Gorbachev's Perestroika and Glasnost: Why Hopes Failed", *Athens Journal of Mass Media and Communications*, 7, 4 (October 2021): 242.

2 *Komsomol'skaia Pravda*, 1 August 1987, 3.

3 A. Novikov, "Eshe raz o SPIDe", *Komsomol'skaia Pravda*, 28 October 1987, 3.

4 GARF, f. 8009, op. 51, delo 2959, l. 43.

Notes

5 Aleksei Novikov, "Sindrom 'Trekh obez'ianok'", *Molodoi Kommunist*, December 1988, 68.
6 Novikov, "Sindrom 'Trekh obez'ianok'", 69.
7 Novikov, "Sindrom 'Trekh obez'ianok'", 70.
8 Novikov, "Sindrom 'Trekh obez'ianok'", 71.
9 Novikov, "Sindrom 'Trekh obez'ianok'", 71.
10 Novikov, "Sindrom 'Trekh obez'ianok'", 71.
11 Novikov, "Sindrom 'Trekh obez'ianok'", 71.
12 Novikov, "Sindrom 'Trekh obez'ianok'", 71.
13 Novikov, "Sindrom 'Trekh obez'ianok'", 72.
14 Novikov, "Sindrom 'Trekh obez'ianok'", 73.
15 Novikov, "Sindrom 'Trekh obez'ianok'", 74.
16 Novikov, "Sindrom 'Trekh obez'ianok'", 74.
17 Novikov, "Sindrom 'Trekh obez'ianok'", 74.
18 Novikov, "Sindrom 'Trekh obez'ianok'", 70.
19 Novikov, "Sindrom 'Trekh obez'ianok'", 75.

Chapter 24

1 N. Boiarkina, "SPID i deti: prokuratura nachala rassledovaniie", *Komsomol'skaia Pravda*, 28 January 1989, 1.
2 Boiarkina, "SPID i deti: prokuratura nachala rassledovaniie", 1.
3 David Remnick, "Unwashed Needles Infect 27 Infants with AIDS", *Washington Post*, 29 January 1989. www.washingtonpost.com/archive/politics/1989/01/29/unwashed-needles-infect-27-infants-with-aids/8ffcd771-7810-48bc-a7f3-c3b6f2f3f34c/.
4 Moroz, *Gruppa riska*, pp. 51–52. The letter has been abridged.
5 Moroz, *Gruppa riska*.
6 Moroz, *Gruppa riska*, p. 65.
7 Moroz, *Gruppa riska*, p. 66.
8 Moroz, *Gruppa riska*, p. 68.
9 Moroz, *Gruppa riska*, p. 68.
10 Moroz, *Gruppa riska*, p. 69.
11 Moroz, *Gruppa riska*, p. 71.
12 Moroz, *Gruppa riska*, p. 72.
13 Moroz, *Gruppa riska*, p. 74.

Epilogue

1 Gessen, *The Rights of Lesbians and Gay Men*, p. 27.
2 Gessen, *The Rights of Lesbians and Gay Men*, p. 28.

Notes

3 Gessen, *The Rights of Lesbians and Gay Men*, p. 29.
4 Gessen, *The Rights of Lesbians and Gay Men*, p. 32.
5 Gessen, *The Rights of Lesbians and Gay Men*.
6 Elena Milashina, 'Ubiistvo chesti: Kak ambitsii izvestnogo LGBT-aktivista razbudili v Chechne strashnyi drevnii obychai', *Novaia Gazeta*, 3 April 2017. www.novayagazeta.ru/articles/2017/04/01/71983-ubiystvo-chesti.
7 Healey, *Russian Homophobia*, p. 174.
8 Healey, *Russian Homophobia*, p. 175.

Acknowledgements

I would like to thank Emma Brennan, the editorial director of Manchester University Press, who met my book proposal with great enthusiasm, as well as the whole team of Manchester University Press along with two anonymous reviewers for their support in making this book possible. I would also like to express my gratitude to June Colbert, who has been my grammar guardian and the first reader of this book as well as my previous written works over the last few years.

This book was written in two different cities – Brisbane and Moscow. I would like to thank my friends Harry Jamieson and Craig Dows who kindly allowed me to stay in their house in Brisbane for several months and also for taking me for trips to beautiful Noosa and the Sunshine Coast, where, surrounded by pristine beaches and scenic sunsets, I often drew my inspiration.

A large part of my book was written in Russia and I would like to thank my family, my mum, dad and my older brother, for letting me stay in their flat without paying rent and for seeing to my comfort, while I was fully immersed in my work. Although my mum and dad still don't know about the kinds of books I am writing, they knew I was working on something important to me and respected my need for time alone.

I would like to dedicate this book to Russians of all sexual orientations, who deserve to live in a free and democratic Russia, safe from discrimination of any kind. And I hope that one day they will be able, if they choose, of course, to read this book in our native language.

São Paulo, 2022

Index

Index